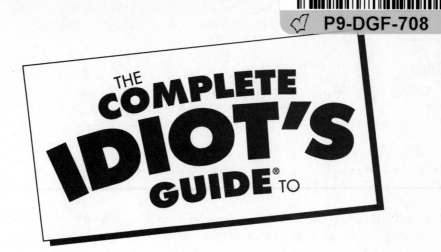

THE
COMPLETE
IDIOT'S
GUIDE® TO

Economic
Indicators

by R. Mark Rogers

ALPHA

A member of Penguin Group (USA) Inc.

To my dear wife, Linda, for encouraging me and putting up with me while I took time away for this project.

ALPHA BOOKS

Published by the Penguin Group

Penguin Group (USA) Inc., 375 Hudson Street, New York, New York 10014, USA

Penguin Group (Canada), 90 Eglinton Avenue East, Suite 700, Toronto, Ontario M4P 2Y3, Canada (a division of Pearson Penguin Canada Inc.)

Penguin Books Ltd., 80 Strand, London WC2R 0RL, England

Penguin Ireland, 25 St. Stephen's Green, Dublin 2, Ireland (a division of Penguin Books Ltd.)

Penguin Group (Australia), 250 Camberwell Road, Camberwell, Victoria 3124, Australia (a division of Pearson Australia Group Pty. Ltd.)

Penguin Books India Pvt. Ltd., 11 Community Centre, Panchsheel Park, New Delhi—110 017, India

Penguin Group (NZ), 67 Apollo Drive, Rosedale, North Shore, Auckland 1311, New Zealand (a division of Pearson New Zealand Ltd.)

Penguin Books (South Africa) (Pty.) Ltd., 24 Sturdee Avenue, Rosebank, Johannesburg 2196, South Africa

Penguin Books Ltd., Registered Offices: 80 Strand, London WC2R 0RL, England

Copyright © 2009 by R. Mark Rogers

International Standard Book Number: 978-1-59257-922-8
Library of Congress Catalog Card Number: 2009924912

11   10   09   8   7   6   5   4   3   2   1

Interpretation of the printing code: The rightmost number of the first series of numbers is the year of the book's printing; the rightmost number of the second series of numbers is the number of the book's printing. For example, a printing code of 09-1 shows that the first printing occurred in 2009.

Printed in the United States of America

Publisher: *Marie Butler-Knight*
Editorial Director/Acquisitions Editor: *Mike Sanders*
Senior Managing Editor: *Billy Fields*
Development Editor: *Ginny Bess Munroe*
Senior Production Editor: *Janette Lynn*
Copy Editor: *Sonja Nikkila*

Cartoonist: *Chris Sabatino*
Cover Designer: *Bill Thomas*
Book Designer: *Trina Wurst*
Indexer: *Brad Herriman*
Layout: *Chad Dressler*
Proofreader: *John Etchison*

Contents at a Glance

Contents

Introduction

Economic news affects everyone. During the past recession, all were touched by economic news. Whether your job situation changed, your retirement wasn't what you thought it was, or your business had to scramble a lot more than you expected, the economy made a difference in everyone's life. Wish you had a better heads up? I explain to you where all of the key economic indicators fit so you can make better decisions with your money, business, or even career. You can be a better-informed purchaser of stocks, plan more carefully for your business, decide whether it's a good time to change jobs, or even be better prepared for retirement by understanding where the economy is headed.

Never set foot into the world of economic indicators? Well, you couldn't have picked a more exciting time than now to jump in. While writing this book, the U.S. economy was in the deepest recession since the 1930s, and the Federal Reserve (the decision maker for U.S. interest rate policy) had adopted a course of action that had never been taken in the United States. The good news is that this book will ease you into the world of economic indicators and tracking the Federal Reserve step-by-step. But you'll quickly find yourself becoming quite an expert on how to read the economy.

This book will teach you much of what I have learned tracking the economy for well over a quarter century. I began my professional economics career at the Federal Reserve Bank of Atlanta and a major part of my responsibilities was to track, analyze, and forecast the U.S. economy. I currently keep my finger on the pulse of the U.S. economy as Senior Economist for Econoday, Inc.—a company that focuses on providing timely economic insight for investors.

What were some of the big lessons for me? The first lesson might be a little surprising. The first thing you need to know is how to get in the game. That is, what is it that financial traders watch to keep up with the economy and how do you watch along with them? I'll put you in the middle of the game with website links that give you up-to-the-minute news on financial markets and economic indicators.

Next, you need to be able to see the big picture of how the major pieces interact. For example, how important is the consumer sector? What makes a difference on whether the consumer sector is strong or weak? Next, you need to know where the economic indicators fit in with different parts of the overall economy. Which indicators focus on the consumer sector versus housing or some other sector? Then, what does each indicator mean and what do you have to watch out for in news releases? Guess what? These are the questions that this book answers.

Now, here's the really good part. Yes, this book carefully eases you into the world of economic indicators—and puts you on the path to becoming an expert. But what else?

The really good part is that there is a lot of really neat stuff out there in the world of economic indicators. By the time you finish this book, not only will you be able to explain why the first Friday of every month is such a big deal but also what fed funds futures are predicting about interest rates. Yes, you will understand the important insights on economic indicators known by Wall Street economists. You'll be the neighborhood Fed guru. And you'll love getting in the game of economic indicators!

How to Use This Book

The Complete Idiot's Guide to Economic Indicators teaches you to understand how financial traders and economists think about economic indicators. You will learn the big picture about how different sectors fit in with the economy. For each economic report, the book teaches you the key definitions and what to look for when news is released and impacts stocks, bonds, currencies and other financial markets.

This book is organized into six parts:

Part 1, "Economic Indicators and You," jumps right in, giving you an overview of indicators tracked by traders. You learn about business cycles and about the indicator that pulls it all together—gross domestic product. And this section puts you in the game with websites that stay on top of financial markets and economic indicators and provide commentary on the status of the economy.

Part 2, "The Consumer in the Economy," explains the number-one economic report on earth—the employment situation report. Plus, you'll find out how to track what most businesses care about consumer spending—including whether households have the income to keep it up.

Part 3, "Inflation Numbers," focuses on consumer and producer prices. These reports play a big role in affecting interest rates and how far your paycheck goes. And this section covers special topics, including oil and gold prices which lead to constant chatter in the financial news.

Part 4, "Housing and Construction," gives you the basics on the number-one housing report, housing starts, and shows you how to track home sales. Plus, there is extra emphasis on a topic that has risen in importance to bankers and investors—home prices.

Part 5, "Manufacturing and International Trade," explains how to track the manufacturing sector—from new orders, to production, to inventories. And this section provides key insight into tracking exports and imports in the economy—something that affects us all, but especially currency traders.

Part 6, "Fed Watching: The Best for Last," gives you insight into how monetary policy is made in the United States. You find out everything from who the key players are, what they think about when deciding interest rates, how to understand Fed reports, and how to track how the financial markets view Fed policy.

You'll come across lots of terms about economic indicators and the economy. If you see terms you don't recognize or acronyms that look like alphabet soup, you can look them up in the Economic Indicators Glossary.

Extras

Along the way, you'll see sidebars throughout the chapters. These point out the meanings of everyday terms about the economy, special tips, and insider information from the view of economists.

def•i•ni•tion

Economic terms can be like speaking Greek to most. These boxes put the meanings of economic indicators and their environment into plain English.

Trader Tip

Financial traders know that economic news can turn markets. These tips teach you some of the inside information on economic indicators that traders focus on.

Only from an Economist

Economists have a different view on the world. These tidbits give you economist insights into everyday life as well as the economy.

Acknowledgments

I would like to thank Cynthia Parker and Anne D. Picker at Econoday, Inc. for encouraging me during my hectic times while writing this book. I cannot thank enough those editing and improving this work—Beverly Harzog, Danielle Chapman, Ginny Bess Munroe, Janette Lynn, and Sonja Nikkila. Thanks to Mike Sanders for keeping everything organized and on track.

Trademarks

All terms mentioned in this book that are known to be or are suspected of being trademarks or service marks have been appropriately capitalized. Alpha Books and Penguin Group (USA) Inc. cannot attest to the accuracy of this information. Use of a term in this book should not be regarded as affecting the validity of any trademark or service mark.

Part 1

Economic Indicators and You

The first part of this book introduces you to what economic indicators are and how they create so much excitement in the financial markets. You see so much of the economy around you every day, but now you'll see how economic indicators capture that information and become part of the world of economists, investors, traders in the financial markets, policymakers—and now, you!

There are rhymes and reasons to the apparent madness of economic data whirling in the financial media, and we are going to make quick sense of it. We start with a big picture of the economy, called gross domestic product. You see how all the sectors fit together—yes, it will make sense. Here's the first adventure—dive into the world of economic indicators and financial markets and keep up with the pros!

Economic Indicators: A High Impact on Markets and You

In This Chapter

♦ How economic indicators create a lot of action in financial markets

♦ The monthly recurrence of economic indicators

♦ How to get in the game by tracking economic indicators

♦ Tips to help prepare for market reactions

♦ The key markets affected by economic indicators

Have you ever watched a World Series baseball game where the pitch count is 3-2, the bases are loaded, and there are two outs? It's also game seven. Well, that kind of tension is nothing compared to the feeling financial analysts and brokers get two seconds after the employment situation report comes out. There's more tension before—and action afterward—in the financial markets when a key economic indicator comes out than during a decade of World Series games. And there's more money at stake, too.

Before an economic news release, financial traders have their fingers on the trigger, ready to trade as soon as they know whether the economic news is good or bad. Within seconds of the news, millions of traders and investors pull the trade trigger. By the time you finish this book, you'll know what's going on in this exciting world. You'll also understand how economic indicators can make or break your retirement savings and even determine whether you have a job!

Are you ready to change channels from the World Series to the excitement of economic indicators? Find a comfortable chair, relax, and read on. And who knows? You might just learn enough to hit a financial home run of your own!

Getting in the Game

Let's start with the basics: what exactly are *economic indicators*? Economic indicators are statistics that reveal the growth (or lack thereof!) and direction of our economy. Examples of economic indicators are gross domestic product, unemployment rate, and money supply.

def•i•ni•tion

Economic indicators are key statistics about the economy. These statistics are economic measures that help predict growth rates and trends in the economy.

So when news about economic indicators is released and we get clues about where the economy is headed, financial markets start buzzing and reacting.

How do traders and investors use economic indicators? There are two general approaches:

◆ To see how economic indicators impact the stock market, the bond market, and other financial markets at the immediate time of release to the public.

◆ To see how economic indicators portray the economy over the long term and short term and how that might affect your career, business, or investments.

First-Tier Economic Indicators: The A Team

What's a first-tier indicator? These are the market movers that nearly every trader tunes in to at release time. The list varies from analyst to analyst as to what is tier one, but here's my list: employment situation, the Federal Reserve's FOMC (Federal Open Market Committee) policy announcement, *gross domestic product (GDP)*, personal income report, housing starts, retail sales, consumer price index, producer price index, industrial production, durable goods orders, international trade, and the ISM (Institute for Supply Management) manufacturing report. You probably do not recognize all of these terms but we will cover them in coming chapters. If you are in a hurry, jump to Appendix A for short definitions.

Second- and third-tier are arbitrary levels of how much attention an indicator gets. One example of a second-tier indicator (relative to the more important employment situation report) might be initial jobless claims; these are important, but not everybody watches them. Third-tier might be the natural gas inventory report, which is mainly watched by specialists.

def•i•ni•tion

Gross domestic product (GDP) represents the market value of goods and services produced in the United States. In other words, GDP represents the total production for a country.

Your Ticket to the Action: Economic Calendars

Want to get in on the excitement when news releases on economic indicators come out? You'll be pleased to know that there's a regular pattern to when economic indicators are made public. The general schedule for indicators has been developed over decades and reflects when the underlying information for an indicator is available and how long it takes the government agency responsible for a given indicator to process that information.

The government agencies that create the economic indicators generally announce a schedule for news releases a year in advance. The timing of a release is generally within the same three or four days each calendar month. For example, the employment situation report is the first Friday of each month and the industrial production report is mid-month.

The following table is a typical calendar of releases. For the monthly and weekly indicators, the timing each month is roughly the same. Only first- and second-tier indicators are listed and are just for monthly or quarterly indicators.

The Monthly Pattern, Selected Economic Releases, April 2009

Apr. 1	Motor vehicle sales
	ADP employment report
	ISM manufacturing index
	Construction spending
	Pending home sales
	EIA petroleum status report
Apr. 2	Factory orders
Apr. 3	Employment situation
	ISM nonmanufacturing index
Apr. 7	FOMC minutes
	Consumer credit
Apr. 9	International trade
	Import and export prices
Apr. 14	Retail sales
	Producer price index
	Business inventories
Apr. 15	Consumer prices
	Empire State manufacturing survey
	Industrial production
	Beige Book
Apr. 16	Housing starts
	Philadelphia Fed manufacturing survey
Apr. 17	Consumer sentiment
	EIA petroleum status report
	FOMC minutes
Apr. 20	Leading indicators
Apr. 23	Existing home sales

Apr. 24	Durable goods orders
	New home sales
Apr. 28	S&P Case-Shiller home price index
	Consumer confidence
Apr. 29	GDP
	FOMC announcement
Apr. 30	Personal income and outlays report
	Employment cost index
	NAPM-Chicago business activity index

Why does it matter which indicators come out first each month? Because some indicators help forecast other indicators. Throughout this book, you will learn which economic indicators are used to predict others. Also, when you track the economy each month, each new indicator adds to your view about the strength of the economy. In addition, the strength of different sectors becomes noticeable. For example, is housing improving? How much are consumers spending and on what? Each month's worth of data refines your view of the economy.

Economic Calendars on the Web

Now that you've decided to keep up with the economy, find a website you like that has an economic calendar of events, preferably one that forecasts the main economic indicators and even second- or third-tier indicators. There are at least four types of relevant content to look for: the key numbers from the announcement, analysis of the indicator, a consensus forecast before the announcement, and streaming headline news.

Premium websites have a streaming headline news service. This means that as soon as the indicator announcement is made public, the site streams headlines about key information on that economic indicator. This happens almost instantaneously with the announcement because news providers have reporters in the "lock up" in the agency newsroom prior to release. Statistical agencies allow cleared reporters early access (about 30 minutes prior) to the news release. They are "locked up" in the sense that they are not allowed access to the outside world until the release time. The agency newsroom gives the reporters a chance to review the numbers and write the story. When the release is officially distributed, reporters simply click "send" on their laptops.

Two top news services in this premium category are Market News International (MNI) and Reuters IFR Markets. They have calendars and real-time news headlines that appeal to traders. The catch? Full service is a little pricey if you are a student, a beginning investor, or a casual market junkie.

A competing, but not as comprehensive, real-time headline service is Need to Know News (NTKN). NTKN is affordable and has plenty of headline detail for the casual trader or plain ol' market junkie. Starting with NTKN, here's a list of sites to check out:

- Need to Know News: www.needtoknownews.com

- Bloomberg: www.bloomberg.com/markets/ecalendar/index.html

- CNBC: www.cnbc.com/id/15839153

- Econoday: www.mam.econoday.com

- Interbankfx.com: www.ibfx.com/News/EconomicCalendar.aspx

- CNN Money: www.money.cnn.com/data/irc/index.html

- MarketWatch: www.marketwatch.com/news/economy/economic_calendar.asp

If you do not want to subscribe to a headline news service, the previous websites may be close enough. You can also catch real-time news by watching the financial networks on TV. You'll hear about "breaking news" alerts for the major indicators, but not for second-tier indicators. These networks include Bloomberg, CNBC, and Fox Business Network, and some carry live, streaming video of the breaking news on their websites, too.

Consensus Forecasts: The Experts Weigh In

Each week, major news services covering the business sector call or e-mail economists who forecast what they think the week's upcoming indicators are going to be. These economists perform a statistical analysis of where the next indicator value is headed. They usually work for major banks or investment houses, but some also work as independent investment advisors or even for major nonfinancial corporations. The surveys of these economists are compiled into summaries for the upcoming week and are usually published the Friday before. The consensus forecast is really the median forecast for the indicator value. From Statistics 101, the median forecast is the one that is in the middle with half of the numbers above and half below. It basically is the forecast that others cluster around. Remember, the median is different from the average. The average value can be skewed by one very atypical forecast number, while the median is not.

The following table is a portion of the consensus forecasts put out by Thomson Reuters IFR Markets on Friday, February 6, 2009.

Reuters News Weekly Economist Poll—U.S. Indicators

Date	Day	Time	Release	Unit	Period	Low	Median	High	Previous
11 Feb	Wed	08:30	International Trade	$ billions	Dec	−45.0	−36.0	−31.0	−40.4
11 Feb	Wed	14:00	Treasury Budget	$ billions	Jan	−126.0	−79.5	−72.4	−17.8
12 Feb	Thu	08:30	Initial Claims	thousands	02/07	510	610	650	598
12 Feb	Thu	08:30	Continuing Claims	thousands	01/31	4750	4800	4880	4788
12 Feb	Thu	08:30	Retail Sales	month-ago %	Jan	−2.2	−0.8	0.3	−2.7
12 Feb	Thu	08:30	Retail Sales Excluding Autos	month-ago %	Jan	−2.3	−0.5	0.6	−3.1
12 Feb	Thu	10:00	Business Inventories	month-ago %	Dec	−2.0	−0.8	0.0	−0.7
13 Feb	Fri	09:55	U. of Mich. Consumer Sentiment	Index	Feb	56.5	61.0	64.0	61.2

Source: Thomson Global Markets, Inc., www.ifrmarkets.com

The consensus forecast tables that other websites post are similar to the previous one. All cover the major economic indicators, but they vary according to the second- and third-tier indicators covered. Because the various news services survey mostly the same economists (there are not a lot of economists paid to forecast monthly indicators), the median forecasts for the major indicators are usually very close to each other.

Trader Tip

Traders don't wait on the actual news release to make their move. The median forecast is what moves the markets before the indicator comes out. Markets move on the news release only if the actual number in the news release differs from the consensus number.

Traders position themselves before the release based on beliefs about whether an indicator is going to be at, above, or below market expectations. So it's not whether an indicator is good or bad at the time of release that moves markets, it is whether the indicator is above or below expectations!

While the key information in a consensus forecast is the consensus number (the median forecast), the range for the forecast is also important. The range is from the lowest to the highest forecast. If an indicator comes out above or below the forecast range, that means the monthly change is way outside expectations and, if it is a key indicator, markets may move significantly. So you need to pay attention to the forecast range in addition to the median.

How about an example of an economic news release messing with the financial markets? On March 7, 2008, the employment situation report for February 2008 was released. The market consensus expected a 25,000 boost in jobs. But the actual number was a 63,000 drop! Markets had to reconsider the still unproven idea that just maybe the economy was in recession. The Dow composite stock index fell 1.2 percent on the belief that the economy and company revenues were worse than expected.

News Affecting the Impact of Economic Indicators

Other news can cause markets to go in a different direction than an indicator suggests. What other financial news can override the impact of an economic indicator on financial markets? Well, the first thing would be another indicator that is either more important or had bigger unexpected movement and that came out at the same time or on the same day. For example, if housing starts come out on a Thursday morning at 8:30 A.M. EST, that indicator has to compete with the weekly initial jobless claims report. It is not uncommon that more than one indicator is released at the same time.

Here's an example: Company news—especially on earnings—can override economic indicator news. If Ford announces a cut in production plans, that can be seen as a reflection on the economy overall and can pull other stocks down—not just Ford's.

Earnings season is a time when company news can impact the stock and bond markets. Earnings season is the period shortly after the end of a quarter, in which companies that have publicly traded stock announce their earnings and revenues for the quarter just ending. Stock analysts have expectations for earnings and revenues and company stock prices have those expectations built in before the company announces the quarterly numbers. So approximately the first six weeks of a quarter are considered the heavy duty portion of earnings season. But earnings reports do trickle out throughout the following quarter.

Some financial websites keep calendars depicting when major corporations release their quarterly earnings statements. For example, CNBC.com has an events calendar for company earnings announcements and consensus expectations for many companies, which can be found under CNBC.com's "Earnings" link. Another good website with free access to earnings is rttnews.com.

What else can trump an economic indicator? A big one is FedSpeak. FedSpeak is when a high-ranking Federal Reserve official (such as the chairman or a regional Fed bank president) makes a speech on the economy and interest rate policy. A speech with new insight on whether the Fed is going to raise or lower interest rates can move markets. FedSpeak is another reason you might want to subscribe to a headline news service—they carry key comments as they happen.

Only from an Economist

On December 5, 1996, then-Fed Chairman Alan Greenspan was giving a rather dry economic speech to the American Enterprise Institute. But then he asked: "But how do we know when 'irrational exuberance' has unduly escalated asset values, which then become subject to unexpected and prolonged contractions as they have in Japan over the past decade?" Greenspan seemed to be implying that if the Fed didn't stick a pin in the stock market balloon by raising interest rates, the stock market would overexpand, burst, and lead to a long recession. The stock market tanked after Greenspan's comment was posted on the news wires. "Irrational exuberance" is now part of the stock market dictionary!

What's another example of economic indicators being overshadowed? On February 6, 2009, the January 2009 jobs report came out. The market consensus had expected a 524,000 drop in payroll employment, but the actual number was even worse: a 598,000 plunge in jobs. What happened to the stock market? A key measure of stock market value—The Dow index—jumped 2.7 percent! Traders pushed up the value of the Dow companies by 2.7 percent in just one day. Why? Market expectations had actually changed after the consensus projection had been published a week earlier.

An earlier released private survey on employment was really bad two days before the employment situation release and initial jobless claims had spiked the day before. The clincher was that major progress had been made in enacting a fiscal stimulus package to get the economy out of recession. All of these factors offset the actual employment situation number being worse than the published consensus.

So, What Am I Looking For?

Whenever an economic indicator is released, the markets focus on key numbers, but there are few indicators for which markets focus on only one number. Either the report has several key facets or, frequently, there are indicators that have one or two volatile subcomponents. An example is auto sales, which we talk more about shortly. The consensus forecasts usually have the break-downs for what is important.

Examples of indicators with more than one area of focus include GDP, the employment situation, and the personal income report. For GDP, the overall GDP growth rate and the price index get market attention. For employment, there are two numbers that stand out—the unemployment rate and payroll job growth—because they come from two separate surveys in the report. For the personal income report, analysts care about the personal income number, the spending figure, and the *inflation* rates in the report.

def•i•ni•tion

Inflation is a trend of rising prices for goods and services in general in the economy.

Other economic reports have a "headline" number and then a second series, because one or more components can create a lot of monthly volatility. Markets need to see the underlying trend in the data, not noise related to volatility. Two standout examples are durable goods orders and retail sales. Durable goods orders are orders to manufacturers for goods that last three years or longer. A very volatile component for durables orders is transportation, because that's where aircraft orders are found. Aircraft orders can be very large one month if a major purchase is made, such as when a commercial airline makes additions to its fleet or when Uncle Sam buys more fighter jets. But those kinds of orders don't happen every month and they distort the underlying trend. So the headline number is total durable goods, but the "core" number is for durable goods excluding transportation.

In retail sales, motor vehicle sales can jump and fall sharply because of off-and-on dealer and manufacturer sales incentives. So the headline number is total retail sales but the core number is for retail sales excluding motor vehicles.

As we learn about each economic indicator, pay attention to the key series and what series may often be excluded due to volatility. Remember, the consensus forecasts help you keep up with this!

The Key Financial Markets

Economic indicators impact all facets of the financial markets and the real economy. The "real economy" is a term used to contrast with financial or price aspects of the economy. The real economy includes manufacturing output, housing construction, employment, sales, inventories, and other nonfinancial aspects. The following sections discuss the primary financial markets that economic indicators affect and thus are closely followed: stocks, bonds, currencies, and commodities. Yes, there's a lot going on, but hang in there. We'll look at them one at a time!

Stock Market

A vital tool that companies use to raise money to operate or expand their business is the stock market. Companies issue shares, which are pieces of ownership in the company. These shares are bought by investors, who are either individuals or companies. Stocks allow issuing companies to be publicly traded, which means the general public can buy into the company. Stocks also are called equities because when you buy stock you have ownership or equity in the company. The value of the stock depends on the public's perception of how profitable the company is and will be in the future. Investors make money on stocks when the value of the stocks rise, or from regular payments from the company called dividends—neither of which is guaranteed.

Only from an Economist

What about those animals you hear about on the news—bull markets and bear markets? A "bull market" is when the stock market is on an upward trend and there is a general mood of optimism about continued gains in the future. In contrast, a "bear market" is on a downward trend and there is broad-based pessimism about losses continuing in the future.

According to Investopedia.com, the use of "bull" and "bear" to describe markets comes from the way the animals attack their opponents. A bull thrusts its horns up into the air while a bear swipes its paws down. These actions are metaphors for the movement of a market. A problem with this labeling of trends is that the stock market is so volatile, it's hard to tell sometimes what direction the trend is.

Bull and bear markets are most commonly used for describing equity markets, but can also be used for other markets.

Economic indicators enter the picture because they can point which way company revenues, costs, and profits are likely headed. Indicators showing healthy growth tend to boost the stock market, while those in decline suggest that the stock market is headed down. While overall growth in the economy is the primary factor behind the direction stock prices take, other factors include interest rates, commodity costs, labor costs, equipment costs, and rent. This leads to a very significant characteristic of the stock market—it is risky. Stock values can go up and down very sharply over the business cycle.

> ### Only from an Economist
>
> What's in the Dow Industrials? Thirty of the largest publicly traded companies in the United States are in the Dow Industrials. The list varies each year, but here's a partial list of companies on the Dow at the beginning of 2009: 3M Company, Alcoa, American Express, AT&T, Bank of America, Boeing, Caterpillar, Chevron, Citigroup, Coca-Cola, DuPont, Exxon Mobil, General Electric, and General Motors.

When tracking equities, you can keep up either with stock prices for individual companies or with stock market indexes. Individual companies would be, for example, General Electric, McDonald's, or Wal-Mart. A stock market index is a composite of the stock prices of a number of companies. Popular stock market indexes include the Dow-Jones industrial average ("the Dow" for short) and the S&P500. These two indexes are produced by information companies, Dow-Jones and Standard & Poor's, respectively.

Bond Market

The bond market is one portion of the credit markets. A bond is a fancy IOU sold by companies or governments, and the bond market is where these debts are bought and sold. Bonds can have varying maturities, ranging from one month to 30 years. Short maturities are called "bills" while medium-length maturities are called "notes." Bills range in maturity from one month to one year. Notes range from two years to ten years. Any maturity over ten years is called a bond.

While there are many types of bonds (including company bonds and city and state bonds, among others), the most popularly traded bonds are those issued by the U.S. Treasury, called "Treasuries" or "Treasurys." Generally, when we talk about the bond market, we are talking about the market for Treasuries.

Here's an example that explains a key point about the interest you get from a bond. Let's say you're buying $1,000 worth of a one-year bill and you pay for the bond according to the market. (Let's say the interest rate is 5 percent.) When you purchase the $1,000 bill, you pay a discount for it. That is, you get $1,000 back in a year, so you pay a discounted amount now, taking into account the 5 percent interest you get later. The question becomes, how much money today at a 5 percent annualized interest rate results in $1,000 in a year? The simplified answer is that you divide $1,000 by 1.05 and get $952.38. This amount plus 5 percent interest ($952.38 x 0.05) gives you $1,000 in a year.

The bottom line is that price and interest rates are in an inverse (opposite) relationship. If you want to trade a bond on the market after buying it, its price goes up when interest rates go down. When interest rates go up, the value of the bond goes down. So, if you trade bonds, losing money is a definite possibility. However, if you buy a bond and hold it to maturity, you still get the full amount you bargained for.

From an indicator perspective, strong economic growth boosts interest rates and causes bond prices to fall, while weak growth eases interest rates and leads to higher bond prices. Higher inflation numbers boost interest rates while lower inflation numbers soften interest rates. If this seems a little complex, don't worry. You'll learn more about bonds in Chapter 22.

Commodities Markets

Commodity exchanges are found in the United States and around the world, and commodities are sometimes seen as the glamorous part of the financial markets; these include oil and gold. But commodities also include "unglamorous" products, such as tin and copper. Commodities range from energy commodities (oil) to metals (gold) to agricultural products (wheat) to other categories (salt). Commodities are goods for which there are buyers, but which are supplied without any qualitative differentiation across the market. That is, you can't tell who produced the product because it is identical from producer to producer.

While most traders see the stock market as one general market (as is also the case for Treasuries), that is hardly the case for commodities. Many of the commodities markets are quite distinct—gold is quite different from cocoa.

What's the bottom line about how economic indicators impact commodity prices? Essentially, stronger economic growth raises demand for commodities and boosts prices. Lower economic growth does the opposite. This applies across the board for the various commodities, from oil to gold to orange juice. It's important to note that growth overseas matters as much as U.S. growth. Economic growth in China and in India can dramatically impact oil and other commodity prices. Selected commodities are discussed in Chapter 12.

Currency Markets

In currency markets, traders exchange currencies from different countries or currency zones. Currencies are exchanged for a wide variety of reasons. These include enabling businesses to import and export goods and services, allowing investment in foreign assets (anything from foreign stocks and bonds to real estate and outright purchases of businesses), and enabling individuals to travel in foreign countries.

There are dozens of currencies that are traded worldwide, but the major currencies that are traded are the U.S. dollar, the euro, the Japanese yen, and the British pound. The euro is a relatively new currency that came into existence on January 1, 1999, as part of the integration of many European countries into a common economy. This economy was based on the 1992 *Maastricht Treaty* among members of the European Union. A large majority of countries in the European Union now use the euro as their official currency. As of early 2009, the countries using the Euro as official currency (called the Eurozone) were Austria, Belgium, Cyprus, Finland, France, Germany, Greece, Ireland, Italy, Luxembourg, Malta, the Netherlands, Portugal, Slovakia, Slovenia, and Spain. A key member of the European Union that did not adopt the euro as its currency, among others, is the United Kingdom, which retained the British pound.

def•i•ni•tion

The **Maastricht Treaty**—formally called the Treaty on European Union—led to the creation of the European Union and eventually the use of the euro currency in most European nations. This treaty was signed on February 7, 1992, in Maastricht, the Netherlands, between the members of the European Community. It took effect on November 1, 1993. The primary motivation for the treaty was to improve trade and economic efficiency within Europe by lowering trade barriers, using common accounting rules, and using a common currency. But the treaty also has some political and judicial aspects. The euro was first introduced to the world as an accounting currency on January 1, 1999—companies kept their financial records in euros rather than in local currencies. The euro began circulating as coins and banknotes on January 1, 2002.

How do economic indicators impact currency exchange rates? Countries with strong economic growth are attractive to investors. So strong economic data in the United States will tend to boost the value of the dollar compared to other countries. A special indicator, however, is the international trade report. The larger the trade gap (deficit) between the United States and other countries, the weaker the dollar is going to be in general because too many dollars have gone overseas.

Tracking the Markets

Many free websites post data for stock indexes, bonds, currencies, and commodities. Commonly used sites are Bloomberg.com, money.cnn.com, and CNBC.com. Modestly priced premium sites include WSJ.com (Wall Street Journal) and FT.com (Financial Times), and are also options.

Is This Good News or Bad News?

Oddly, this is a question financial traders ask themselves at turning points in the economy. Sometimes bad economic news is actually good news for equity markets. And sometimes good news is bad news. And no, I'm not kidding.

When the economy is at a potential turning point in monetary policy, markets may react to economic news in a manner opposite to "normal." For example, if the economy is slowing and the Fed has been reluctant to cut interest rates, unexpectedly weak economic data (especially on the job front) can lead markets to believe that the Fed will reevaluate its view of the economy and lower rates. The lower rates boost the value of stocks, which can result in higher stock prices even though the economic data were negative. Similarly, if retail sales numbers are running hot well into economic expansion, it likely means the economy is strong, but it also means that the Fed is going to raise interest rates to keep inflation from spiking.

Prepping Before an Indicator News Release

Now that you're an official market junkie, you'll like watching the financial market action on a daily or weekly basis. So what are the key pieces of information you should have before an indicator news release, so that you can make the most out of the report? Here's your "official market junkie" checklist:

♦ The consensus forecast

♦ The consensus forecast range

♦ The key components the markets focus on

♦ Potential quirks in the data

♦ Other economic news due out at the same time that could impact market direction

For fun (and maybe even profit), start thinking like a professional trader. What do you think the actual number for an indicator will be? Where do you fit in the consensus range? What are the headline numbers the markets will focus on? How do you think the markets will react if the indicator is stronger or weaker than expected?

Now look ahead of the indicator news release. Do you think bonds or stocks are a good bet? What about gold, oil, or other commodities?

We've covered a lot about how markets react to news releases for economic indicators. Chapter 2 discusses the longer-term impact and business cycles.

The Least You Need to Know

- There is a regular cycle each month for economic indicator news announcements. The cycle includes monthly and weekly reports as well as an occasional quarterly indicator.

- To track indicator news, pick a website with an economic calendar, find a business channel you like, and keep up with what market expectations are before the release.

- For each indicator report, learn what the top one or two components are that the markets and media follow.

- The key markets affected by economic indicators are stocks, bonds, currencies, and commodities.

- Strangely enough, sometimes bad economic news is actually good news for equity markets.

2

Basics About Indicators and Business Cycles

In This Chapter

◆ Understanding recessions and business cycles

◆ How leading indicators give insight into business cycles

◆ Economic data come in a variety of forms

◆ Seasonal aspects of economic data

You're ready to learn the basics about what causes recession and how indicators might give you warning. For you to appreciate the informational content of economic indicators, you need to understand that the economy goes through cycles of expansion and recession. And guess what? Some indicators have more forecasting ability than others, and a key one is the index of leading indicators.

By the time you finish this chapter, you will know what business cycles are and how number formats for indicators differ (and there are some subtle differences!). You should also know why seasonally adjusted data is important. So let's get started! Get comfortable and let's dive right into business cycles.

Business Cycles Matter

The economy doesn't always operate smoothly. The *business cycle* is the recurring ups and downs in economic activity experienced by an economy over the long run. And these swings affect your investments, your business, and maybe even your job. What are the key parts of the business cycle? The National Bureau of Economic Research (NBER), the official business cycle dating committee in the United States, identifies four key points in the business cycle: *peak, recession, trough,* and *expansion.*

def•i•ni•tion

> The **business cycle** refers to the recurring ups and downs in economic activity experienced by an economy over the long run.
>
> The business cycle **peak** is the last month in which the economy is growing overall.
>
> A **recession** is a significant decline in economic activity that permeates the economy and lasts more than a few months.
>
> The **trough** of a business cycle is the last month that economic activity declines.
>
> **Expansion** starts when economic activity resumes growing after the trough of recession.

A business cycle ends when economic activity reaches a high, or peak. Following the peak, the overall economy shrinks. This is the recession part of the cycle.

The next phase in the business cycle is when the economy stops contracting. The final phase of the business cycle is expansion, which is when positive growth resumes after the bottom of recession. The bottom is also known as the trough. However, expansion is the normal state of the economy. Recessions are typically short and normally last about a year.

Many economists like to split the NBER's expansion phase into two informal phases (not defined or dated by the NBER). These are *recovery* and a differently defined *expansion.* Recovery is simply when the economy is growing after the end of the recession but the level of activity is still below that of the prior peak. Then, according to many economists expansion begins when the level of economic activity exceeds the prior peak. While there is no agreement by the media or economists about which definition of expansion is better, the main point is to understand the frequently used term of recovery—which is not part of the NBER's official definitions.

def•i•ni•tion

Recovery is considered part of the expansion phase and it occurs immediately after the business cycle trough, in which the economy is growing but has not reached a level of activity matching the prior peak.

Expansion, as a complementary definition to recovery and according to some non-NBER economists, is the growth period after the end of recession when the level of economic activity exceeds the prior peak.

Picking the Start and End of Recession

The peaks and troughs of the business cycle in the United States are determined by a special committee of the NBER—a nonprofit research organization. Yes, this is the group that says when recession has started and ended. The Business Cycle Dating Committee of the NBER announced the start of the most recent recession on December 1, 2008, saying the previous expansion ended in December 2007 and recession started in January 2008.

How does this business cycle committee decide when recession starts? Many think it is a simple rule of two consecutive quarters of decline in overall economic growth in an indicator called gross domestic product, or GDP (stay tuned for details on gross domestic product in Chapter 3). However, GDP is a quarterly number and is not very timely.

The NBER focuses on two key monthly indicators to set turning points in the economy: payroll employment and personal income, excluding government transfer payments such as unemployment benefits. For determining the start of the recession in 2008, the large loss of employees on company payrolls was the key factor, but the process is still flexible and the dating committee looks at a variety of data. If you are interested in more details on how the NBER thinks about business cycles, go to www.nber.org.

Take a look at the payroll employment chart that follows. When payroll jobs start to decline consistently (that is, if the monthly changes are negative), this is usually the start of a recession. But other indicators also weigh in on the decision.

Payroll employment defines recessions.

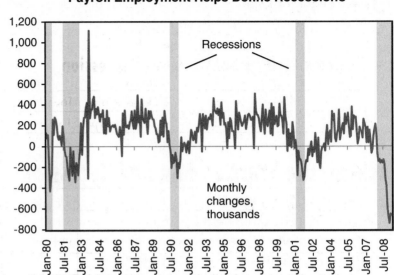

Payroll Employment Helps Define Recessions

Why do we care about business cycles? They affect how well our investments, businesses, and jobs are doing. And economic indicators give us status reports on how the economy is doing and where it's headed.

Only from an Economist

Was the Great Depression really the "greatest" recession? The Great Depression recession lasted from September 1929 through March 1933—a 43-month contraction. But the 1873–1879 recession lasted from November 1873 through March 1879—a 65-month drop in the economy! At the time it was called the "Long Depression." Yes, the Great Depression had the worst impact on the economy by far, but it comes in a distant second in terms of how long it lasted. You've heard President Herbert Hoover being blamed for the Great Depression, but when was the last time you heard President Ulysses S. Grant being blamed for starting the longest recession? For more on the longest recession, do a web search on "the panic of 1873."

What Causes a Recession?

Every business cycle and each recession is different. But there are some recurring causes of recession. These include the Federal Reserve slowing the economy to stop rising inflation, business inventories getting out of hand leading to production cuts, asset bubbles bursting, oil price shocks, and loss of exports.

In the next few sections, we talk about each of these so you get a good understanding of how a recession might get kick-started.

U.S. Business Cycles Since the Great Depression

Duration in Months					
Peak	**Trough**	**Contraction**	**Expansion**	**Cycle**	
Quarterly dates are in parentheses		*Peak to Trough*	*Previous Trough to This Peak*	*Trough from Previous Trough*	*Peak from Previous Peak*
Aug 1929 (III)	Mar 1933 (I)	43	21	64	34
May 1937 (II)	Jun 1938 (II)	13	50	63	93
Feb 1945 (I)	Oct 1945 (IV)	8	80	88	93
Nov 1948 (IV)	Oct 1949 (IV)	11	37	48	45
Jul 1953 (II)	May 1954 (II)	10	45	55	56
Aug 1957 (III)	Apr 1958 (II)	8	39	47	49
Apr 1960 (II)	Feb 1961 (I)	10	24	34	32
Dec 1969 (IV)	Nov 1970 (IV)	11	106	117	116
Nov 1973 (IV)	Mar 1975 (I)	16	36	52	47
Jan 1980 (I)	Jul 1980 (III)	6	58	64	74
Jul 1981 (III)	Nov 1982 (IV)	16	12	28	18
Jul 1990 (III)	Mar 1991 (I)	8	92	100	108
Mar 2001 (I)	Nov 2001 (IV)	8	120	128	128

Rising Interest Rates and the Fed

At times, the economy is so strong that inflation gets out of control. At this point, the Federal Reserve has to step in and raise interest rates to cool the economy and bring down inflation. Normally, the Fed tries to balance interest rates and economic growth so neither extreme occurs, but the Fed does not always manage this. The worst recent inflation-fighting induced recession was in 1981–1982. Annual consumer price inflation hit a high of 13.5 percent in 1980 and the Fed jacked up interest rates (we discuss the Fed's role more in Part 6).

Inventory Build-Up

When businesses build up too much inventory, it's either due to excessive optimism or because demand eases somewhat. This is the college textbook scenario for recession. To bring inventories back in line, manufacturers cut production. These cuts lower employment and income, and the impact spreads to other sectors. But even though an inventory cycle is what is typically cited in textbooks as the cause of recession, it is not the biggest or most common cause. In fact, inventory cycles tend to result in slowdowns rather than recession. A slowdown is simply a period of lower but still positive growth.

When Asset Bubbles Burst

When irrational demand drives up prices for some type of asset, an asset bubble occurs. That is, prices are driven up by investors taking on a herd mentality rather than based on a careful evaluation of value. In the past, numerous recessions have been caused by a run-up on a variety of types of assets that is then sharply reversed. The reversal leads to a drop in confidence and a seizing of credit markets. Lenders become wary of the value of assets behind loans—and these assets can be stocks, multifamily housing, commercial real estate, single-family housing, and others. A massive drop in the stock market played a key role in the four-year recession that started in 1929 and is nicknamed the Great Depression. More recently, a sharp drop in home prices was the initial cause of the recession that started in 2008.

Oil Price Shocks

Oil price hikes have also played a role in recessions. For example, back in 1973–1975 and in 1981, a spike in oil prices cut into consumer spending power and raised business costs, leading to recession.

Inflation got out of control during the late 1970s and at the start of the 1980s, with consumer price inflation hitting an annual high of 13.5 percent in 1980. The Federal Reserve—charged with keeping inflation under control—hit the economic brakes in 1981 and 1982 by boosting interest rates sharply to bring inflation down. A key interest rate controlled by the Fed even topped 19 percent in 1981! In contrast, during the current decade, this short-term rate ranged typically between 1 to 5 percent. This higher interest rate brought the economy into recession, but also tamed the inflation tiger.

Decrease in Exports

Loss of exports is not a major factor for causing recessions in U.S. business cycles; however, a decrease in exports can play a major role in other countries' economies. Exports are bigger sources of income for other emerging or even developed economies. A sharp drop in exports was a major reason for Japan and Germany falling into recession in 2008. However, the United States did see a decline in exports starting in the fourth quarter of 2008. Although exports did not start the recession in early 2008, the fall later did make the recession worse.

Key Facts About Leading Indicators

The good news is that economic indicators can sound the alarm bell as recessions or recoveries begin to develop! Different economic indicators do have different properties relative to the business cycle. Some tend to lead the business cycle (they have forecasting value), whereas others tend to reflect where the economy is right now.

To gain some insight into business cycles, let's look at a report that specifically focuses on forecasting business cycles: the Conference Board Leading Economic Index report.

Here's what's in the report:

- ◆ Official name: The Conference Board Leading Economic Index for the United States, and Related Composite Indexes

- ◆ Release date: Monthly, in the last week of the month for the prior month's data (July release has June data)

- ◆ Produced by: The Conference Board, a nonprofit research organization for businesses, located in New York, New York

- ◆ Form of data: Indexes

- ◆ Market watchers focus on: Monthly percentage changes (view reports at www.conference-board.org/economics/bci)

Key Data Series

The report focuses on the composite index of *leading indicators* and its components. There are two other composite indexes in the report: *coincident indicators* and *lagging indicators*. The three different indexes have different purposes. These are:

◆ The leading index helps to predict peaks and troughs in the business cycle.

◆ The coincident index is a key basis for determining peaks and troughs in the business cycle.

◆ The lagging index largely is used to confirm peaks and troughs as suggested by the coincident index. The lagging index is a second way of bracketing the business cycle.

def•i•ni•tion

Leading indicators are those that typically lead changes in the business cycle.

Coincident indicators typically have changes in strength and weakness in line with the timing of the economy's business cycle.

Lagging indicators are those that have peaks and troughs that typically occur after the highs and lows of the overall business cycle.

◆ The leading index is designed to give advance warning of turning points in the economy.

◆ The coincident index helps to define the peaks and troughs of the business cycle. It measures current production.

◆ The lagging index contains indicators that tend to change long after the overall business cycle changes. For the NBER Business Cycle Dating Committee, it acts to confirm the turning points suggested by the coincident index.

The indexes are composites; they are made up of numerous component indicators. This is because any given indicator can behave differently (timing wise) for any given business cycle. Also, any given indicator can have sharply erratic movements in any given month or two and can give false signals. That's why we use composite indicators—there is safety in numbers to provide the proper economic signals!

What's in Each Composite Index?

We can't go into every detail for each component of the indexes or you'd never finish this chapter! Let's talk a bit about each one, and if you're interested in finding out more, go to the Conference Board's website, www.conference-board.org/economics/bci.

◆ Leading economic index components are: average weekly hours in manufacturing; average weekly initial claims for unemployment insurance; manufacturers' new orders for consumer goods and materials; the index of supplier deliveries, a measure of how fast manufacturers can fill orders; manufacturers' new orders for nondefense capital goods; building permits for new houses; stock prices for 500 common stocks; money supply; an interest rate comparison between a short-term rate and a long-term rate (a large gap generally means the short-term rate has fallen, boosting the economy); and the index of consumer expectations.

◆ Coincident economic index components are: employees on nonagricultural payrolls; personal income less transfer payments from government (such as welfare or Medicaid); industrial production; and business sales.

◆ Lagging economic index components are: average duration of unemployment; inventories to sales ratio for manufacturing and trade; labor costs for manufacturing; the average prime rate charged by banks; commercial and industrial loans; consumer installment credit to personal income ratio; consumer price index for services.

Next, let's look at a few components and see what the business cycle characteristics are.

What Are Important Cyclical Characteristics?

What we find in each of the composite indexes gives us clues about the nature of other indicators that we should look for. What should you look for in other indicators so you can anticipate how the economy affects you?

First, interest-rate-sensitive indicators definitely are more cyclical, but are not necessarily leading. They are leading if changes in interest rates lead to a quick response by businesses or consumers. An example is building permits since lower mortgage rates lead homebuilders to believe that home sales will be up soon. But some sectors take a long time to respond to changes in interest rates because of other factors. An example is nonresidential construction, because such projects are far more expensive than merely building houses and companies wait until building expansion is needed.

Indicators for discretionary purchases can lead and are more cyclical. Necessities are more stable. The timing of home purchases is mostly discretionary, and building permits reflect that. Orders for consumer goods generally change the most for motor vehicles and appliances—the durables portions of this indicator—reflecting spending discretion.

We also see that goods-producing industries (manufacturing and construction, although mining also is a goods-producing sector) tend to lead the business cycle, whereas services lag and are less volatile. This is seen in the inclusion of manufacturing orders and building permits in the leading index while the consumer price index for services is in the lagging index.

Finally, measures of current production are coincident indicators while those portending changes in production (such as factory orders) are leading indicators.

Market Focus on the Leading Economic Indicators Report

The leading index actually does not get much attention in the financial markets except when the economy appears to be teetering on recession, or is in recession with everyone hoping for signs of recovery. When financial markets do care, they focus on percentage changes in the leading index. The coincident index is important for those wanting to know when a recession actually starts and ends. But markets generally look to the future and don't worry much about the coincident or lagging index.

When does the leading index tell us a recession or recovery is coming? Traditionally, there has been a rule of thumb that three consecutive monthly gains after entering the recession phase indicates pending recovery (typically in six to nine months) and three monthly declines in a row after entering expansion points toward pending recession. But studies indicate that this rule of thumb can give false signals sometimes. The three consecutive changes in a new direction may not be very large and may revert to the previous pattern.

Now, however, it's believed that to make the most of the leading index you also have to look at the components. Many economists use the "3 Ds" to evaluate the leading index movement: duration, depth, and diffusion. This just means they look at how long the turnaround has been, how big the changes in the index are, and how many components are participating in the turnaround. So to make the most of the leading index, you really have to look further into the components.

Trader Tip _____

Three of the easiest economic indicators to track for predicting turning points in the economy are motor vehicle sales, building permits, and initial jobless claims.

Key Forms of Economic Data—Starting with Levels

The reports for economic indicators have a variety of forms for the data. There is a particular format for the basic data and then a general monthly change format. The original form for most economic indicators is some type of "level," but these come in many types. Levels typically are expressed as units, dollars, or index levels. Examples of units are (using initial estimates): payroll employment for August 2008 stood at 137.473 million and housing starts were 895,000 for August 2008.

Indexes express the level of an indicator for any particular period relative to a base period. One of the most recognized examples is the consumer price index (CPI). The CPI currently has a base period of January 1982 through December 1984 being equal to 100. That is, the average of the values of consumer prices over this three-year period is set equal to 100.

Values of the CPI are indexed to the base period. The level of the CPI for any period indicates how much higher or lower that period was compared to the 1982–1984 base period. If a CPI value is 100, that means it is equal to the base period. For August 2008, the CPI was 218.880. This means that this month's value was 118.880 percent higher than the average of 1982–1984. The government agency in charge of the CPI changes base periods infrequently—about every 30 years. The basket of goods and services going into the CPI (what consumers buy) is kept updated more frequently—about every five years.

Types of Measures

Data expressed as levels may represent a *stock* type measure or a "flow" type measure. For example, the level of employment is a stock measure. Housing starts are actually a flow, representing how many starts took place during a given month (or other time frame, such as quarter or year).

def•i•ni•tion

A **stock** is a measure for a specific point in time, whereas a flow represents how much economic activity has occurred over a particular time frame.

Economic indicators that are flow measures typically come in one of two forms: simple measures of what was produced, sold, etc., during that month (or quarter), or measures expressed at an annual rate. The retail sales series is an example of a simple measure of sales for the month and only for a one-month time span.

However, some flow measures for a month or quarter are commonly expressed at an annual rate. That is, for a given month, the amount is expressed as if the actual pace for that one month were to continue for a full year. Common economic indicators that are expressed as annualized levels are gross domestic product, personal income, personal consumption expenditures, housing starts, housing permits, existing home sales, and new home sales, among others.

Percent Changes and Other Change Formats

For most economic reports, the key information is not so much the level for a given month or quarter, but how much the indicator changed from the previous period. The focus of analysis is on percentage changes or some other measure of change from month to month or quarter to quarter. Most economic reports focus on simple percentage changes. This merely means dividing the latest month's level by the prior month's level, subtracting 1, and then multiplying by 100 to get the result in percentage form.

Here's an example: The consumer price index level for June 2008 was 217.403 and the value for July 2008 was 219.181. Here's the calculation of a simple percentage change between June and July 2008:

- 219.181 ÷ 217.403 = 1.00818

- 1.00818 − 1 = .00818

- .00818 × 100 = 0.8%

Another common format for some economic indicators is annualized percent changes. These are compound percent changes as if the growth rate continued for a full year. The percentage changes are calculated using the ratio of the latest period level divided by the prior period level. This ratio is then raised to the power of the number of periods in the year (12 for monthly data; 4 for quarterly data). After this compounding, it is put into percentage form by subtracting 1 and then multiplying by 100.

Real GDP is the most prominent example of a measure that's expressed in annualized percentage changes. The final estimate for second quarter 2008 real GDP was $11,727.4 billion (base year 2000 chain dollars) and first quarter real GDP was $11,646.0 billion. The second quarter annualized growth rate is calculated as follows:

- $11,727.4 ÷ $11,646.0 = 1.00699 (rounded)

- $1.00699^4 = 1.2825$

- 1.2825 − 1 = 0.2825

- 0.2825 × 100 = 2.8% annualized (rounded to one decimal place)

Whether the basic form of the data (the level) is annualized or not is a separate issue from whether the monthly change is typically viewed as an annualized percent change or simple percent change. New home sales, existing home sales, housing starts, housing permits, and monthly personal income are stated in levels at an annualized rate for the month. The common percent change that is used for their monthly comparisons is a simple monthly percent change.

A final key monthly change format for economic indicators is simply a monthly difference. This is the current month's level minus the prior month's level. Probably the most noted indicator that is discussed in terms of monthly differences is payroll employment. An example of monthly difference can be created using nonfarm payroll employment numbers for the United States. At the initial release of employment numbers for August 2008, nonfarm payrolls for that month stood at 137.473 million while the July figure was 137.557 million.

Analysts typically discuss the monthly changes in thousands:

- ◆ 137,473,000 − 137,557,000 = −84,000

The monthly difference is minus 84,000, which means that nonfarm payroll employment fell by 84,000 in August 2008.

As a final note on data formats, there is something called a "diffusion index," which we talk about in Chapter 17 on manufacturing surveys.

What Are Seasonally Adjusted Numbers?

Most economic indicators have strong seasonal patterns. The time of year has a larger effect on monthly changes than on the growth trend for the economy. Financial markets are most concerned about the growth trend. Sure, retail sales jumped in December, but how did the numbers compare to a trend? We see similar problems with a drop in housing sales in January and a jump in May—those patterns happen almost every year. To sort out the growth trend from the "noise" of seasonal swings, most economic data are seasonally adjusted. *Seasonal adjustment* is a statistical technique for taking into account typical seasonal pattern of economic data.

def•i•ni•tion

Here's how the Bureau of Labor Statistics (BLS) defines **seasonal adjustment** for employment data:

"Seasonal adjustment is a statistical technique that attempts to measure and remove the influences of predictable seasonal patterns to reveal how employment and unemployment change from month to month."

Over the course of a year, the size of the labor force, the levels of employment and unemployment, and other measures of labor market activity undergo fluctuations due to seasonal events including changes in weather, harvests, major holidays, and school schedules. Because these seasonal events follow a more or less regular pattern each year, their influence on statistical trends can be eliminated by seasonally adjusting the statistics from month to month. These seasonal adjustments make it easier to observe the cyclical, underlying trend and other nonseasonal movements in the series.

As a general rule, the monthly employment and unemployment numbers reported in the news are seasonally adjusted data. Seasonally adjusted data are useful when comparing several months of data.

You can swap employment and unemployment in the previous paragraph for just about any indicator and see the point.

The retail sales chart in the following figure shows both seasonally adjusted and not seasonally adjusted numbers for the United States in some recent years. Notice that for the unadjusted data, sales spike each December and fall sharply in January. Of course, this represents Christmas sales and then the winter slowdown that follows.

If sales typically surge in December, what a market analyst wants to know is whether sales are stronger or weaker than is normal for that month. One can calculate a year-ago percentage change to offset seasonal swings, but year-ago percentages are slow moving and do not give much information about what is happening "right now."

As a simplification, seasonal adjustment is based on calculating a trend line (a moving average of several years' data) and then calculating each month's ratio to the trend line. The unadjusted data are converted to seasonally adjusted numbers by applying each month's ratio to the unadjusted data. Again, as a simplification, if the ratio of unadjusted sales in December to the trend is 1.4 over a number of years, then December data are seasonally adjusted by dividing that month's numbers by 1.4.

This ratio approach is called "multiplicative seasonal adjustment." For some economic indicators, it makes sense to compare the differences between a month and its trend, instead of comparing ratios. Thus, one adds or subtracts this typical difference from unadjusted data to get seasonally adjusted numbers. This version is called "additive seasonal adjustment."

The bottom line? Most economic indicators are seasonally adjusted so market watchers can better determine whether that part of the economy is getting worse or improving in terms of the business cycle. Market watchers prefer to look at seasonally adjusted data.

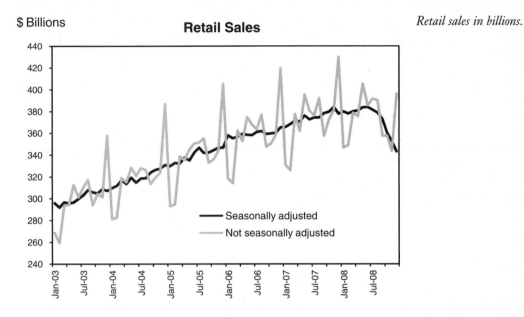

$ Billions

Retail Sales

Retail sales in billions.

Only from an Economist

Seasonality in economic data can show up in some unexpected places. Many companies have sales that are seasonal. Pizza sales, in fact, have big spikes certain days of the year. According to Papa John's Pizza, sales jump on Super Bowl Sunday. Guess what their next two biggest days of the year are? Halloween and the night before Thanksgiving Day! Seasonality is important and can show up in ways you might not expect.

The Least You Need to Know

◆ Key business cycle phases are expansion, peak, recession, and trough.

◆ Recessions can be started by Fed interest rate hikes, asset bubbles bursting, inventory corrections, oil price shocks, and other things.

◆ Leading indicators tend to be interest-rate sensitive, in goods-producing industries, and for discretionary items.

◆ Seasonally adjusted economic indicators are usually best for analyzing the economy.

Gross Domestic Product: The Big Picture

In This Chapter

♦ GDP represents the big picture of economic health

♦ Understanding how GDP reflects a country's production

♦ Three different ways to measure GDP

♦ The four major spending components of GDP

♦ Learning to think about how the economy behaves

Why should you care about *gross domestic product (GDP)*? Because once you understand GDP, you'll start to understand what constitutes a healthy economy, providing you with insight into what makes each component of GDP (such as personal spending and investment) tick. The major point about GDP is that it helps you think about how the economy behaves.

And if you think that kind of insight works to your advantage when it comes to investing your money, you're right! Overall economic growth of the economy affects all of the financial markets. Financial traders have an advantage because they understand the likely direction of the markets. Read on and learn about GDP so that you can gain that advantage, too.

def•i•ni•tion

Gross domestic product (GDP) represents the market value of goods and services produced in the United States. In other words, GDP represents the total production for a country.

The Big Picture

First, let's talk about how the Commerce Department measures the overall economy by calculating GDP. U.S. GDP consists of the total market value of goods and services that are produced by U.S. labor and property located in the United States. So GDP is the measure of total production for the nation for a given time period. GDP is measured quarterly, but comes in an annualized format.

Measuring GDP is a tough job. Why? Because during the production process, value is added at each step of the way by manufacturers, wholesalers, retailers, importers, and exporters. With so many cooks in the kitchen, you can see how hard it is to keep track of all the "added value."

GDP is measured in three different ways:

◆ By adding up total spending in the economy

◆ By adding up all of the income received in the economy

◆ By adding up the "value added" along each step of production and distribution

As you can imagine, this measurement creates a huge accounting system in the government and it even has a name: the National Income and Product Accounts (NIPA).

The first two approaches to calculating GDP receive the most attention. In fact, these two approaches make up two sides of this economic ledger—spending and income—and both sides should end up with the same number.

Using different data sources can lead to some differences in the final tally. But most "economy watchers" focus on the first one, total spending in the economy. The spending components also go by other names: product accounts or, more commonly, expenditure categories. We focus on the spending components shortly.

Key Facts About the GDP Report

Where's all the spending in the economy? GDP adds it up by sectors, with different types of behavior for each. In the GDP expenditure accounts, there are four major sectors: consumer, investment, government, and international trade. Yes, this sounds complex. But the formula for GDP breaks it down nicely:

$$GDP = C + I + G + X - M$$

Here's how each component in the formula is defined: C = total spending by consumers, I = total investment by businesses, G = total spending by government on current expenditures and investments, X = exports, and M = imports. So now you have a picture of how GDP is calculated. Don't forget the formula. While this GDP accounting seems a little detailed, keep in mind that this accounting system helps you think about how the economy behaves! You will be more comfortable with the GDP components as we get into more everyday examples of what each sector is about.

Here's what's in the official Gross Domestic Product report:

◆ Official name: Gross Domestic Product

◆ Release date: During the last week of each month. The data are quarterly, with the initial estimate known as the "advance" estimate. The first revision is known as the "preliminary" estimate.

◆ The second revision to a quarter is called the "final" estimate. The advance estimate is released the month after the end of the quarter, with the next two estimates the following two months. For example, the first quarter advance GDP is released in April, Q1 preliminary in May, and Q1 final in June.

◆ Produced by: Bureau of Economic Analysis (BEA), U.S. Department of Commerce

◆ Form of data: GDP and its components are in annualized dollars and are in both current dollars and in inflation-adjusted dollars. GDP, components, and price indexes are seasonally adjusted. GDP and components also are published as percent changes. Inventory investment and net exports, however, are in dollar levels and dollar differences (change from prior quarter).

◆ Market watchers focus on: Annualized quarterly percentage changes for overall GDP and major components (view reports at www.bea.gov/National/Index.htm)

> ### Only from an Economist
>
> Did you know that the United States—with current-dollar GDP of $13.8 trillion in 2007—was the number-one economy in the world, followed by Japan as number two and Germany as number three? Even though the United States has only about 5 percent of the world's population, it contributes about 25 percent of the world's output. Sources: U.S. Department of Commerce and the CIA Factbook.

Top three GDP gross world product.

Top 3 GDP as Shares of Gross World Product, 2007

U.S.
25%

Japan
8%

Germany
6%

Rest of World
61%

Real GDP vs. Fake GDP

Let's talk about *real GDP* because that's what most economy watchers focus on in the GDP report. Does that mean there's fake GDP? No, not really. But what is real GDP?

Here's an example: We can measure motor vehicle sales in dollars or in units sold. Units sold gets around the problem of inflation, which distorts the count in dollars. Essentially, real GDP is inflation-adjusted GDP. Real GDP is expressed in dollar terms, but the real dollars are given after adjusting for inflation

The base year for real GDP currently is the year 2000 since that is the baseline for the price index used to deflate current-dollar GDP. Real GDP is essentially the dollar value of GDP as if there was no inflation before or since the year 2000. Changes in dollar value of GDP represent only growth (or contraction) in the economy. Because the price index has the year 2000 for its base period, real GDP is said to be expressed in year 2000 dollars or chain dollars. Why "chain dollars"? The statistical technique to deflate to real GDP actually chains together the deflated dollars from one quarter to the next. This is why another name for real GDP is chain dollar GDP. Nearly all economists and media just call it GDP or real GDP, though.

When you compare real GDP dollar amounts from quarter to quarter or from year to year, you can tell if output is higher or lower by comparing real dollar levels, and comparing how much (such as percent higher). With current-dollar GDP, you do not know how much physical output is higher or lower in different time periods, since inflation has not been taken into account. Current-dollar GDP is more commonly called *nominal GDP.*

Today—as in decades past—most economy watchers focus on real GDP instead of nominal GDP. But it used to be that everyone would specifically say "real GDP" when they meant inflation-adjusted GDP. Now, almost everyone assumes that when you say GDP, you mean real GDP.

def•i•ni•tion

Real GDP is actually inflation-adjusted GDP. **Nominal GDP** is current-dollar GDP.

The following table shows items included in the GDP report for real GDP.

Real GDP Components by Percentage Shares, 2007

Component	Chain $	% Share
Gross domestic product	**$11,523.9**	**100.0%**
Personal consumption expenditures:	**8,252.8**	**71.6**
Durable goods	1,242.4	10.8
Nondurable goods	2,392.6	20.8
Services	4,646.2	40.3
Gross private domestic investment:	**1,809.7**	**15.7**
Fixed investment	1,808.5	15.7
Nonresidential	1,382.9	12.0
Structures	304.6	2.6
Equipment and software	1,078.9	9.4
Residential	453.8	3.9
Change in private inventories	–2.5	–0.0

continues

Real GDP Components by Percentage Shares, 2007   (continued)

Component	Chain $	% Share
Net exports of goods and services:	**−546.5**	**−6.6**
Exports	1,425.9	12.4
Imports	1,972.4	−17.1
Government consumption:		
Expenditures & gross investment	2,012.1	17.5
Federal	752.9	6.5
State and local	1,259.0	10.9

Consumer Spending: The Economy's Heavy Lifter

The consumer sector typically makes up about two thirds of spending in the economy. If the consumer sector stumbles, so does the overall economy. The official name for this expenditure category is *personal consumption expenditures*, or PCEs.

Within personal consumption expenditures, there are three broad categories that have very different characteristics in terms of how they behave over the business cycle. These broad components are durable goods, nondurable goods, and services.

def•i•ni•tion

Personal consumption expenditures (PCEs) are the purchases of goods and services by persons and nonprofit institutions that primarily serve households.

Here's a quick overview:

♦ **Durable goods are goods with expected lifetimes of three years or longer.** Examples are motor vehicles, furniture, and appliances. The durables component is the most cyclical (with the largest ups and downs over business cycles) for two main reasons: first, the longer lifetimes enable you to postpone purchases during difficult economic times; second, durable goods are sensitive to fluctuations in interest rates.

♦ **Nondurables are goods with expected lifetimes of less than three years.** Examples are food, clothing, gasoline, and fuel oil. Nondurable goods are largely considered necessities, and thus, aren't very cyclical.

◆ **Services PCEs cover a wide range of services purchased or consumed by households.** Examples are housing services, household operation (including electricity and natural gas), transportation services, medical care, education, personal care, recreation, and lodging. Services PCEs are less sensitive to interest rates and so vary only moderately over the business cycle.

Let's stop and think a second about why differing cyclical behavior is something that is important to understand. If the economy is about to move into a new phase of the business cycle, that likely will affect your investments in varying degrees. For example, if a recession is pending, it is good to know which sectors are likely to be harder hit and which are going to be safer. For example, homebuilders and automakers typically suffer significantly in recession. Meanwhile, health-care providers generally do not lose business as much.

What Are Real Investments? (Hint: Not the Stock Market!)

The official name for the investment spending component of GDP is "gross private investment." The word "gross" is used because the investment numbers do not include a deduction for depreciation. Investment in terms of GDP is not the same as the purchase of stocks on the New York Stock Exchange.

Here, we're talking about the actual physical production of buildings, business equipment, investment in software, and goods on store shelves. Now, let's take a look at the "subcomponents" in gross private investment.

Only from an Economist
Attention! Investment in GDP is not the same thing as what your stock broker tries to sell you, such as stocks in a company or bonds. In GDP, investment reflects physical assets used for production. This includes business equipment, structures, and inventories. Also, residential investment is considered part of business investment in GDP because homeowners are treated as businesses. Houses also "produce" housing services—the use of the house-but use of the house goes into personal consumption.

Fixed Investment

The first major break in investment components is between fixed investment and inventory investment. Fixed investment measures additions and replacements in the stock of private fixed assets. By fixed assets, we mean they stay with the company. Some fixed investment assets certainly move around (for instance, aircraft for airlines and cars and trucks used by businesses), but they are still retained by the company.

Inventory investment is not fixed because these assets are not retained by the company in the long run—they move on as they are sold.

Again, fixed investment refers to physical assets, not the stock market. Within fixed investment, there are two divisions: nonresidential and residential. First, let's talk about nonresidential fixed investment.

The real GDP growth chart that follows shows how two of the more volatile components—PCEs on durables and residential investment (we talk about this later in this chapter)—move up and down during expansions and recessions more than other components.

Real GDP growth and cyclical components.

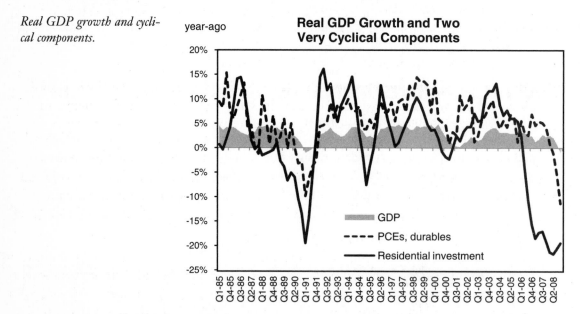

Nonresidential Fixed Investment

Nonresidential fixed investments have two major components: structures, and equipment and software. Nonresidential structures are expenditures by businesses on structures. Examples are office buildings, retail stores, hotels and motels, private hospitals and education facilities, manufacturing plants, warehouses, public utilities, mining exploration, and farm buildings. Some of these types of investments are also done by the government, but they go in the government spending category (Veterans Administration hospitals and public schools are examples).

What are some characteristics of this component? Nonresidential structures investment is cyclical for three key reasons. First, it is sensitive to interest rates: when rates are high, new projects are deferred. Second, businesses generally invest in new structures only when existing structures are at (or approaching) full capacity. You don't build a new building when the one you are using is half empty! Reaching full capacity depends on the business cycle; investment in nonresidential structures generally picks up speed late in economic expansions. Typically, it also follows business investment in equipment.

Finally, the decision to make an investment in structures is usually made late in expansion because it is such a major commitment. Generally, big bucks are required for this type of investment and funding the construction requires big decisions. Even if the company has a lot of cash lying around, the decision may not be an easy one. The board of directors may argue over whether there are better uses for the cash, such as buying another company or building a new structure. When there isn't a lot of cash lying around, the company might have to issue new stock or bonds, which are also big decisions. So investing in nonresidential structures typically occurs only when there truly is a demand for it—and late in expansion.

After structures, the second major category in nonresidential fixed investment is business equipment and software. The equipment series covers purchases of equipment by private businesses and nonprofit institutions for the production of other goods and services. Examples are information processing equipment and software, medical equipment, office and accounting equipment, industrial equipment, and transportation equipment. Note that the information processing category includes both software already *included* with a computer purchase and software purchased *separately* by the business. Transportation is a key category and includes business purchases of cars, trucks, and even aircraft.

As you can see in the following equipment and software chart, over the business cycle, investment in business equipment and software and in nonresidential structures has larger ups and downs than GDP. Equipment investment is easier to start up or cut back than nonresidential structures. Therefore, it typically leads the structures component during expansions and recessions.

The business equipment and software series is cyclical because purchases are interest-rate sensitive. Their long lives also mean that new purchases can be postponed if needed. This category typically has higher ups and downs than nonresidential structures. There are more companies buying equipment than companies needing additional building space.

During an expansion, equipment investment rises more quickly than nonresidential structures. Why? It's simple. Expanding capacity with equipment is cheaper and less of a long-term risk than adding a structure. And during economic downturns, equipment investment can be turned off faster than stopping the construction of new structures. Once there's a signed contract, construction of a nonresidential structure generally continues, even if at a slower pace, during a recession.

Equipment and software investment.

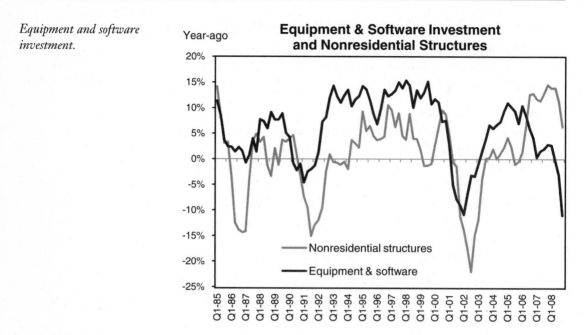

Where Residential Housing Investment Fits In

The Commerce Department treats housing investment in GDP as being entirely in the business sector. Residential investment doesn't include the purchase of a house, but rather the construction of the housing. Examples include single-family and multi-family buildings, mobile homes, brokers' commissions, home improvements, and net purchases of existing structures. The vast majority of residential investment is new construction for single-family homes, followed by multi-family homes.

You're probably not surprised to hear that residential investment is cyclical. New construction is sensitive to how strong home purchases are, which in turn are sensitive to mortgage rates, unemployment, and income growth. When economic conditions are not good, home purchases are deferred, resulting in an excess supply of new homes. But when the economy perks up, many new households are eager to buy houses. Early in an economic recovery, there's often a surge in both housing purchases and residential investment. At that point, interest rates have fallen and income prospects have improved.

Inventory Investment: The Tail That Wags the Dog

Wondering where inventories fit in GDP? The portion of business investment that doesn't fall under the fixed category is "inventory investment." What are inventories? These are basically things sitting on company shelves, ready for sale. But there is more to it than that. It's not just retailers that have inventories but also manufacturers and distributors. *Inventories* include production materials held by manufacturers as well as partially completed manufactured goods and factory goods not yet shipped out. Inventories also include goods for sale or resale in retail stores and in wholesale warehouses.

Now, why do we care about inventories? Inventories provide key signals on the direction of the economy. Businesses that sell products need goods to put in warehouses or on store shelves. But from a GDP perspective, it's the change in inventories that is counted as new investment each quarter or year. Remember that GDP

def•i•ni•tion

According to the Commerce Department, private **inventories** consist of materials and supplies, work in process, finished goods, and goods held for resale.

is a measure of current production for a given time period, so it's the difference in inventory levels at the end of the period compared to the start of the next period that matters. If GDP included the total levels of inventories, that would "double count" what was produced in an earlier period.

If inventories decrease (a negative change), the difference still must be included in GDP. It's included in GDP as a negative because the inventory decline shows up as expenditures for consumers, businesses, or the government. Again, looking at the changes in inventories avoids double counting—either between new and existing inventories or between inventories and spending in other categories.

Only from an Economist

It's not simply inventory changes that affect the upcoming strength of GDP. It's the unplanned changes in U.S.-produced inventories that make the difference. It isn't always easy to tell the difference between planned and unplanned changes and how much of inventories is being imported versus coming from domestic producers.

Businesses want inventories to be in line with sales. This is key. Unexpected increases or decreases in inventories often suggest changes in the business cycle. For example, strong sales and declining inventories suggest a needed boost in production. But weak sales and increasing inventories point toward production cuts until inventories are back in line.

Businesses often anticipate changes, and if they expect demand to pick up they will build inventories to meet the expected demand. When demand then matches inventories, there's no impact on the production trend. Take a look at the real GDP growth and business inventories chart that follows. It's actually the unplanned changes in inventories that can boost or lower production. And planned or unplanned inventory changes can only be determined within the context of spending trends.

Real GDP growth and business inventories.

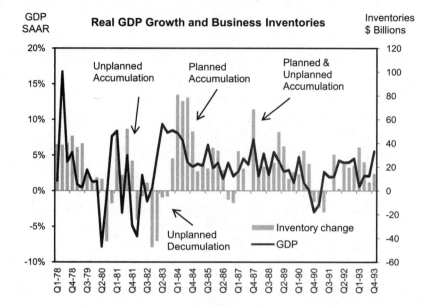

Within GDP, the way to compare sales trends is to look at *final sales of domestic product*. Want another way to look at final sales? They are equal to the sum of personal consumption expenditures, gross private fixed investment, government consumption expenditures and gross investment, and net exports. Are final sales strengthening or weakening? Are inventories changing to meet that trend or did inventories misjudge the trend? What is the momentum of each of those components in GDP?

Before we move on, let's touch on how inventories are affected by imports. Because more inventories are imported than in decades past, inventory swings have less impact on production changes than they used to. Today, if inventories exceed final sales needs, the cutback in production is felt by both U.S. producers and by manufacturers overseas. What this means is that changes in GDP are usually less pronounced than unplanned changes in inventories.

def•i•ni•tion

Final sales of domestic product is equal to GDP less the change in private inventories.

Trader Tip

A quick way to see if inventory growth is out of line with demand is to compare growth rates for final sales with GDP. If GDP growth is outstripping final sales, inventory accumulation may be a problem.

Government Purchases

The complete name for the government component in GDP is "government consumption expenditures and gross investment."

Current consumption expenditures are broken down into durables, nondurables, and services. The durables component includes items such as spare parts. The nondurables component includes items such as petroleum, office supplies, food, clothing, and ammunition. The services component is primarily employee compensation but also includes these subcomponents: research and development, travel, consulting services, rents, and utilities expenses.

Gross investment at the federal level includes equipment such as aircraft, tanks, missiles, ships, and trucks. Structures investment is also included in government gross investment, and it covers military construction, buildings, highways, and streets. At state and local levels, spending on services is mainly for employee compensation, but also includes education and law enforcement. Structures investment covers items such as expenditures on highways and bridges, correctional facilities, and waste treatment facilities.

Net Exports

The net exports component in GDP is the difference between exports and imports of goods and services. Put simply: net exports equals the stuff we sell to other countries minus the stuff we purchase from overseas. This also includes services that are exported and imported. Services cover a lot; examples are travel (tourism), consulting services, banking, and even electricity sold across national borders.

Now back to where exports and imports fit into how GDP adds up. Exports are added to GDP because they were produced in the United States, but are not included in the other measures of final expenditures (C+I+G). Imports are subtracted from GDP because they were produced outside of the United States, but are included in portions of personal consumption, business equipment investment, inventory investment, and even parts of the government components. Remember, GDP is a measure of domestic production.

You've been introduced to basic concepts in GDP in this chapter. We build on that knowledge in the next chapter by looking at how monthly economic indicators relate to GDP components. We also look at how the economy behaves—you're starting to think like an economist!

The Least You Need to Know

◆ GDP measures overall production in the economy and is the broadest measure of economic output.

◆ Forward momentum in GDP growth is determined by how healthy the fundamentals are for each sector.

◆ Unplanned inventory swings can lead to a spurt or drop in GDP growth.

◆ The most cyclical components of GDP are consumption of durables, residential investment, durables equipment investment, and nonresidential structures investment.

4

GDP and Monthly Indicators

In This Chapter

- ◆ Understanding monthly indicators
- ◆ Key indicators and sector fundamentals
- ◆ Tracking down source data for GDP
- ◆ Price indexes and GDP
- ◆ Measuring GDP by income

In Chapter 3, you got an introduction to the big picture of GDP. Now you're going to learn some fascinating details about monthly indicators' relationships to GDP. By the time you finish this chapter, you'll have a solid grasp on how these indicators lend insight into GDP components ... and it's not as complex as you might think.

You already understand some basics of GDP, so we're going to hit the ground running. Grab your beverage of choice, get comfortable, and hop back onto the path of becoming a savvy market watcher!

Monthly Indicators and GDP Components

The bottom line is that we want to know how monthly economic indicators give us the big picture for the economy. GDP paints a broad picture of what's going on and actually condenses the major sectors into four manageable parts. Now we want to learn which monthly indicators impact those four parts (C + I + G + Net Exports or personal consumption plus private investment plus government expenditures plus net exports). How do we start to tie together the monthly indicators to get the overall direction of the economy? We tie them in with GDP components!

There are two basic ways to view monthly indicators and their relationships to GDP components. First, some series are *source data* for GDP. The Commerce Department uses these indicators to estimate portions of GDP. Second, other monthly indicators suggest how strong or weak a particular GDP component will be in coming months. The expenditure approach to GDP (C + I + G + Net Exports) helps you think about how other economic indicators fit into the big picture, such as which indicators tell you how strong the consumer sector currently is in GDP.

GDP divides the expenditure view of the economy into relatively tidy categories that have common factors that affect each sector's growth. After you learn the basic GDP expenditure components and their fundamentals, you'll be thinking like an economist! It may seem daunting now, but by the time you finish this book, you'll understand the underlying factors that determine the strength for a sector. These factors are what economists call *sector fundamentals*.

def•i•ni•tion

Source data are economic indicators and surveys that are available early and are used by a statistical agency (such as the Commerce Department) to calculate another economic indicator that is published later.

Sector fundamentals are the underlying factors for each sector that determine sector growth rates.

Here's a quick list of the key indicators that affect the different sectors:

- **Consumer spending:** Employment, unemployment rate, personal income, interest rates, debt, house prices, stock market, inflation, and confidence

- **Business fixed investment:** Capacity utilization rates, interest rates, corporate profits, and cost of construction and new equipment

- **Inventory investment:** Expected demand, inventory-to-sales ratios, and interest rates

◆ **Residential investment:** Employment, personal income, unemployment rate, mortgage rate, and unsold inventories of houses on the market

◆ **Government consumption expenditures and investment:** Overall economic growth, fiscal policy on deficit spending at the federal level, changes in defense spending needs, and the fiscal policy against deficit spending at the state and local government levels

◆ **Exports:** Economic growth overseas, export prices, and the exchange value of the dollar

◆ **Imports:** Economic growth in the United States, import prices, and the exchange value of the dollar

Now let's take a closer look at the key indicators in each sector.

Consumer Fundamentals

What determines consumer spending? The most important factors are job growth and income growth. Both directly affect consumers' budgets. The unemployment rate can not only affect income directly, but it can also have a psychological impact. What do you do when you hear about people losing their jobs? You probably save more because you're worried about losing your own job.

You've already learned that the interest rate has a huge effect on durables PCEs. For instance, higher interest rates make car payments less affordable. Think about it this way: the more money you pay in interest and principal for that car, the less income you have left over for going out to a nice restaurant.

Housing prices affect consumer spending, too. When housing prices rise sharply, it's easier for homeowners to borrow against home equity (a home equity line of credit or HELOC). Declining house prices have the opposite effect. Similarly, for investors household wealth gets a boost when the stock market rises, and when the stock market goes down, investor wealth decreases. Changes in consumers' wealth affect their willingness to spend. Inflation also has indirect effects on consumer spending. For example, a spike in gasoline prices reduces how much money consumers have to spend on other things.

And guess what else affects consumer spending-consumer confidence. We are not talking about how good someone feels about himself or herself—no mirrors needed here. *Consumer confidence* is how optimistic or pessimistic consumers are about the economy currently or in the near future. When consumer confidence is rattled, consumers cut back on spending. We talk more about a lot of these issues in coming chapters on employment, personal income, consumer confidence, and home sales.

def•i•ni•tion

Consumer confidence is how optimistic or pessimistic consumers are about current conditions in the economy or how conditions will be in the near future. Later, we'll discuss surveys that attempt to measure consumer confidence.

Investment Fundamentals

How much businesses spend to expand production capacity depends on many factors. For businesses, fixed investment (structures and equipment), capacity utilization, and expected capacity utilization directly affect investment spending. If a business is operating near full capacity or expects to be operating at full capacity in coming quarters, then a business will likely want to expand.

What else affects investment? Interest rates, corporate profits, and the cost of construction or new equipment. Lower interest rates mean that it's easier for the rate of return from the investment to be higher than the cost of paying for the investment. Corporate profits help fund investment, so low corporate profits mean reduced funding.

When it comes to inventory investment, expected demand—by consumers, other businesses, government, and foreign purchasers—is the biggest factor affecting how much businesses want to put into inventories. One way of determining whether inventories should be boosted or reduced is to look at inventory-to-sales ratios. If demand is expected to rise, then a higher ratio is likely appropriate in the near term. Interest rates also affect inventory accumulation as inventories are usually financed. With lower interest rates, companies can afford larger inventories.

Many of the same factors that affect consumer spending also impact residential investment. These include employment, income, the unemployment rate, interest rates, consumer confidence, house prices, and inventories of unsold houses on the market. If there are a large number of unsold houses, then residential investment will be weaker.

Another big factor affecting how far your monthly paycheck goes is mortgage rates. When mortgage rates go up, household budgets are greatly impacted. Remember how rising interest rates influence your ability (and desire) to buy a car? Well, mortgage rates have an even bigger impact on housing than interest rates do on your purchase of durable goods. It makes perfect sense when you think about it. The mortgage payment is a much bigger chunk of your budget than is your car note payment.

Government Consumption Expenditures and Investment Fundamentals

Did you know that nearly all state and local governments in the United States are not allowed to have deficits? During recessions, state and local governments actually engage in budget cutting to prevent deficit spending.

As you probably do know, however, the federal government is under no such constraint. The federal government is allowed to run budget deficits to boost spending. And at the federal level, spending can be affected by special spending programs, such as an increase or reduction in defense spending. The primary factor affecting the growth rate of government spending in the GDP component, though, is overall economic growth. This boosts both household income and business income, resulting in more personal and corporate tax revenue for states. Other revenues also get a lift—such as sales taxes from stronger retail sales and property taxes from higher real estate values.

Net Export Fundamentals

The main factors affecting exports are economic growth overseas, export prices, and the exchange value of the dollar. U.S. export prices and the exchange value of the dollar determine how much foreigners pay for goods from the United States. Most analysts look at foreign GDP as a basic measure of overseas demand. While it is income growth that directly affects how much consumers overseas can afford to buy, GDP growth is often seen as a more readily available measure that closely tracks income growth. What affects imports into the United States? Imports are determined by income growth in the United States, import prices, and the exchange value of the dollar. Stronger income growth boosts purchases of imports. A stronger exchange value of the dollar and lower import prices raise the demand for imports by consumers and businesses in the United States.

Only from an Economist

Is GDP the best way to judge a country's standard of living? Some think not. While gross domestic product measures output, GDP is not a measure of the well-being of a country's citizens. GDP does not take into account pollution, traffic congestion, stress, health of workers, and similar issues. One country has a different idea of what to measure for well-being. The country of Bhutan prefers to focus on what a former king of that country called gross national happiness (GNH).

Yes, it's more of a philosophy than an actual economic measure, and it's based largely on Bhutan's Buddhist culture. The four pillars of GNH are sharing prosperity broadly, balancing growth against maintaining cultural traditions, protecting the environment, and maintaining good government.

Monthly Source Data for GDP

If you find that you just can't wait to get a glimpse of the GDP before the report comes out at the end of each month, you're in luck. The Commerce Department has an extensive list of economic data used to derive GDP numbers. Some numbers are available early in the estimation process while others become available with a lag (even up to a year later). For the later data, the Commerce Department initially estimates the missing numbers.

But there are a number of monthly economic indicators that GDP watchers track to estimate what the upcoming GDP number is going to be. Any moderately serious economy watcher (that's you!) can track these monthly releases to get an idea as to how components are going to do in the upcoming GDP report.

Here's a list of key monthly source data for GDP:

◆ **PCEs:** New motor vehicle sales (by units) and retail sales excluding motor vehicles (Census data in dollars)

◆ **Nonresidential structures investment:** Construction outlays (private nonresidential component)

◆ **Business equipment:** Shipments of nondefense capital goods in the durable orders report, imports of capital equipment (added in the estimate for producers' durable equipment or PDEs) in the international trade report, and exports of capital equipment (subtracted in the PDEs estimate) in the international trade report

◆ **Residential investment:** Construction outlays (private residential component)

- **Inventory investment:** Monthly business inventories

- **Government consumption expenditures and investment:** Construction outlays (public outlays component) and monthly Treasury report

- **Net exports:** Exports and imports in the monthly international trade report

GDP Price Indexes

Okay, we've talked about real GDP merely being current-dollar GDP deflated by price indexes. But for economy watchers, the price indexes have their own value as broad measures of inflation for the economy. Key monthly inflation indexes (you'll learn more about this in a later chapter) are the consumer price index and the producer price index. They cover far less than the overall economy. The consumer price index measures how fast prices are rising for consumers while the producer price index shows how quickly prices received by manufacturers are going up. Many financial traders care more about economy-wide inflation than inflation simply at the consumer or producer levels. Economy-wide inflation affects interest rates and profits, for example.

Not only do GDP price indexes cover the consumer sector, but they also cover the other expenditure components, such as investment, government, exports, and imports. The GDP report has broader coverage on inflation than any other inflation measure.

Trader Tip _____

For the inflation part of the GDP report, markets focus on the overall GDP price index, PCE price index, and the "core" PCE price index (which excludes volatile food and energy components).

Inflation measured by the GDP price index is not as volatile as that based on the price index for PCEs. The latter can have large swings due to changes in oil prices (which affect gasoline and heating oil). Also, inflation for investment goods in GDP tends to be more subdued.

During 2008, the BEA shifted its focus regarding what is best to look at for overall inflation. In the GDP report, the BEA now calls the price index for gross domestic purchases its "featured" index for inflation. Why the change in focus? It's simple. The sharp swings in oil prices really messed up some quarterly movements in the GDP price index. Using the domestic purchases price measure gives a better picture of quarterly changes in inflation because it does not include the oil imports component which has unusual effects in the overall GDP price index.

GDP versus PCE price indexes.

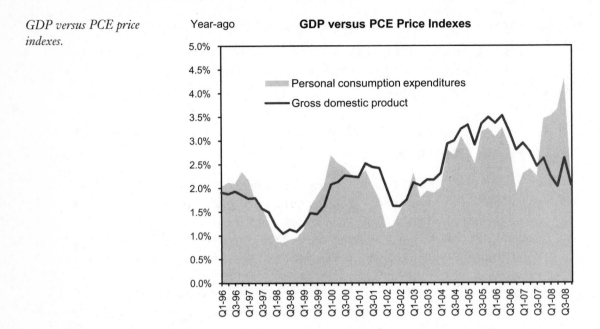

As a simplification, the price index is based on weighting the price changes for each of the components, but the import component is a subtraction because of how GDP is defined (C + I + G + X - M). If you take out exports and imports of the calculation of GDP, you are left with domestic purchases, and this eliminates the quirks that come from swings in oil import prices.

The following GDP Price Indexes chart (which includes gross domestic purchases price indexes) makes the economy-wide inflation in 2008 more clear, illustrating the mid-year surges in oil prices and the drop at year end. Looking only at the GDP price index would not reveal how high inflation really had been in the middle of 2008 because the accelerating import price component was subtracted from the rest of the index. But by excluding export and import prices, the gross domestic purchases price index picked up the surge in inflation felt by consumers, businesses, and even government.

For a better perspective, the BEA also has unpublished numbers for the price index for gross domestic purchases but excluding food and energy. The ex-food and energy gross domestic purchases inflation measure can be seen as portraying the underlying inflation trend for the economy, while the overall gross domestic purchases price index indicates where the trend is headed, provided that food and energy price changes are more than just a temporary blip.

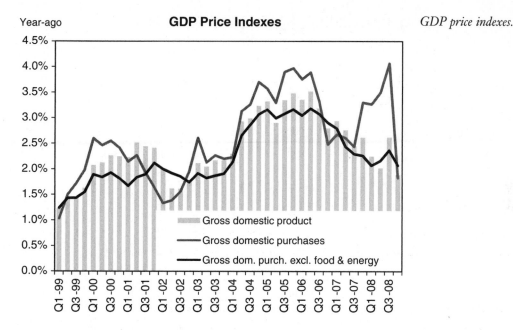

GDP price indexes.

It is interesting that the financial media has not yet picked up on the fact that the BEA has the gross domestic purchases price index as it "featured" index and continues to highlight the overall GDP price index. So the next time you read a news story on the latest GDP report, look to see if the media has gotten the news that the BEA has a new and improved version of the GDP inflation measure.

GDP Measured by Income

There are two primary methods of measuring GDP: by expenditures and by income. We've talked about the expenditures side. Now let's take a look at the income side. One of the key ideas about measuring GDP by income is that income equals expenditures (including investment expenditures, which cover how savings are used).

GDP is basically made up of national income, income from outside the United States less income paid to rest of the world, consumption of fixed capital, and the statistical discrepancy between income-based GDP and expenditure-based GDP. Check out the following table.

Nominal (Current-Dollar) GDP by Income, 2007

	$ Billions	% of GDP
Gross domestic product	$13,807.5	100.0
Plus: Income from the rest of the world	861.7	6.2
Less: Income payments to the rest of the world	759.3	5.5
Equals: Gross national product	13,910.0	100.7
Less: Consumption of fixed capital	1,720.5	12.5
Less: Statistical discrepancy	–81.4	–0.6
Equals: National income	12,270.9	88.9
Compensation of employees	7,812.3	56.6
Wage and salary accruals	6,355.7	46.0
Supplements to wages and salaries	1,456.6	10.5
Proprietors' income	1,056.2	7.6
Rental income of persons	40.0	0.3
Corporate profits with IV & CCA*	1,642.4	11.9
Net interest and miscellaneous payments	664.4	4.8
Taxes on production & imports less subsidies	963.2	7.0
Business current transfer payments	100.2	0.7
Current surplus of government enterprises	–7.9	–0.1

Inventory valuation and capital consumption adjustments

Note that the largest part of GDP by income is national income, which makes up about 90 percent of nominal GDP. Within national income, the two components that have the biggest impact on the strength of GDP growth are the income series related to personal income and to corporate profits. The GDP income accounts do break out personal income separately from national income (you'll learn more about this in Chapter 8). Personal income is the key driver behind the strength of personal spending.

In 2008, corporate profits made up about 10 percent of nominal GDP. But this component is very volatile, so the percentage share can vary. You should know that corporate profits are important to the economy because they fund—either directly or indirectly—interest income and dividend income.

Finally, corporate profits play a key role in funding business investment. The three biggest factors affecting business investment are profits, interest rates, and utilization rates of plants and equipment. Strong corporate profits can be a source for upgrading or expanding business equipment, or even boosting structures investment. Profits generally lead business investment during economic expansion and recession.

The following business fixed investment chart shows that corporate profits are more volatile than business fixed investment, but changes in corporate profits generally lead business fixed investment over the business cycle. Additionally, the equipment investment subcomponent leads nonresidential structures investment. Equipment generally costs less than structures and is more readily purchased or financed.

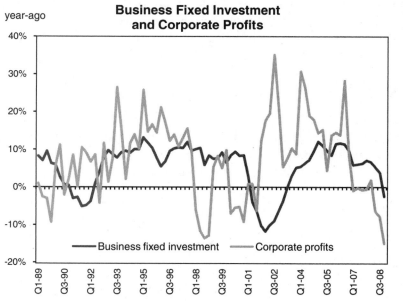

Business fixed investment and corporate profits.

Market Reaction to the GDP News Release

Now that you've read Chapters 3 and 4, you're on your way to becoming a savvy market watcher. You now understand what you're reading or hearing about GDP in the news. The next step is to learn how to interpret what the market reaction will be when the GDP news release comes out. So let's talk about a few things that market watchers focus on.

If GDP growth is stronger than expected, this is generally good news for the stock market and interest rates tend to stabilize. But if economic growth is too strong and inflation starts to build, this can be bad news for the stock market because the Fed might decide to raise interest rates.

The comparison between final sales growth to real GDP is also scrutinized. Why? Because this can indicate whether or not there are unplanned changes in inventories. If there appears to be an unplanned jump in inventories, then the market watchers look at whether there was a jump in similar components in imports. If so, then this suggests production cutbacks will be shared with overseas producers as imports are cut to reduce inventories.

On the price front, market watchers look to see whether there is acceleration or deceleration in overall GDP inflation and in the headline PCE price index and core PCE price index. If there is sharp movement in the PCE price index, the PCE index for nondurables can suggest whether or not it is energy related. But for economy-wide inflation, look at the index for gross domestic purchases to make sure statistical quirks in the GDP price index aren't misleading the markets.

For the income components, market watchers look to see if there is healthy growth in personal income and in corporate profits. Personal income is reported on a quarterly basis in the GDP report, but on a more current monthly basis in the personal income report, which follows the GDP report typically by one business day.

The Least You Need to Know

- ◆ Forward momentum in GDP growth is determined by how healthy the fundamentals are for each sector.

- ◆ Learn which key monthly indicators are tied to each component of GDP.

- ◆ Unplanned inventory swings can lead to a spurt or drop in GDP growth.

- ◆ GDP measures inflation at the broadest level.

- ◆ GDP is also measured by income, and the two key income components are personal income and corporate profits.

- ◆ Generally, strong GDP growth is good for stocks, but also tends to bump up interest rates.

Part 2

The Consumer in the Economy

You'll feel right at home in this part of the book, because it's talking about you, the consumer! But just because you're in it, don't take it lightly—the consumer makes up about two-thirds of the economy, and that gets the attention of financial markets. Consumers make or break the economy.

In this part, we'll see how economists box up all this information about consumers. We'll start with the number-one economic report in the known universe (but we'll keep you in suspense on that until you turn the page)! Then we'll move on to see how the government measures the money going into our wallets and where we spend it. And you can certainly believe financial markets want to know that! Finally, believe it or not, financial markets indeed do care about your feelings—they just call it consumer confidence and consumer sentiment. Stay tuned to see just how much markets care!

Chapter 5

The Employment Report

In This Chapter

- ◆ The two main employment surveys
- ◆ How the two main employment surveys differ
- ◆ The most timely measure of wage inflation
- ◆ How employment data affect other economic reports

The employment report is the most closely followed economic report on earth. No, that isn't a typo! It is the most timely and comprehensive economic report for the world's largest economy.

Because of its broad and timely scope, this report sets the tone for what investors and traders expect for economic releases for the rest of the month. To be sure, there are a number of other employment indicators that provide different perspectives on the labor market. But the employment report is the Big One and so we talk about that one first.

The Employment Report Sets the Tone

On the first Friday of each month, the Department of Labor releases the employment situation report. This is the most comprehensive and timely update on the economy each month. In many ways, GDP is more comprehensive, but it's also a lagging report in terms of timeliness. In sharp contrast, the employment report has data for the prior month, covers every major nonfarm sector of the economy, *and* is timely.

In addition, because employment is a fundamental underlying factor for many sectors of the economy, the information in this report can project the direction of the economy better than most indicators. Not only are numbers provided for jobs created or lost, but also for wages, earnings, and unemployment. Also, several key employment series are used as source data for several indicators that are released later. For investors and traders in the financial markets, the employment situation is the most anticipated economic indicator.

Key Facts About the Employment Report

The employment situation report is based on surveys taken by the government. However, a key fact about the employment situation report is that it contains data from not one ongoing survey but two. The first survey in the report is the Household Survey, which is conducted by the Bureau of the Census. This is a survey of households and is from the worker's perspective. The second survey in the report is the establishment survey, which is conducted by the Bureau of Labor Statistics (BLS), part of the Department of Labor. It is a survey of businesses and it's basically a job count from the employer's perspective. This survey is also informally called the payroll survey.

Here's what's in the employment situation report:

◆ Official name: The Employment Situation

◆ Release date: Monthly, the first Friday in the month for the prior month's data (July release has June data)

◆ Produced by: U.S. Bureau of Labor Statistics (BLS), U.S. Department of Labor

◆ Form of data: *Unemployment rates* are calculated in percentages. Household employment, unemployment, labor force, and payroll employment are in thousands. Average hourly earnings are in dollars. The average workweek is in hours. There are other formats (such as diffusion indexes) for miscellaneous series. Data are available as seasonally adjusted and not seasonally adjusted.

◆ Market watchers focus on: Percentages for the unemployment rate and monthly differences in employment (household and establishment Surveys), the number of unemployed, and the labor force (view reports at www.stats.bls.gov/news.release/ empsit.toc.htm)

def•i•ni•tion

The **unemployment rate** is the percent of the labor force who are unemployed.

Key Data Series

In the household survey, the most important indicators are the unemployment rate, household employment, the number of unemployed, the *civilian labor force*, and those *not in the labor force*. In the following table, we see levels for August, September, and October 2008 (with the unemployment rate a percentage). The last column is what markets focus on—the monthly change in the numbers. We see a 297 thousand drop in household employment for October 2008 and a 0.4 percentage point spike in the unemployment rate to 6.5 percent.

def•i•ni•tion

Not in the labor force are those who aren't in either the employed or unemployed categories. The **civilian labor force** is simply the sum of employed and unemployed persons.

Employment Status of the Civilian Population

	Aug. 2008	Sept. 2008	Oct. 2008
Civilian labor force	154,853	154,732	155,038
Employed	145,477	145,255	144,958
Unemployed	9,376	9,477	10,080
Unemployment rate	6.1	6.1	6.5
Not in labor force	79,253	79,628	79,575

Numbers are in thousands except unemployment rate

In the establishment survey, the key series are total employment, private employment, goods-producing employment, service-providing employment, employment by major industries, average hourly earnings, and the average workweek. The first three columns in the following table are for employment levels—the number of payroll jobs. The fourth column shows the monthly change in employment for October 2008. Total nonfarm payroll jobs fell 240 thousand in October 2008 to 136.899 million.

In the last part of the following table are data for average weekly hours and for average hourly earnings. The first three columns show how many hours per week the average worker worked and the average hourly earnings in dollars. The fourth column shows the change in the average workweek (latest month minus prior month) and the percentage change in average hourly earnings for the most recent month.

Nonfarm Payrolls, Selected Industries, in Thousands, Seasonally Adjusted

	Monthly Change			
	Aug. 2008	Sept. 2008	Oct. 2008	Oct. 2008
Total nonfarm	137,423	137,139	136,899	–240
Total private industries	114,909	114,666	114,403	–263
Goods-producing industries	21,367	21,284	21,152	–132
Natural resources and mining	788	796	803	7
Construction	7,153	7,118	7,069	–49
Manufacturing	13,426	13,370	13,280	–90
Service-providing industries	116,056	115,855	115,747	–108
Private service-providing industries	93,542	93,382	93,251	–131
Trade, transportation & utilities	26,346	26,278	26,211	–67
Wholesale trade	6,007	6,005	5,984	–21
Retail trade	15,275	15,230	15,192	–38
Transportation & warehousing	4,505	4,481	4,472	–9
Utilities	559	561	563	2
Information	2,984	2,981	2,981	0
Financial activities	8,196	8,180	8,156	–24

	Monthly Change			
	Aug. 2008	Sept. 2008	Oct. 2008	Oct. 2008
Professional & business services	17,854	17,815	17,770	–45
Education & health services	18,997	18,981	19,002	21
Leisure & hospitality	13,639	13,618	13,602	–16
Other services	5,526	5,529	5,529	0
Government	22,514	22,473	22,496	23
Monthly Change				
Average weekly hours, total private	33.7	33.6	33.6	0.0
Monthly Change				
Average hourly earnings	$18.14	$18.17	$18.21	0.2

The Household Survey

The Household Survey gives us the unemployment rate. The general public probably recognizes this indicator best. But before we go into detail about the key indicators in this portion of the employment report, let's talk about how the Household Survey is conducted.

Just a heads up—for the household survey, two government bureaus are involved. The Census Bureau collects the data and then the Bureau of Labor Statistics makes adjustments for use in the employment situation report. The household survey is taken from data that the Bureau of the Census has collected from its Current Population Survey. The household survey is based on a sample of roughly 72,000 housing units from which a sample of about 60,000 households is selected. The samples are from the civilian noninstitutional population (those who are in prison or institutionalized are excluded). Each month, data are collected for about 110,000 persons age 16 and older. The Bureau of Labor Statistics then uses the Census data for the household survey part of the employment situation report. The BLS weights the data to reflect the full population of the United States. The survey asks interviewees about their work status for the Sunday-through-Saturday calendar week that includes the twelfth of the month. However, the survey is conducted the following week.

For the initial interview, the Census Bureau sends field representatives to the household to make an in-person visit—this is largely to encourage participation and to ensure reliability of the answers (by making sure the questions are understood). After the initial interview, follow-up surveys are generally done by telephone. The Household Survey is based on a gradual rotation of survey panels with each household being on a four-month on, eight-month off, four-month on schedule before being dropped from the survey. This rotation plan reduces the burden of reporting and provides significant overlap in the data each month. Any two consecutive months have an overlap of about 75 percent of their samples. Samples that are a year apart have about a 50 percent overlap. The household survey numbers are not revised other than for an updating of seasonal factors.

The Primary Categories for Work Status

How do we get to the unemployment rate numbers? The Household Survey classifies people interviewed into one of three categories: employed, unemployed, or not in the labor force (in this case, they don't fit into either employed or unemployed status). You've probably also heard the term "civilian labor force." This refers to those 16 and over who are available and able to work (meaning they aren't in the military or in an institution).

What does it take to fit into the employed category? According to the BLS, people are classified as employed if they …

- Did any work as paid employees during the reference week.

- Worked in their own business or profession, or on their own farm.

- Worked without pay at least 15 hours in a family business or farm.

People are also counted as employed if they were temporarily absent from their jobs due to illness, bad weather, vacation, labor-management disputes, or personal reasons.

Now, the tricky category is being unemployed. It actually takes work to be unemployed. That is, your work is looking for work. You can't just sit on the sofa watching TV to be considered unemployed! People are classified as unemployed if they meet all of the following criteria:

- They had no employment during the reference week.

- They were available for work at that time.

- They made specific efforts to find employment sometime during the four-week period ending with the reference week.

Those laid off from a job and expecting to be recalled do not need to be looking for work to be counted as unemployed. Being classified as unemployed in the household survey does not depend on the person being eligible for receipt of unemployment insurance benefits.

And now we come to the headline number for the household survey. The unemployment rate simply is the number unemployed as a percent of the labor force:

Unemployment Rate = Number of Unemployed ÷ Labor Force × 100

The Unemployment Rate over the Business Cycle

Since the unemployment rate is probably the most visible economic indicator to the public, it's often touted by the news media as the predictor for how strong or weak the consumer sector is. But the unemployment rate doesn't provide much advance warning regarding where the economy is heading. When the economy is going into recession, the unemployment rate tends to worsen at the same time as the rest of the economy, and even lags the economy during economic recovery.

Take a look at the civilian unemployment rate chart below. The unemployment rate tends to be a coincident indicator at the start of recession, but a lagging indicator at the start of recovery. The unemployment rate typically continues to rise after recovery has begun.

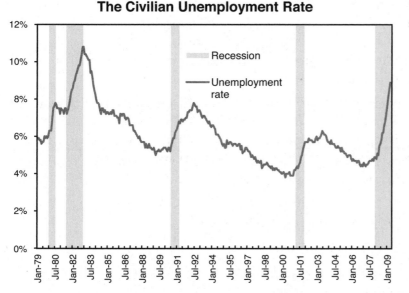

The civilian unemployment rate.

The Establishment Survey

The establishment survey is informally known as the payroll survey. For many years, the markets and the public gave more attention to the household survey than to the establishment survey because of the then-headline figure of the unemployment rate. But in recent years, financial analysts and even mainstream news reporters have switched headline focus to the nonfarm payroll employment number from the establishment survey. This survey is now seen as a better measure of the overall economy than the unemployment rate. Of course, the best approach is to take in all of the information—but that is a separate issue from what the headline number is.

Trader Tip

Today, the first number that the markets react to at the release of the employment situation report is the latest month's change in total nonfarm payroll employment. In decades past, the markets' initial reactions focused on changes in the unemployment rate.

The primary types of data in the establishment survey portion of the employment situation report are employment, average hourly earnings, and average workweek. Indexes of production hours and aggregate weekly earnings are in the report but aren't frequently followed. Also, various series from the payroll survey are used as source data for other important economic indicators.

To be counted as part of the payroll survey, an employee must be paid by a work establishment. The "being paid" part is the key portion of the definition. Therefore, the payroll survey includes workers that are working but also many who are not working but are being paid. These include workers on paid leave, such as for sick leave, paid holiday, or paid vacation. Also, the worker only needs to be paid for part of the pay period—not the entire period. Similarly, if a worker is not paid during a pay period, that worker is not counted as employed according to the establishment survey.

The employment numbers do not distinguish between full-time and part-time employment, but they are limited to the nonfarm sector. Each job held by an individual is counted separately except when an individual holds multiple jobs in the same establishment (meaning just one paycheck). Temporary workers are included in the job count.

> **Only from an Economist**
>
> Even though the main numbers in the payroll survey are called "employment" or "employees," the data represent a job count rather than the number of employees. The job counts include multiple job holders—each job held by an individual is counted separately. Multiple jobs are counted separately only if they are for different employers.

Behind the Establishment Survey Numbers

The establishment survey employment numbers are derived from the Current Employment Statistics (CES) program of the BLS, which is a cooperative effort between the BLS and state employment security agencies. The initial estimates for the payroll numbers come from surveys of about 150,000 businesses and government agencies, representing approximately 390,000 individual worksites. The sample for the monthly surveys is taken from 8.9 million establishments that pay into unemployment insurance (UI) accounts. Civilian government workers are included but not the military or national security agency employees.

The initial payroll estimate is for the prior month's data. That is, June data are released in July. However, the survey numbers trickle in and are updated for the next two months after the initial release.

Establishment data are revised annually and these are benchmark revisions. Each year, the sample-based March data are realigned with comprehensive March data from the state-provided unemployment insurance data. The UI data provide the benchmark for the sample-based monthly estimates. Essentially, the UI data represent almost the full universe of employment data that go into the employment situation report. The monthly data going back to the prior March benchmark revision are adjusted so that monthly data gradually merge and match the new March data.

One of the controversial issues about the benchmarking process for payroll numbers is that the BLS must estimate births and deaths of firms during the year, especially for small firms. The controversial part is whether the estimates are very reliable. The BLS states that the birth/death relationship is stable and predictable. However, some economists believe that the BLS overestimates the net birth and death of new firms when the economy is starting to slow or decline, and underestimates new firms when the economy is starting to accelerate. So when the economy is slowing, some analysts build in an assumption that job growth (or decline) is actually worse than initially reported in the payroll survey data.

The Components of Payroll Employment Data

The payroll data are divided into two broad categories: goods-producing industries and service-providing industries. The service-providing sector accounts for the greatest share of jobs by far—83.8 percent of the total in 2008. The industries in the service-providing sector include: trade, transportation & utilities; information services, financial activities, professional & business services, education & health services, leisure & hospitality, other services, and government. Goods-producing industries make up about 16.2 percent of total nonfarm employment while service-providing industries are about 83.8 percent of the total.

What stands out about the goods-producing industries is that they are the more cyclically sensitive industries (natural resources & mining, manufacturing, and construction). So goods-producing industries typically lose a greater percentage of jobs during recession than do service-providing industries. But these industries also typically rebound more strongly during economic recoveries.

In the following goods-producing and service-providing job growth chart, you can see how the goods-producing industries are more cyclically volatile than services. Also, growth in services employment has had a stronger long-term trend than goods-producing industries.

Job growth for goods-producing versus service-providing industries.

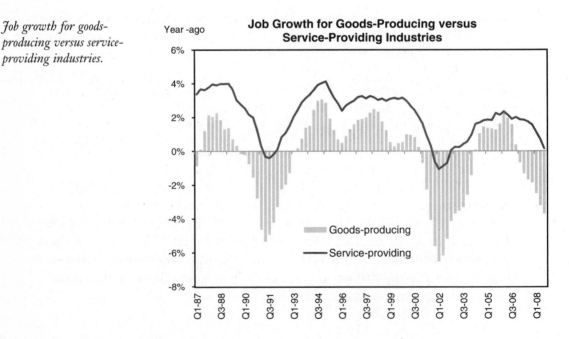

Comparing Household and Establishment Employment

The following table gives the key differences between the two employment measures. It's commonly believed that the biggest difference is that the Household Survey includes the farm sector while the Establishment numbers do not. In reality, the biggest difference is that the Household data include the self-employed and proprietors while payroll (establishment) data do not.

On a monthly basis, the household employment numbers are more volatile than the payroll employment numbers because of the household survey's much smaller sample size. This is a key reason that many economy watchers prefer the payroll employment numbers to the household survey data.

Over the long run, household and payroll employment closely track each other. However, after the 2001 recession, household employment outpaced payroll jobs because more workers found they could not rely on getting a salaried job and became self-employed (and thus aren't counted in payroll jobs).

Comparison of Household and Establishment Employment Surveys

We've covered a lot of information about the two different employment surveys in the employment situation report. The following table will help you keep the differences and similarities sorted out.

Household Survey	Establishment Survey
Survey is from the perspective of households; measures work status of individuals	Survey is from the perspective of businesses; it is the job count of payrolls
Survey covers week including the 12th day of the month	Survey covers the pay period that includes the 12th day of the month
Sample size of about 60,000 households	Sample size of about 390,000 business establishments
Covers nonfarm and farm sectors	Covers only nonfarm sectors
Includes the self-employed, proprietors, and some unpaid workers in addition to payroll workers	Includes only payroll workers

continues

(continued)

Household Survey	Establishment Survey
Includes workers on unpaid leave	Does not include workers on unpaid leave
Includes workers age 16 and older	Age is not an issue; all payroll workers are counted regardless of age
Data are organized by socio-economic characteristics (age, gender, race, education, and other)	Data generally are organized by industry
Has unemployment rate measures	No unemployment numbers
Individual workers counted only once	Each job counted separately even if held by same person
Work stoppages (strikes) do not affect job status	Striking workers not counted on payroll; counted upon return
Separate job count for part-time workers	Just one job count; full-time and part-time workers counted the same

Other Key Payroll Series

Three other notable indicators found in the establishment survey portion of the employment situation report are average weekly hours, average hourly earnings, and the index of aggregate weekly hours.

The average weekly hours series is also known as the average workweek. It's a measure of the length of the workweek for the average worker. The importance of the average workweek is that it provides an additional indication of how tight—or strong—labor markets are; that is, whether there is a shortage of workers. A long workweek indicates that the labor market is tight. Also, changes in the workweek can help forecast turning points in the economy. Businesses tend to boost or lower the workweek before hiring or firing employees. A long workweek indicates a strong economy.

Average hourly earnings are seen as a measure of labor cost inflation. The Fed watches this series for signs of rising or easing inflation pressures. Average hourly earnings numbers come from payroll data and are on a before-tax basis. They include earnings for overtime, holidays, vacation, and sick leave. Sometimes this series is called "wages" but technically the numbers include both salary and wage income.

One warning about the average hourly earnings numbers is that they are not based on fixed component weights the way most inflation series are (such as the consumer price index). So monthly changes in this wage series are affected both by actual changes in earnings and by changes in the composition of total employment between high- and low-earnings workers. During recession, if low-income workers are laid off faster than high-income workers, average hourly earnings growth can get stronger when you would think wage pressures would be easing.

The index of aggregate weekly hours reflects the sum of total hours worked in the nonfarm payroll sector. Indexes are available for major sectors and industries. This index for manufacturing is used by the Federal Reserve in its initial estimates of monthly industrial production.

Average Hourly Earnings of Production and Nonsupervisory Workers, October 2008

Total private	$17.59		
Natural resources & mining	21.05	Financial activities	$19.78
Construction	21.07	Professional & business services	20.31
Manufacturing	17.34	Retail trade	12.86
Wholesale trade	15.94	Education & health services	18.34
Transportation & warehousing	17.86	Leisure & hospitality	10.60
Utilities	28.32	Other services	15.59
Information	24.10		

Use of Payroll Employment Data in Other Economic Indicators

Because the employment situation numbers come out so early, some components are used in other, later-released indicators. The key reports that use payroll data for source data are industrial production, personal income, and the coincident indicator in the leading indicators report.

As already noted, the Federal Reserve uses the manufacturing aggregate weekly production hours series for its initial estimates of the manufacturing portion of industrial production. Basically, the Fed used statistical analysis of percentage changes in manufacturing production hours to estimate percent changes in manufacturing industries. For later releases, the Fed uses specific output data obtained from manufacturers.

For personal income, the Bureau of Economic Analysis uses the average weekly earnings numbers as primary inputs to estimate the private wages and salaries components of personal income.

The payroll employment numbers tell us a lot about where we are in the business cycle—recession or expansion. You may remember that the coincident index (part of the leading indicators report) helps to define the business cycle peaks and troughs. Nonfarm payroll employment is one of the four components of the coincident index.

Not only is the employment situation report an important update on the economy during the first Friday of each month, but components help make up some key indicators throughout the month.

How Financial Markets React to the Employment Report

When the employment situation report is posted on financial websites at 8:30 A.M. EST the first Friday of each month, market attention zooms in on two key numbers: first, on how much payroll jobs rose or fell, and second, on whether the unemployment rate went up or down. Getting a little less attention—but still important—is the average hourly earnings (wages) number. Markets see that indicator as a measure of wage inflation that could affect business costs and whether the Fed decides to tighten or ease monetary policy. Equity markets see moderately strong wage growth as good since it helps fuel consumer spending. But wage growth that is very strong for an extended period of months can lead to higher interest rates from the Fed, which cuts into economic growth and stock gains.

The Least You Need to Know

- The employment situation report is the most important economic news each month.

- Markets primarily focus on monthly changes in payroll employment, followed by changes in the unemployment rate.

- Within payroll employment, the most cyclically sensitive industries are manufacturing and construction. They are important because they reflect high-wage jobs and high-value production activity.

- Average hourly earnings tell us whether wage inflation is strong or not.

- The unemployment rate tells us how tight labor markets are.

6

More Employment Indicators

In This Chapter

- ◆ Why unemployment claims are a leading indicator
- ◆ What you'll find in the ADP Employment Report
- ◆ Why the Monster Employment Index is important

The Employment Situation report grabs the spotlight each month, but there are a number of other employment reports that either help you antic-ipate what the numbers will be in the employment situation report or that give you a view of the jobs market from a different angle.

These three employment indicators we are going to cover come out before the all-important employment situation and get a fair amount of market attention. You'll even be pleasantly surprised to see that economists are keeping up with the times, creating an Internet-based employment index.

Other Employment Data

There are a number of labor market indicators that financial markets track on a monthly or even weekly basis. Each indicator provides information on many facets of the labor market that are not covered by the employment situation report. In this section, we take a peek at *unemployment claims*, the ADP Employment Report, the Monster Employment Index, and the Mass Layoffs report.

def•i•ni•tion

Unemployment claims are made by unemployed persons who wish to receive unemployment benefits.

Key Facts About the Unemployment Claims Report

Probably the most closely followed labor market report after the employment situation is the unemployment claims report. Markets particularly like this release because it's extremely timely. The data are weekly and released each Thursday morning for the week ending just the prior Saturday for initial unemployment claims. For continuing unemployment claims, the data are for one week later than for initial claims.

Here's what's in the unemployment claims report:

◆ Official name: Unemployment Insurance Weekly Claims Report

◆ Release date: Weekly, on Thursdays for the week ending on the Saturday immediately prior to the release, for initial claims. Continuing claims data lag initial claims data by one week.

◆ Produced by: Employment and Training Administration, U.S. Department of Labor

◆ Form of data: Levels and weekly changes (differences). Data are available seasonally adjusted and not seasonally adjusted.

◆ Market watchers focus on: Weekly changes in initial claims, but also in levels (view reports at www.dol.gov/opa/media/press/eta/main.html)

Key Data Series

The primary data series in this report are initial claims and continuing claims (officially listed as "insured employment"). The continuing claims data lag initial claims by one week.

The report does not make available comprehensive state data. However, it does include highlights of which states had the largest gains or losses in initial claims.

The following table shows typical headline numbers in the weekly report. We see in the first two columns the latest initial claims number and the same for the prior week. The third column is the change in initial claims for the latest week from the previous week. For longer-term comparison, the final column has the claims number for a year ago. Both seasonally adjusted (SA) and not seasonally adjusted (NSA) data are reported but markets focus on the seasonally adjusted figures.

The weekly initial claims data can be volatile from week to week and many market watchers like to follow a four-week average of the claims to see the underlying trend.

The report also gives the claims number as a percentage of workers covered under state unemployment insurance programs. This unemployment rate is going to be lower than that in the employment situation report since the household survey covers all of the labor force while the claims unemployment rate is based on only workers covered by unemployment insurance.

In the following initial unemployment claims chart, you can see that initial claims are a leading indicator for the economy, rising before recession and falling before recovery starts for the overall economy.

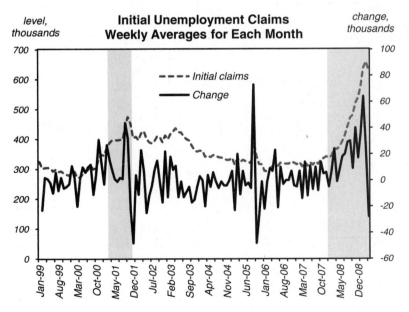

Initial Unemployment Claims, first line; Weekly Averages for Each Month, second line.

Initial Claims and Insured Unemployment Rate, November 29, 2008

Regular State Programs

Week Ending	Nov. 29	Nov. 22	Change	Nov. 15	Prior Year
Initial Claims (SA)	509,000	530,000	21,000	543,000	340,000
Initial Claims (NSA)	529,941	608,915	−78,974	513,000	462,902
4-Wk Moving Average (SA)	524,500	518,250	+6,250	507,000	340,000

Week Ending	Nov. 22	Nov. 15	Change	Nov. 8	Prior Year
Ins. Unemployment (SA)	4,087,000	3,998,000	+89,000	4,016,000	2,611,000
Ins. Unemployment (NSA)	3,649,809	3,781,878	−132,069	3,521,971	2,725,542
4-Wk Moving Average (SA)	4,001,750	3,938,000	+63,750	3,868,750	2,609,250
Ins. Unemployment Rate (SA)	3.1%	3.0%	+0.1	3.0%	2.0%
Ins. Unemployment Rate (NSA)	2.7%	2.8%	−0.1	2.6%	2.1%

Behind the Claims Data

The jobless claims numbers are collected and published by the Employment and Training Administration (ETA) as part of a cooperative effort between state and local unemployment agencies. The data originate when an unemployed worker files a claim for unemployment benefits with the local office of a state unemployment agency. The data are for unemployment claims made under state programs—not federal programs. Local agencies compile claims data over the weekend and forward the numbers to state agencies. In turn, the state agencies forward the information to the ETA.

This report also has lesser-followed data on claims filed under federal programs, which cover federal employees and veterans. The federal data are released with a one-week lag after the state claims data. Markets generally do not track this part of the claims report because it is not as timely and the federal government sector is relatively stable. The state agency claims data more closely reflect changes in the strength of the overall economy.

There are two major categories in the state program data: initial unemployment claims and continuing claims. The initial claims actually reflect applications for unemployment benefits. An applicant might not necessarily receive unemployment benefits because of various legal disqualifications. Markets like to track the initial claims numbers because they are an early indicator for labor markets. Initial claims tend to rise before overall recession sets in and tend to fall prior to economic recovery. Some market analysts also like to use the claims data to try to predict changes in the unemployment rate or in payroll employment in the upcoming employment situation report.

The big drawback to the initial claims series is that it is very volatile. It is difficult to seasonally adjust weekly numbers. Data collected from weeks with national holidays are notoriously volatile. To counter some of this volatility, many market watchers like to focus on four-week moving averages of initial claims and continuing claims, which are published in the official report and by many news reporters.

Key Facts About the ADP Employment Report

The payroll data in the employment situation report get much attention in the financial press. Based on this, one company decided to create its own version of the payroll survey for marketing purposes. Automatic Data Processing, Inc. (ADP) is one of the nation's top providers of payroll-related services, and it releases estimates of national payroll employment based on data from its own massive database of payrolls.

Intended to maximize market attention, the ADP National Employment Report is released two days before the Employment Situation. In turn, traders and investors often adjust their market positions to take into account the ADP job gains or losses, headed into the first Friday Employment Situation numbers.

Here's what's in the ADP National Employment Report:

- Official name: The ADP National Employment Report

- Release date: Monthly, on Wednesday prior to the release date for the BLS employment situation (first Friday of the month), with data being for the same reference month as the employment situation report. Data typically are for the prior month, but if the first Friday is on the first or second, then ADP data are released at the end of the reference month.

- Produced by: Automatic Data Processing, Inc., with Macroeconomic Advisors, LLC, doing the actual creation of the employment numbers from ADP client payrolls (on an anonymous basis)

- Form of data: Levels and monthly changes (differences). Data are available seasonally adjusted.

- Market watchers focus on: Monthly changes (www.ADPemploymentreport.com)

Key Data Series

The series highlighted in the news release are total nonfarm private, goods-producing, and service-providing employment, with manufacturing as an addendum. Except for manufacturing, the aggregate components are broken down into three categories for firm size (small, 1–49 employees; medium, 50–499 employees; and large, greater than 499 employees).

Derived from ADP Payroll Data: Employees on nonfarm private payrolls by selected industry sector and size (in thousands)

November 2008 Initial Estimates

Industry/Size of Payroll	Aug. 2008	Sep. 2008	Oct. 2008	Nov. 2008	Change from: Oct. 2008–Nov. 2008
Total nonfarm private	115,981	115,955	115,776	115,526	–250
Small (1–49)	51,319	51,337	51,298	51,219	–79
Medium (50–499)	45,512	45,476	45,381	45,251	–130
Large (> 499)					
Goods-producing	21,598	21,518	21,386	21,228	–158
Service-providing	94,383	94,437	94,390	94,298	–92
Addendum:					
Manufacturing	13,484	13,431	13,344	13,226	–118

Note: the goods-producing and service-providing sector data are also available by size of payroll.

The following chart compares ADP and BLS payroll employment using monthly changes. Traders in the financial markets often like to use the earlier-released ADP employment numbers to forecast the change in payroll jobs in the employment situation report. You can see that the earlier released ADP employment changes each month are similar to the later-released payroll employment numbers. But there can be sizeable missed forecasts by the ADP data on occasion.

ADP versus BLS payroll employment, first line, monthly changes second line.

(Source: ADP, Inc., and Macroeconomic Advisers, LLC. Use prohibited without express permission from ADP. Questions/ comments to: doug_offer@adp. com.)

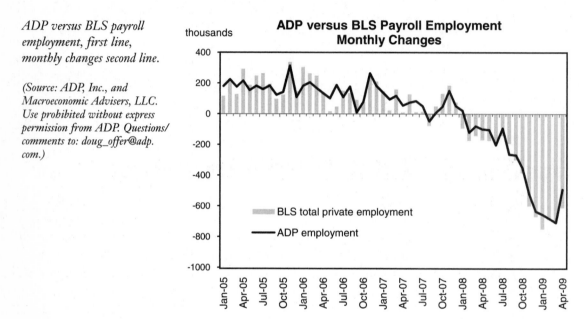

Behind the ADP Numbers

According to ADP, the company processes over 500,000 payrolls. A subset of this database is used to construct ADP's own estimates of national payroll numbers. However, ADP does not do the number crunching. The firm has hired Macroeconomic Advisors, LLC, to create and maintain the numbers in the ADP National Employment report. Macroeconomic Advisors analyzes anonymous data on payrolls collected by ADP from its customers. For the last six months of 2008, the subset sample averaged about 400,000 U.S. businesses, covering roughly 24 million employees.

In contrast to the BLS's sample for the employment situation report, the ADP sample does not include government employees. The ADP payroll data are for private payrolls only, but do cover all major private sectors and geographic regions. Government agencies generally do not outsource payroll functions to private agencies such as ADP.

As a simplification of the process used by Macroeconomic Advisors, estimates are based upon a statistical comparison of ADP growth rates to BLS payroll employment growth rates at the industry level. ADP also adds in the BLS initial claims data for the week just prior to the employment report as part of its estimation procedure. Industry levels are calculated from the estimated growth rates. That is, the estimated percent changes for industries this month are applied to last month's industry levels. Then, industry levels are totaled to get a national private payroll employment number.

Trader Tip

If you want to compare monthly changes in ADP employment with BLS payroll employment changes, be sure you only use private employment data in the BLS numbers since ADP does not cover the government sector.

How Financial Markets View ADP Employment

First, investors and traders like the fact that the ADP numbers come out two days before the Employment Situation report. It helps them plan for the first Friday jobs report. However, the ADP data do not always track the private employment portion of payroll employment as well as hoped. Still, the ADP numbers are a good addition to looking at initial claims numbers when trying to figure out the upcoming BLS payroll numbers.

Key Facts About the Monster Employment Index

Remember those "Help Wanted" ads in the newspaper? Today, employers and job seekers alike both jump to the Internet for the latest job openings. In the past, economists would count job openings in major newspapers as a measure of labor market health. But the Conference Board admitted the irrelevance of newspaper job ads when it quit publishing its long-revered "help wanted" index in the middle of 2008. Remember, the Conference Board is a private research group for business that is best known for publishing the index of leading indicators.

What's the modern-day replacement for the help wanted newspaper ad? It's the Monster Employment Index. Yes, this index was created by the Internet heavyweight for job placement, Monster.com. Basically, Monster.com uses its search engines to tally up not just its own job offerings but those posted on many other job-posting websites.

The Monster Employment Index is a measure of employer online recruitment activity and is seen as a leading indicator of changes in the strength of the job market. Changes in aggregate company hiring plans are seen early in changes in the movement of online job listings.

Here's what's in the Monster Employment Index:

 ◆ Official name: The Monster Employment Index

 ◆ Release date: Monthly, on the day before the BLS employment situation release date (first Friday of the month), with data from the same reference month as the Employment Situation report. Data typically are for the prior month, but if the first Friday is on the first, then Monster data are released at the end of the reference month.

 ◆ Produced by: Monster Worldwide, Inc., which owns Monster.com

 ◆ Form of data: Index levels, not seasonally adjusted

 ◆ Market watchers focus on: Index levels, and changes in levels as well as monthly and year-ago percent changes (view reports at www.corporate.monster.com/Press_Room/MEI.html)

Behind the Monster Employment Index

The Monster Employment Index is put together by Monster Worldwide, Inc., an Internet-based, jobs-posting company. The data go back to October 2003 and are based on "a real-time review of millions of job opportunities culled from a large, representative selection of career sites and job boards, including Monster," according to Monster Worldwide. Data are available by Census Bureau region, industry, occupation, and by an extensive list of metropolitan areas. Each month, accuracy of the data is verified through an independent, third-party audit conducted by Research America, Inc.

Key Data Series

There is only one key national index in the report and it is simply called the Monster Employment Index. Further in the report are series for Census regions, occupations, industries, and selected cities.

The Monster Employment Index

Oct 08	Sep 08	Aug 08	Jul 08	Jun 08	May 08	Apr 8	Mar 08	Feb 08	Oct 07
150	160	159	157	163	166	174	167	165	188

The national index's baseline value of 100 represents the average number of online job ads measured monthly during the first 12 months of the index, which was from October 2003 to September 2004.

Take a look at the following chart, which compares the Monster Employment Index and Payroll Employment Survey. With its limited history, the Monster Employment Index has led changes in payroll employment during the past expansion ending in late 2007 and the recession that began in January 2008.

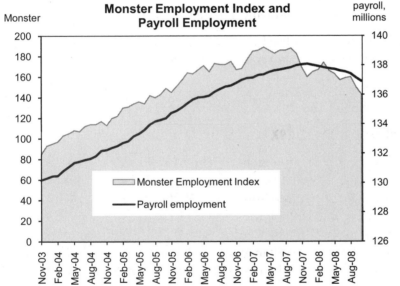

Monster Employment Index and Payroll Employment.

(Source: Monster Worldwide Inc., Monster.com.)

Market Focus on the Monster News Release

The financial markets look at monthly changes in index levels as well as year-ago percent changes. Many market analysts use this report to make day-before adjustments in their forecast for the payroll employment numbers in the next day's employment situation report. So when you are looking at the published consensus numbers for the employment situation report, think about whether the Monster Employment Index may have made traders more optimistic or more pessimistic.

The Least You Need to Know

♦ The initial unemployment claims report is a leading indicator and is the second most closely followed report on the labor markets.

♦ The ADP employment report is used by many market analysts to predict changes in the private-sector portion of the Labor Department's monthly payroll employment numbers.

♦ The Monster Employment Index gives you an early picture of job openings— whether they are rising or falling.

Chapter 7

Retail Sales: Going Malling and More

In This Chapter

◆ Why retail sales are an important economic indicator

◆ The key components for retail sales

◆ Where motor vehicle sales fit in

◆ The early indicators for retail sales

Have you shopped at the mall lately? This may seem like an odd question, but consumer spending at key hangouts tells us how retail sales are doing. The consumer (that's you!) is a big part of the economy. So when people stop shopping at places like Macy's or Target, that affects the economy because it indicates a decrease in spending.

GDP may be the ultimate "big picture" of economic indicators, but retail sales give us a really good look at the health of the consumer spending sector. At mid-month, the Commerce Department releases the Retail Sales and Food Services report for sales for the prior month. This provides the first data on how various retailers are doing. It's the most watched report on the consumer sector by financial markets, the public, and policy makers.

Let's take a look at the details and you'll understand how all this works.

Key Facts for the Retail Sales Report

The retail sales report is particularly important to traders in the financial markets (especially equities) because the report provides details on industries that a trader might be tracking for investment purposes. Here's what's in the official report:

- ◆ Official name: Advance Monthly Sales for Retail and Food Services

- ◆ Release date: Monthly, mid-month for the prior month's data (July release has June data)

- ◆ Produced by: U.S. Bureau of the Census, U.S. Department of Commerce

- ◆ Form of data: Dollar levels and percent changes (available seasonally adjusted and not seasonally adjusted). Levels are for sales during a given month and are not annualized.

- ◆ Market watchers focus on: Monthly percentage changes (and year-ago percent changes to a lesser degree). View reports at www.census.gov/marts/www/marts. html.

The retail sales table that follows shows 2008 retail sales by major sales groups:

Retail sales by major sales groups 2008.

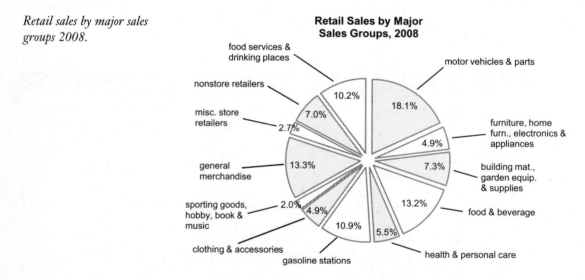

Retail Sales by Major Sales Groups, 2008

What Are Retail and Food Services Store Sales?

According to the Commerce Department, *retail and food services store sales* are sales within U.S. firms that sell merchandise and related services to final consumers. Direct sales to consumers by wholesalers or manufacturers are not included.

Sales are categorized by the kind of business instead of by the kind of product. Many times the kind of product and kind of business are essentially the same, but not always. For example, clothing stores sell mainly clothes and accessories. However, department stores sell many types of products. And most gasoline stations sell not just gasoline, but all kinds of snacks and other convenience goods.

def•i•ni•tion

Retail and food services store sales are sales of firms within the United States that sell merchandise and related services to final consumers.

What's in the Components?

Let's take a look at each component. The primary components are based on the North American Industry Classification System (NAICS). This is a trade classification system that is relatively new and was intended to help simplify some accounting aspects of trade between the United States, Canada, and Mexico. If you read any official reports on retail sales, you'll see NAICS referenced. Now you know what they are talking about.

Only from an Economist

NAICS sounds like an exotic disease, doesn't it? Well, it isn't! The NAICS, or North American Industry Classification System, was developed jointly by statistical agencies in the United States, Canada, and Mexico so that the three countries would have highly comparable business statistics. NAICS determines which industry a business is classified as for statistical purposes. (For more information on NAICS, go to www.census.gov/eos/www/naics/.)

Yes, retail sales include purchases at your nearby mall, but that's not how the numbers are organized. There are two broad types of retailers: *store retailers* and *nonstore retailers*. Store retailers operate fixed point-of-sale locations and often attract a high volume of walk-in customers. The point-of-sale is the location of a purchase. Store retailers typically sell to the general public for personal or household consumption, but some also serve business clients. Examples of the latter include office supply stores, building materials dealers, and electrical supply stores.

Because nonstore retailers do not have fixed point-of-sale locations, these businesses reach customers with marketing methods such as infomercials on TV, direct-response advertising on radio or TV, Internet catalogs, door-to-door sales, selling from portable stalls (street vendors), and vending machines.

Let's take a closer look at each component of retail sales:

◆ Motor Vehicle and Parts Dealers: Includes new and used car dealerships; "other" vehicle dealerships also are included such as those for recreational vehicles, motorcycles, boats, and utility trailers. The "Automotive Parts and Accessories Stores" subcomponent includes tire dealers.

◆ Furniture and Home Furnishings Stores: Made up of establishments mainly selling new furniture, such as household furniture and outdoor furniture; office furniture (except that sold in combination with office supplies and equipment); and/or furniture sold in combination with major appliances, home electronics, home furnishings, and/or floor coverings.

◆ Electronics and Appliance Stores: Includes stores selling household appliances, radios, televisions, computers and software, cameras, and photographic supplies to the general public.

◆ Building Material and Garden Equipment and Supplies Dealers: Made up of building material and supply dealers, paint and wallpaper stores, hardware stores, and lawn and garden equipment stores.

◆ Food and Beverage Stores: Include stores where consumers purchase the products for later use at home or some other location. Examples are grocery stores, convenience stores, specialty food stores, meat markets, fish and seafood markets, fruit and vegetable markets, baked goods stores, and beer, wine, and liquor stores.

◆ Health and Personal Care Stores: Include pharmacies, drug stores, and cosmetic, beauty supply, perfume, optical goods, and vitamin supplement stores.

◆ Gasoline Stations: Primarily sell gasoline, but some are also convenience stores and/or provide automotive repair services. Gasoline sales make up the bulk of sales (nongasoline sales aren't listed separately in the data).

◆ Clothing and Clothing Accessories Stores: Includes family clothing stores, women's clothing, men's clothing, clothing accessory stores, and shoe stores. Also includes jewelry stores and luggage & leather goods stores.

◆ Sporting Goods, Hobby, Book, and Music Stores: Pretty much covers what each says.

◆ General Merchandise Stores: Include stores that sell a wide range of goods. The biggest subcomponent is department stores. Department stores sell a wide range of goods and there isn't one merchandise line dominating store sales. Outside of department stores are warehouse clubs, such as Sam's Club, supercenters, and variety stores.

◆ Miscellaneous Store Retailers: Include unique stores that sell from fixed locations. Examples are florists, used merchandise stores, pet and pet supply stores, office supply stores, art dealers, tobacco stores, and even manufactured (mobile) home dealers.

◆ Nonstore Retailers: Includes direct sales to households. Examples are home delivery newspaper routes, home delivery of heating oil, frozen food and freezer plan providers, coffee-break services providers, bottled water or water softener services, and even eBay.

> **Only from an Economist**
>
> Believe it or not, according to the Census Bureau, a briefcase is a clothing accessory. So tote it in style!

◆ Food Services and Drinking Places: Businesses that prepare meals, snacks, and beverages to customer order for eating and drinking, either on or off the premises. Examples are full-service restaurants, limited-service restaurants, ice cream shops, bagel shops, coffee shops (can't leave out Starbucks!), food service contractors (such as for government institutions or even sports facilities), caterers, and drinking places serving alcoholic beverages.

> **Only from an Economist**
>
> In 2007, American households spent an average of $2,668 on food away from home. Think about it: That's about $51 dollars a week going toward McDonald's, Wendy's, and other restaurants. Source: www.bls.gov/news.release/cesan.nr0.htm.

For the advance numbers of the retail sales report, the Census Bureau mails questionnaires to a sample of approximately 5,000 employer firms each month. Later, annual data are updated according to results from the Census Annual Retail Trade Survey. Participation in this annual survey is required by law and the results are better than the sample based on initial monthly estimates for retail sales.

Retail Sales, the Business Cycle, and Price Factors

In Chapter 3, you learned that stores selling durable-type goods tend to have larger cyclical volatility. Examples of these stores are motor vehicle dealerships, building materials and garden supplies, and furniture and appliance stores. Want to better anticipate sales at these kinds of stores? Track the unemployment rate (higher is worse, of course), interest rates (lower is better), and housing starts (higher starts are good for building materials and for furniture and appliances).

The price of gasoline affects dollar volume sales at service station stores. Oddly, higher gasoline prices can make overall retail sales look good, even though consumers have less money to spend on other things after filling the gas tank. Eventually, high gasoline prices hurt retail sales outside of gasoline. Lower gasoline prices boost the real spending power of consumers; this ends up boosting retail sales outside of the service station component.

Although it does not get as much play in the media as the impact of gasoline prices, discounting or lack of seasonal discounting in apparel stores can affect overall retail sales. During recession, apparel stores generally discount more than usual. But some unexpected swings in seasonally adjusted apparel prices can occur during transition months between spring/summer and fall/winter seasons. At the end of a season, retailers cut prices sharply to move out old inventories to make way for the new season. But if inventories are much higher than usual, then the discounting will be unusually deep, perhaps causing dollar sales volume to fall since a smaller share of sales were at regular price. The reverse happens—there is less discounting—if sales have been stronger than usual.

Take a look at the two retail sales charts that follow. In the first one, note how retail sales get battered during recession as consumers hold on to their wallets. And in the second chart, note how price changes affect some retail sales components, especially service station sales.

Retail Sales as Source Data

Retail sales are source data for the durables and nondurables components in the personal consumption expenditures of the personal income report and GDP report. However, the BEA does not use the motor vehicle dealer sales from Census retail sales, but substitutes data directly from the automakers (you learn about this next). Economists who are in the business of forecasting this month's personal consumption expenditures numbers eagerly await the retail sales numbers to crunch into their statistical models.

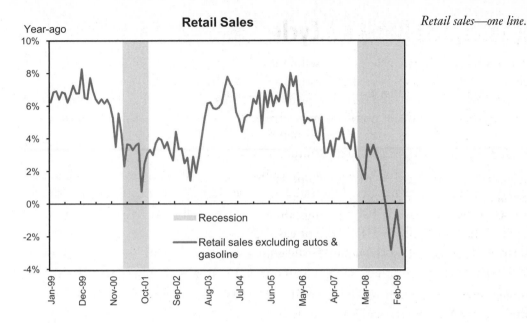

Retail sales—one line.

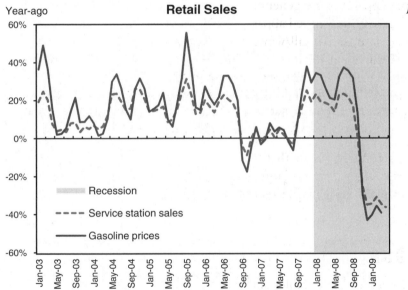

Retail sales—two lines.

How Markets Move on the News Release

Generally, when retail sales are higher than expected, stock prices jump—especially for retailers—and interest rates rise. When sales are lower than expected, the opposite happens.

What do economy trackers home in on when the retail sales report is released each month? Financial markets focus on these three primary series:

- Total retail sales

- Total sales excluding motor vehicle and parts dealers

- Total sales excluding motor vehicle and parts dealers and service station sales

Why do analysts want to look at sales excluding motor vehicles and service station sales? Traditionally, motor vehicle sales have been taken out of the total to look at the underlying trend in retail sales. Auto sales can have large swings due to off-and-on discounts and rebates. Taking out autos creates a less volatile series that shows more of the underlying strength in retail sales.

What else do analysts think about when poking around the details, trying to figure out the true strength of retail sales? The monthly retail sales numbers get revised for two additional months. So a big issue can be whether the revisions for the prior two months were significant.

How's the Weather?

Unseasonable weather can affect retail sales. Warm weather in the winter can lead to a drop in winter apparel sales. Extremely wet winters or springs can lead to a decrease in sales at building materials and garden equipment stores. Bad weather during critical sales times also affects sales. For instance, during the final days before Christmas, extended snow storms in heavily populated areas of the United States can lead to a big drop in retail sales.

The Number of New Motor Vehicle Sales

The sales activity of cars, trucks, and SUVs is a big part of the economy. Also, motor vehicle sales dramatically affect stock prices for automakers such as General Motors and Ford, and even foreign producers such as Toyota and Honda. The first hard numbers out are motor vehicle sales, which are released by automakers the first week of the month for the prior month. During the government bailout period of General Motors and Chrysler during 2008 and 2009, investors and traders closely tracked the monthly sales numbers of the automakers—U.S. and imports alike. Chrysler and General Motors eventually went into bankruptcy in 2009. These events make the sales numbers even more important after the companies come out of bankruptcy and investors track how well consumers buy into the idea that the newly emerged auto companies are new and improved.

Yes, there is also a component for sales by auto dealers in the mid-month retail sales report by the Census Bureau. But there are two big differences between the motor vehicle sales data that come out the first week of the month and the Census retail sales for auto dealers at mid-month.

The motor vehicle sales that are released the first week of the month are unit sales—the number of motor vehicles sold—whereas the auto dealer component of the broad retail sales report is in dollars, not units sold. The second difference is that the Census numbers are based on a small sample of auto dealers. In contrast, the unit sales come from manufacturers and represent all of the units sold—not a sample-based number.

There actually is more than one report on unit new motor vehicle sales. The first numbers dribble out from each of the manufacturers and then financial reporters tally them up. The first published compilation of the totals is by Autodata Corporation, a private company in Detroit, Michigan. Meanwhile, the U.S. Bureau of Economic Analysis culls the numbers and puts them together for their own estimates of personal consumption expenditures and gross domestic product. Then, a week or so after manufacturers release their numbers, the BEA makes special tables of unit new auto sales available on their website.

Key Facts from the Vehicle Sales Reports

Autodata Corporation has specific numbers for individual manufacturers while the BEA only makes available industry totals for cars and light trucks. There is some detail, however, on sales of vehicles from Mexico and Canada. Here's what's in the Autodata Corporation report:

- ◆ Official name: U.S. Light Vehicle Retail Sales

- ◆ Release date: Monthly, first week of the month for the prior month's data (July release has June data)

- ◆ Produced by: Autodata Corporation

- ◆ Form of data: Units sold and percent changes. Data are available seasonally adjusted and not seasonally adjusted. Levels are for sales during a given month. Some data are annualized.

- ◆ Market watchers focus on: Monthly percentage changes and units sold (view reports at www.motorintelligence.com/m_frameset.html)

Follow what is in the Commerce Department reports:

- Official name: Supplemental Estimates, Motor Vehicle Unit Retail Sales

- Release date: Monthly, mid-month for the prior month's data (July release has June data)

- Produced by: U.S. Bureau of Economic Analysis, U.S. Department of Commerce

- Form of data: Units sold and percent changes; data are available seasonally adjusted and not seasonally adjusted. Levels are for sales during a given month. Some data are annualized.

- Market watchers focus on: Monthly percentage changes and units sold (view reports at www.bea.gov/national/index.htm)

Motor Vehicle Sales and the Economy

Why do investors and traders watch unit new motor vehicle sales? First, the sales have a direct impact on automaker profits and stock prices. Motor vehicle sales and stock prices of automakers go up and down together. Motor vehicle sales are cyclical and typically go up and down more than the overall economy during boom periods or recessions.

In Chapter 3, you learned that autos are durables—purchases that are often postponed during difficult economic times. These purchases are also typically financed and sales strength is affected by the level of interest rates. This is another factor that not only makes motor vehicle sales very cyclical, but also makes them a leading indicator. Take a look at the following automaker stock prices chart and notice that auto sales typically go up before the rest of the economy during recovery and go down sooner when heading into recession.

Light Trucks: A Heavier Category Than You Think

There are two broad categories within motor vehicles: passenger cars and light trucks. Light trucks are vehicles that weigh 10,000 pounds or less. Heavy trucks, such as dump trucks, are not included in these sales numbers. The light trucks category includes pickup trucks, vans, minivans, and SUVs. The inclusion of minivans and SUVs in this category is a big part of the long-term trend for light trucks becoming a larger share of vehicle sales. Until the massive spike in gasoline prices in 2008, the light trucks' share of total shares had been rising steadily.

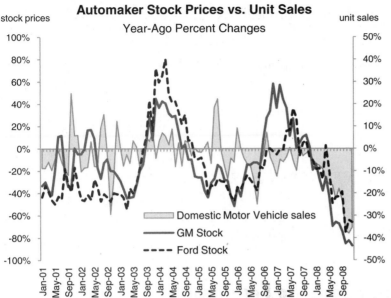

Automaker stock prices vs. unit sales.

(Source for sales: Autodata Corp., www. motorintelligence.com. Source for stock prices: Data provided by www.csidata. com.)

Only from an Economist

Did you know that the light trucks share of the monthly total vehicle share topped 50 percent for the first time in 1997? This share peaked at 67 percent during 2007 and has been slipping since then because of concern over high gasoline prices.

Truck Sales and the Price of Gasoline

In Economics 101, there's typically a discussion about so-called *complementary goods* and how the price of a complementary good affects the price of the main good. Complementary goods are items that are used or consumed together. An example would be gasoline and motor vehicles; or more specifically, gasoline and SUVs. In case it's been a while since you studied economics, the idea is that when the price of a complementary good goes up, the demand for the main good goes down.

Remember what happened with gas prices in 2008? The price spiked from about $2 per gallon to over $4 per gallon at mid-year. And sales of gas-guzzling pickup trucks and SUVs fell like a lead balloon! Not all consumers have studied economics, but they all sure know how to react to high prices for gasoline—dump the SUV.

def•i•ni•tion

Complementary goods are products that are used together.

In the following domestic-made motor vehicle sales chart, notice that higher gasoline prices led to a decline in the light trucks' share of motor vehicle sales.

Domestic-made motor vehicle sales.

(Source for sales: Autodata Corp.)

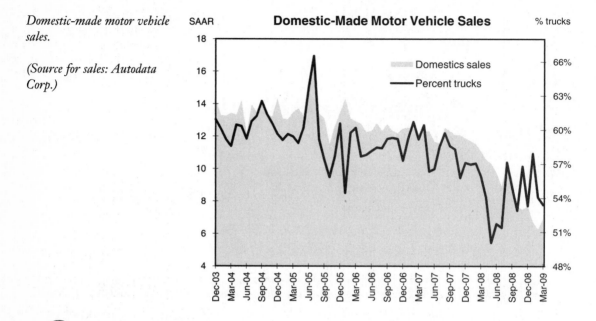

Domestic-Made Motor Vehicle Sales

SAAR ... % trucks

Trader Tip

Consumers delay buying new cars when the job situation does not look good and when interest rates are high. Why should you wait for lower interest rates? Here's what monthly payments would be for a $20,000 car loan over a four-year term: 4 percent interest rate, $451.58 monthly payment; 5 percent, $460.59; 6 percent, $469.70; 7 percent, $478.92; 8 percent, $488.26; 9 percent, $497.70; and 10 percent, $507.25.

Unit New Motor Sales as Related to Other Indicators

The unit new motor vehicle data also are important to economy watchers. Here are four reasons why:

◆ Unit new motor vehicle sales are source data for portions of the personal consumption expenditures for durables in the monthly personal income report.

◆ This source data, in turn, goes into the personal consumption expenditures portion of gross domestic product and the producers' durable equipment portion, and, to a lesser degree, into government purchases. Motor vehicle sales are allocated between the consumer, business, and government sectors based on information from motor vehicle registrations.

♦ Many financial traders use the motor vehicles numbers to help predict the over-all retail sales data that come out at mid-month.

♦ Sales of domestic vehicles have a direct impact on industrial production. Motor vehicle production is a key part of manufacturing output in the monthly industrial production report at mid-month.

Buy American—Even If It's an Import!

Many politicians—and, of course, U.S. automakers—scream that consumers should buy American-made cars to support the U.S. economy. So does that mean buy just General Motors, Ford, and Chrysler? There are two trends that have made it tough to tell exactly what an American-made car is and what it is not.

♦ **Trend #1:** Over the last few decades, foreign producers have built production facilities in the United States. These include, at a minimum, Nissan, Honda, Toyota, BMW, and Mazda. Other foreign producers are also considering buying unused U.S. auto manufacturing plants.

♦ **Trend #2:** U.S. producers have increasingly outsourced parts production over-seas. According to Chicago Federal Reserve Economist Thomas Klier, who specializes in tracking the auto industry, about 25 percent of the parts in cars and light trucks put together in the United States came from overseas. And another 25 percent came from "foreign owner" parts manufacturers located in the United States. Therefore, many U.S. nameplates have a high content of foreign parts even though the final vehicle was assembled in the United States.

Can you guess which cars have mainly U.S. content and which ones do not? According to data disclosed by manufacturers under the American Automobile Labeling Act, only about 35 percent of the parts in the Mercury Milan came from the United States or Canada (next door to Detroit). In contrast, 80 percent of the parts in Toyota's Sequoia SUV are U.S. made. Source: *Wall Street Journal*, January 26, 2009.

So to "buy American," do you buy the American nameplate which may have a big percentage of imported parts, or do you buy the import nameplate which may have been made in America and with mainly American parts? And, yes, there is a lot of in between.

To learn more about domestic and import content of cars and trucks you are thinking about buying, go to the National Highway Traffic Safety Administration website at www.nhtsa.dot.gov. Then click the link to "Vehicles/Equipment."

How Markets Move on the News Release of Unit New Auto Sales

Investors and traders focus on the level of sales and monthly percentage changes in unit new motor vehicle sales. The total numbers are important for gauging the strength of the consumer sector and the overall economy. Traders also look at company detail to judge whether individual stocks for automakers are overvalued or undervalued. On days that motor vehicle sales numbers come out, you may see significant jumps or declines in the price of stocks for companies such as Ford, General Motors, Chrysler, Toyota, Nissan, Honda, and others.

While these sales numbers provide a measure of the strength of the overall economy, you can also see sizeable movement in consumer-related stocks. If sales are stronger than expected, then stock prices are likely to go up, as will interest rates. Rates go up when the economy is strong.

Stock traders who focus on the auto industry know that manufacturer and dealer incentives can cause sharp swings in sales. If car buyers are getting hefty cash rebates one month, sales can jump. But when the rebate incentive ends, sales can temporarily drop. Stock traders try to keep up with what rebate and incentive plans dealers offer month to month, and then try to build that into their expectations before the sales data are made public.

Key Facts for Weekly Numbers on Retail Sales

If you can't wait for the monthly retail sales report from the Census Bureau, you can get a sneak peek at department-store type components with weekly announcements from two well-known chain store reports: the International Council of Shopping Centers (ICSC)-Goldman Sachs and Redbook.

In collaboration with Goldman Sachs, the ICSC produces the Weekly U.S. Retail Chain Store Sales Snapshot. How does ICSC come up with the numbers? A representative sample of major retailers in its membership is used to calculate weekly changes in sales.

However, this report is quite a bit more narrowly focused than the Census Bureau's comprehensive retail sales. Coverage of the retail industry by this index is roughly comparable to the general merchandise portion of Census Bureau's monthly retail sales. Each weekly report compares seasonally adjusted week-ago percentage changes in sales as well as year-ago changes. This is a very timely report. Also, the measure is more narrowly focused in another way. Rather than including total sales from existing and new stores, ICSC measures same-store or comparable-store sales. Restaurant and vehicle sales are not included.

You may have seen this retail sales series under another name. The ICSC-Goldman Sachs store sales series was previously known as ICSC-UBS, prior to Goldman Sachs' involvement with the index. The name change took place with the September 30, 2008, release.

Here's what's in the ICSC-Goldman Sachs Weekly Chain Store Sales report:

- Official name: Weekly U.S. Retail Chain Store Sales Snapshot

- Release date: Weekly, generally on Tuesday for the prior week's data ending on Saturday (January 13, 2009 release is for week ending January 10, 2009)

- Produced by: International Council of Shopping Centers (ICSC) and Goldman Sachs

- Form of data: Percent changes. Data are available seasonally adjusted.

- Market watchers focus on: Weekly percentage changes and year-ago percent changes (view reports at www.icsc.org/cgi/rsrchshow?section=st)

The other well-known report is named after its creator, Edward F. Johnson, who called his weekly report Johnson Redbook. Johnson personally compiled the information from individual stores while working as a researcher at a New York brokerage house during the 1960s and later. The product is now owned by Redbook Research, Inc., of New York City.

Here's what's in the Redbook Weekly Chain Store Sales report:

- Official name: Johnson Redbook Retail Sales Index

- Release date: Weekly, generally on Tuesday for the prior week's data, with weeks ending on Saturday (January 13, 2009 release is for the week ending January 10, 2009)

- Produced by: Redbook Research, Inc., New York, NY

- Form of data: Percent changes. Data are available seasonally adjusted.

- Market watchers focus on: Year-ago percent changes (view reports at www. redbookresearch.com/8733.html)

This index is a measure of sales at chain stores, discounters, and department stores as collected by Redbook from company contacts. While the Redbook releases are as timely as those of ICSC-Goldman Sachs, the weekly numbers are not as useful for determining current strength in chain stores. This is because of the way percent changes are calculated. The weekly numbers are comparisons to the prior month and are not simple, week-to-week changes as is the case with ICSC-Goldman Sachs weekly data. In fact, Redbook's weekly numbers are monthly cumulative-to-prior month comparisons. For example, when a first week of the month is available, it is compared to the full prior month. Then, when two weeks of sales are available, the two-week cumulative is compared to the prior month and so on. So it's hard to tell how strong the latest week really is. But the year-ago comparisons are similar to those from ICSC-Goldman.

How Financial Markets React to Weekly Sales Numbers

Even though weekly numbers are seasonally adjusted, the weekly numbers are extremely volatile. That's why markets mainly watch the year-ago percent changes. Both the ISCS-Goldman Sachs and Redbook reports are proprietary (privately owned) and the companies want you to pay to get any significant detail. You'll only see the most recent week-ago and year-ago percent changes for free—generally in stories put out by financial news services. The numbers do get more market attention during big holiday retail seasons—such as Christmas and Easter—so you'll generally only see these reports cause sizeable market swings when there are big changes in year-ago percentages, or if there are swings in "week-ago" sales for several weeks in a row.

The Least You Need to Know

- The retail sales report is the most-followed economic news on the consumer.
- The biggest swings in retail sales typically are caused by auto sales.
- Service station sales can be jerked around by swings in gasoline prices.
- The numbers (units) of new motor vehicle sales are very cyclical and are a leading indicator for the economy.
- Weekly chain store sales numbers can have an impact on retailer stock values.

Chapter 8

Personal Income: Don't Spend It All in One Place

In This Chapter

◆ How personal income fuels consumer spending

◆ Understanding consumer spending components

◆ The personal consumption expenditure price index is closely tracked by the Federal Reserve

◆ Why the personal income report is more up-to-date than the GDP report

The personal income report provides the broadest picture regarding the health of the household sector. After all, when it comes to spending, it's how many bucks get deposited into your bank account—your income—that plays the key role in how much you purchase. You might be wondering if the personal income report tells us so much about consumers, why doesn't it get as much market attention as the employment situation report? Well, they both get lots of attention but the personal income report is released right at the very end of the month, while the employment situation report is early out of the gate, being released on first Fridays.

What Is Personal Income?

The personal income report is produced by the Bureau of Economic Analysis (BEA) in the Commerce Department and is released to the public late in the month, one business day after the GDP report. There are three main sections in the report:

- Personal income
- Disposition of personal income
- Prices or inflation

We look at each of these sections, starting with *personal income*. What is personal income? Generically, personal income is a monetary payment for goods or services or from property (rent) and investments. But the focus here is on income received by individuals as opposed to businesses or governments. That is why an important part of the definition is "personal."

def•i•ni•tion

The Bureau of Economic Analysis has a more detailed definition of personal income. **Personal income** is the income that persons receive in return for their provision of labor, land, and capital used in current production and the net current transfer payments that they receive from business and from government.

Simplified, personal income is the monies individuals get for their labor (salary and wages), owning their own business (proprietor income), for someone using an individual's property (rent), and for financial investments (interest and dividends)—plus private and government aid. The Bureau of Economic Analysis has a more detailed definition.

You would think you already know what a "person" is, but for these government statistics, "persons" consists of individuals, nonprofit institutions that primarily serve households, private noninsured welfare funds, and private trust funds. This broader definition helps to explain income used by individuals and their spending.

Key Facts About the Personal Income Report

Here's what's in the official report:

- Official name: Personal Income and Outlays
- Release date: Monthly, one business day after the GDP release. This is typically during the last week of the month after the reference month for the data (July release has June data).

♦ Produced by: Bureau of Economic Analysis, U.S. Department of Commerce

♦ Form of data: Personal income and its components are in annualized dollars, both in current dollars and in inflation-adjusted chain dollars (year 2000 base). Price indexes are indexed to the year 2000.

♦ Market watchers focus on: Simple monthly percent changes for income, consumption, and price indexes. Data are seasonally adjusted. (View reports at www.bea.gov/National/Index.htm.)

The Major Components of Personal Income

The following table shows the major components and their shares of total personal income. Personal income is the sum of compensation of employees; proprietors' income; rental income of persons; personal income receipts on assets; and personal current transfer receipts—less contributions for government social insurance. Some of the components sound complicated but we can put them in everyday language. Looking ahead, though, think about why we care about the components. Hint: Some affect near-term spending more than others, and this will become clearer shortly.

Personal Income and Disposition, 2008

	Billions of Dollars	Share of Personal Income
Personal Income	**12,099.0**	**100.0%**
Compensation of Employees, Received	**8,047.6**	**66.5%**
Wage and Salary Disbursements	6,543.2	54.1%
Supplements to Wages and Salaries	1,504.5	12.4%
Proprietors' Income	**1,072.4**	**8.9%**
Rental Income of Persons	**64.0**	**0.5%**
Personal Income Receipts from Assets	**2,040.4**	**16.9%**
Personal Interest Income	1,206.3	10.0%
Personal Dividend Income	834.1	6.9%
Personal Current Transfer Receipts	**1,869.8**	**15.5%**
Less: Contributions for Government Social Insurance	**995.2**	**–8.2%**

The biggest component by far is compensation of employees. It makes up two thirds of personal income! It has two major subcomponents: wage and salary disbursements and supplements to wages and salaries. The names are long, but these are the income components you see regularly. Wage and salary disbursements are simply what businesses pay their employees. This includes salaried income and hourly income.

Supplements to wages and salaries are what employers pay for employees' benefits (such as for employee pensions and insurance) and for employer contributions to a number of federal and state benefit and insurance programs. For the latter group, the biggest contributions are for employer contributions to Social Security and Medicare. But here's the full list of where federal and state and local government program contributions go: old age, survivor, and disability insurance (Social Security); hospital insurance; unemployment insurance; railroad retirement; pension benefit guaranty; veterans' life insurance; publicly administered workers' compensation; military medical insurance; and temporary disability insurance.

Trader Tip

The wage and salary disbursements component is the most important component of personal income in the way it affects consumer spending. This is the income that's most available for household spending. Other components affect ability to spend, but generally not as quickly or by as much as wages and salaries. The other types of income, such as rental income, tend to be saved or reinvested more than wages and salaries.

Proprietors' income is income from businesses owned by individuals (including partnerships) rather than corporations, and includes farm and nonfarm businesses.

Rental income is income to persons from rental of real (physical) property. An adjustment is made, so depreciation is on a current basis. There are some interesting features in the rental component. First, the income of individuals primarily making their living in real estate is allocated to proprietors' income. Next, to cover all of the bases of rental income from a pure economics basis, imputed—or implied—income applies to owner-occupied housing. That is, a homeowner is treated as being a business renting to himself or herself and the BEA attributes rental income to the homeowner solely for statistical purposes as related to going into the personal income report.

Personal income from receipts on assets is made up of personal interest income and personal dividend income. Personal interest income is the interest income from all sources. It includes government interest payments and interest payments from outside the United States. But that interest is net of what persons pay to business, government, and overseas. Mortgage interest is excluded since it is taken into account in rental income. Personal dividend income is the net dividend income of persons from all sources.

Only from an Economist

Warning! The personal income definitions are not intended to mimic income that the Internal Revenue Service cares about. The personal income report focuses on income related to "payment" for current use of labor, management of proprietor businesses, or assets. Increases in the value of assets—or appreciation—are not counted as income. While a capital gain is income for the IRS, it is not income related to current production and is not included in personal income here.

Personal current transfer receipts are income payments to persons for which no current services are performed. These are basically Social Security, Medicare, unemployment insurance, federal old age and survivor benefits, food stamps, disability, earned income credits, and a number of other programs both from the government and businesses. Business write-offs of bad consumer debt are included.

Now, we need to take out one major component to get personal income. This is contributions for government social insurance made by employers, employees, the self-employed, and other individuals who participate in these government programs. These programs include Social Security, hospital insurance, and unemployment insurance, among others. These contributions are deducted from the sources of income so that personal income includes only government social benefits received by the sector rather than both benefits and contributions associated with the same programs.

The What-You-Do-With-It Side of Personal Income

The second side to personal income is what you do with it. That is, you can take your money and do the following: pay taxes, buy things and services, pay interest, make certain transfer payments through nonprofit organizations or directly to persons overseas, and save.

Trader Tip

Want to pay less income tax? Then consider moving to Alaska, Florida, Nevada, South Dakota, Texas, Washington State, or Wyoming. As of 2008, these states do not impose an income tax on individuals. Also, think about New Hampshire and Tennessee. They only impose income taxes on dividends and interest income over a moderate threshold.

Only from an Economist

You may be thinking, where do money gifts to friends or family fit in? And what about charitable contributions? Those aren't in any category mentioned in income or spending. Well, it's all about avoiding double counting. A gift paid by a person to another person does not change total personal income—it just shifts around which individual has that income. Trying to count gifts as income likely would result in counting the same income twice—the gift would likely be reported as paid but not by the person receiving it. Next, charities are seen by the BEA as serving individuals. So charitable contributions are seen as staying in personal income. Because data on charitable contributions are of such poor quality, the BEA decided to not have a special category since the net effect on personal income would be zero if calculated properly.

Personal current taxes are tax payments (net of refunds) by U.S. residents that are not chargeable to business expense. Personal taxes include income taxes and taxes on personal property. Taxes on real estate are not included since those are considered business taxes.

Only from an Economist

The federal income tax was made constitutional with the passage of the Sixteenth Amendment to the Constitution in 1913. In 1913, the tax rate was 1 percent on taxable income above $3,000 ($4,000 for married couples), less deductions and exemptions. The maximum rate was 7 percent on incomes above $500,000. For calendar 2008, the maximum marginal tax rate was 35 percent for taxable income over $357,700 for single taxpayers and those married filing jointly, and over $178,850 for those married filing separately.

So, after taxes, what's left? Why, that's your *disposable personal income*. This is what you get to play with!

While financial markets focus on overall personal income in the monthly reports, it is disposable or after-tax income that drives consumer spending in the long run. Take a look at the disposable personal income and spending chart to see a comparison between disposable personal income and spending.

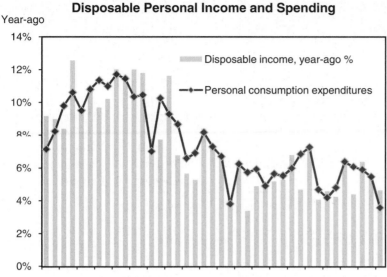

Disposable Personal Income and Spending

Year-ago

Legend:
- Disposable income, year-ago %
- Personal consumption expenditures

Disposable personal income and spending.

Personal outlays are what you do with disposable personal income other than save, such as buy things or services, pay interest, or make a gift or donation. So there are three major components in personal outlays: personal consumption expenditures (PCEs), personal interest payments, and personal current transfer payments.

def•i•ni•tion

Disposable personal income is personal income less personal current taxes. It is the income available to persons for spending or saving.

PCEs are purchases of things and services used by a consumer. Officially, PCEs measure the value of the goods and services bought by persons. PCEs typically make up 95 percent or more of personal outlays. Here are the major goods and services components in PCEs:

- Durable goods: major categories are motor vehicles and parts, and furniture and household equipment. Durable goods are those with expected lifetimes of at least three years.

- Nondurable goods: includes food; clothing and shoes; gasoline, fuel oil, and other energy goods.

- Services: components are housing, household operation (which includes electricity and gas), transportation, medical care, recreation, and other. The other services subcomponent includes personal business services (e.g., brokerage, banking, insurance, legal services) as well as personal care, recreation, education, and religion.

Disposition of Personal Income, 2008

	Billions of Dollars	Share of Personal Income	Share of Personal Consumption Expenditures
Personal Income	12,099.0	100.0%	
Less: Current Personal Taxes	1,462.0	12.1%	
Equals: Disposable Personal Income	10,637.1	87.9%	
Less: Personal Outlays	10,454.7	86.4%	
Personal Consumption Expenditures	10,058.5	83.1%	100.0%
Durable Goods	1,022.7	8.5%	10.2%
Nondurable Goods	2,966.9	24.5%	29.5%
Services	6,068.9	50.2%	60.3%
Personal Interest Payments	251.4	2.1%	
Personal Current Transfer Payments	144.7	1.2%	
Equals: Personal Saving	182.4	1.5%	
Misc. Personal Saving Rate, % of Disposable Personal Income	1.7		

Look at the following personal consumption expenditure chart. Durable goods are the most cyclically sensitive while services are the most stable over the business cycle. Durables include things you can put off buying during tough times (like cars and household appliances) while services have stable demand (such as for housing and medical services). Nondurables are not very volatile and include essentials such as food and gasoline.

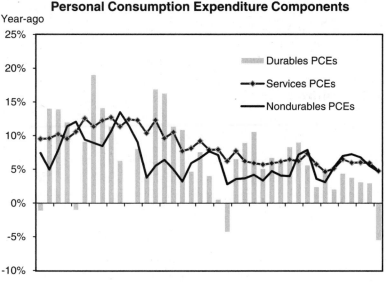

Personal Consumption Expenditure Components

Personal consumption expenditure components.

Personal interest payments are interest payments by persons to businesses. Simply, this is nonmortgage interest paid to businesses—including interest on car loans, credit card debt, and other personal debt. Remember, mortgage interest is considered a business expense.

Personal current transfer payments consist of transfer payments to government and to the rest of the world. Payments to government includes donations, fees, and fines paid to federal, state, and local governments. So these include everything from the entrance fee to your local state park to that speeding ticket you got stuck with. Payments to the rest of the world are largely personal payments to individuals overseas less payments from individuals overseas. For the most part, these payments are immigrants and other workers sending money "back home."

What's Left? Personal Saving

Personal saving (in the personal income accounts) is different from the way you typically think about saving. Here, personal saving is simply the income left over after paying taxes and after personal consumption outlays. It is nothing more than a math formula. While lots of effort goes into estimating personal income and personal outlays, no effort is made to directly estimate personal saving—it's simply a statistical leftover! So how good the estimate is for personal saving depends on whether personal income and outlays are well estimated.

Does personal saving make sense? It does from the view of the BEA, who wants to measure current income and spending. We often think of saving in terms of how much our house is appreciating or in terms of whether the stock market is going up. Appreciation raises the value of assets that we can use for retirement, but appreciation is not based on current production or current payment for the use of an asset. So many of the ways we think of "savings" don't enter into the official calculations for personal saving. This is partly why U.S. official saving rates appear so low. The official BEA saving rate is saving divided by disposable personal income.

Take a look at the personal saving rate and disposable personal income chart below. There has been a long-term downward trend in the personal saving rate as households have increased spending by borrowing through credit cards and home equity lines of credit.

Personal saving rate and disposable personal income.

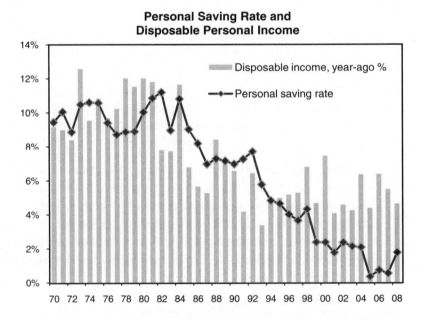

When the stock market was rising, it also boosted spending outside of income. Disposable personal income growth has eased somewhat along with inflation over the years. The recession that started in 2008 worsened in part as consumers realized they were overspending and needed to pay down the debt that had fueled spending during the prior two decades. The personal saving rate in 2008 was boosted in part also by income tax rebate checks. They were intended for fiscal stimulus but much of the money was saved instead of spent. Consumers also cut back on credit card spending and worked on rebuilding retirement funds after the stock market drop during 2007 and 2008.

> ### Only from an Economist
>
> Saving is not as easy as it used to be. A six-month certificate of deposit attracted only a 1.53 percent rate of return in January 2009. It had been as high as 6.91 percent in June 2000 and as much as 17.98 percent in August 1981. Why such a difference in interest rates? Interest rates generally track inflation rates. The CPI inflation rate (looking at twelve-month-ago changes) was minus 0.1 percent in January 2009, compared to 3.7 percent in June 2000 and 10.8 percent in August 1981

What Are the Differences Between PCEs and Retail Sales?

Both retail sales and PCEs measure consumer spending. But they do not move exactly the same. This is because there are some differences in coverage and differences in measurement of components. First, remember that the personal income and retail sales reports have two very different focuses. The retail sales report focuses on sales by retail establishments to individuals but also includes some (modest fraction) of business-to-business sales. The personal income report has spending by households only. While retail sales data are based entirely on market transactions, some PCE components are not. A key example is the spending on use of houses by homeowners which is attributed to homeowners as if they were paying rent to themselves.

A significant difference in coverage is related to services—which PCEs have while retail sales have only durables and nondurables. But due to the overlap in coverage for durables and nondurables, a key point is that much of the retail sales report is the foundation for the durables and nondurables portions of personal consumption expenditures. But the BEA makes adjustments whenever better data are available than what is found in retail sales for certain PCE subcomponents. We'll see an example below.

Here are some significant differences between what's in the major components in retail sales but not in PCEs:

- ◆ Sales of motor vehicles and parts are survey-based. These sales are not just to persons—but also to businesses and to government. PCEs use more reliable and comprehensive data from automakers.

- ◆ Sales of gasoline and oil are survey-based. Similar PCEs components are based on more reliable industry estimates.

- ◆ Retail sales include building materials, hardware, garden supplies, and mobile home dealer sales. These are largely taken out in PCEs since they are more related to business spending on residential investment than to personal spending.

Here are some significant differences between what's in the major components in PCEs but not in retail sales:

♦ Retail sales essentially have no services purchases while PCEs do. The BEA adds in services from other data sources.

♦ Motor vehicle sales are based on sales data directly from manufacturers and are also limited to sales to consumers, and not to businesses and government.

♦ PCEs add in dealers' margins on used car sales.

♦ Gasoline and oil sales are based on data from the Department of Transportation and the Department of Labor.

♦ PCEs include spending abroad by U.S. residents.

♦ PCEs include personal remittances in kind to foreigners.

There are various additional miscellaneous components for each of these, but the above differences are the most notable.

> **Trader Tip**
>
> Many market watchers use the retail sales numbers to estimate portions of PCEs, which are released two weeks later. The retail sales control series—as named by the BEA—is retail sales excluding motor vehicle sales and the broad component for building materials and supply stores. The retail sales control series moves closely with durables and nondurables PCEs, excluding motor vehicles.

PCE Price Indexes: The Fed Is Watching!

The final area of the personal income report that cannot be ignored is that of price indexes—inflation measures. The initial personal income report has price indexes for overall personal consumption expenditures, the three major components of PCEs, and a few specially calculated price indexes with the standout being PCEs excluding food and energy. Later, the BEA makes price indexes for the next level of detail below durables, nondurables, and services, in its publication entitled *Survey of Current Business* and on its website.

To view *Survey of Current Business*, go to www.bea.gov/scb/index.htm. Go to the link for "Charts, Tables, More." See Table 2.3.4.

How do financial markets view the PCE price indexes? Financial markets see the PCE price indexes as the best measures of inflation for the consumer sector. This is largely because the Federal Reserve focuses on the headline PCE price index and the core PCE price index as their preferred measures of consumer price inflation. Financial markets focus on the headline (overall) PCE price index and PCE price index excluding food and energy when evaluating inflation pressures.

We will come across quite often shorthand names for the two primary inflation measures for various inflation reports (yes, there are several in coming chapters). The two most common measures getting market attention are called *headline inflation* and *core inflation*. The first is for overall inflation and the second excludes the volatile food and energy components. Headline inflation is the number that the media gives the most attention.

The obvious shortcoming of the PCE price indexes is that they come out about two weeks after the CPI report. What are their advantages? In the PCE versus CPI chart, you can see how they compare.

Now, there are two main reasons the Federal Reserve sees the PCE price indexes as superior to the CPIs. First, the PCE price indexes have updated weighting of components. The PCE price indexes are chain-weighted indexes, meaning the component weights are updated every year and chained together. In contrast, the CPI has fixed weights from the base year. The fixed weighting means the CPI has an upward bias measuring inflation of about a quarter of a percentage point. That is, the CPI does not take into account that, over time, consumers change their spending patterns away from higher-priced goods. Keeping fixed weights means that the CPI includes inflation numbers for components that consumers aren't purchasing that much.

> ## def•i•ni•tion
>
> **Headline inflation** is the overall or total inflation rate for a given inflation indicator—such as for personal consumption expenditure prices, for the consumer price index, or for the producer price index. (with the latter two discussed in Chapter 10).
>
> **Core inflation** is the overall inflation rate but excluding the volatile food and energy components.

The second and less important reason the Fed prefers the PCE price indexes to the CPI report is that the PCE price index is a little more comprehensive in scope. It includes some minor services components not included in the CPI. The bottom line is that the overall PCE and core PCE price indexes provide a better view as to how the Fed sees inflation than the CPI does. Over time, the PCE price index has an inflation rate that is about a quarter percentage point lower than for the CPI—and the Fed believes the PCE price index is more accurate.

Core inflation measures: PCE vs. CPI.

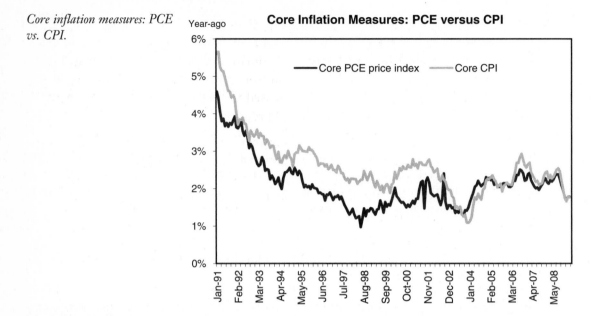

Core Inflation Measures: PCE versus CPI

We'll talk more about it later, but the Fed's implicit inflation target is 1.5 to 2 percent annualized inflation. So watch to see if the PCE and PCE core price indexes are tracking in this range to gauge whether the Fed is willing to cut interest rates or sees the need to raise rates. The implication for monthly numbers is that headline and core PCE price index numbers need to average a little below 0.2 percent monthly increases to keep the Fed happy. That is, we want numbers going between 0.1 percent and 0.2 percent, and only an occasional 0.3 percent monthly gain. No, you can't expect a consistent number every month!

Special Events and Personal Income, Spending, and Price Indexes

There are a number of special events that can cause sudden swings in certain indicators in the personal income report. For instance, natural disasters can have an impact on personal income—with hurricanes being the most frequent such event. When a hurricane is big enough, it can put people out of work for weeks. In the month that a large hurricane hits a major metropolitan area, massive numbers of homes are destroyed and rental income is slashed enough that you actually notice it on a national scale. The rental losses are both for actual rental homes and on the imputed rental income in owner-occupied homes.

Hurricane Katrina devastated New Orleans in August 2005. For that month, rental income decreased $92 billion (annual rate—remember, personal income and components are annualized for monthly numbers), primarily reflecting uninsured damages to residential structures, which is a deduction from rental income. But a partial offset was the current transfer receipts, which increased $72 billion (annual rate), primarily reflecting net benefits for damage to insured property.

In 2008, Hurricanes Gustav and Ike hit major metropolitan areas in Texas and had similar but not as massive impacts on personal income. As of the end of 2008, Hurricane Katrina held the record for causing the most losses in rental income. Previously, the record had been held by Hurricane Andrew, which hit southern Florida and Louisiana in August 1992.

Also sometimes affecting wages and salaries is the annual pay raise for federal employees in January of each year. The timing is well known, but the magnitude is not always easy to seasonally adjust smoothly.

Only from an Economist

Once in a while, even a major corporation can reach out and touch national statistics. This was the case in December 2004 when Microsoft Corporation made a special dividend payment. Personal income spiked a huge monthly 3.7 percent in December 2004 and mainly reflected the payment of a special dividend by the Microsoft Corporation. On July 20, 2004, Microsoft announced that it would pay a special dividend of $3.00 per share to shareholders of record as of November 17, 2004. The total payout, which was made on December 2, 2004, was about $32 billion. This type of impact on personal income by a single corporation is not common. Excluding this special factor, personal income increased a more moderate 0.6 percent.

More recently, fiscal stimulus programs have resulted in occasional sharp swings in personal income. The biggest spike in 2008 personal income was in May 2008 when the first round of income tax rebate checks went out to try to boost the economy.

In addition, sharp changes in oil prices can cause the headline PCE price index to jump or fall. Also, the nondurables component of PCEs tends to move in tandem with oil prices (but not as sharply), since gasoline and heating oil are part of nondurables PCEs. So watch out for weakness that is price induced and should be discounted. The personal income report actually has a specific way to address that issue. PCEs and the three main subcomponents are not only published in current dollars, but in real, chain-weighted dollars. The chain-weighted PCEs are not always discussed in news reports, but they are readily available in the official report.

Sharp swings in oil prices cause the overall (headline) PCE price index to move more sharply than the core PCE price index. Oil prices rose dramatically during mid-2008 but dropped steeply toward year end.

How Markets Move on the News Release

When the personal income report comes out, markets focus on four key numbers and the monthly percent changes in overall personal income, the core PCE price index, the overall PCE price index, and overall personal consumption expenditures. If there are quirks in the headline personal income number, many analysts call attention to the wages and salaries component as more representative of the underlying trend in income.

During most of the business cycle, gains in personal income are positive for the stock market and negative for the bond market (resulting in higher interest rates). But if the economy is at a turning point, the income number could be seen as tipping the Fed's hand to make a policy change in interest rates. During a slowing economy, a particularly weak income number could be seen as causing an interest rate reduction by the Fed, thereby boosting optimism in equity markets. The reverse is true when the economy is starting to heat up too much. High inflation numbers also tend to boost interest rates and cause bond prices to fall.

The Least You Need to Know

- Markets watch the personal income report to see how much spending power consumers have.

- For near-term impact, the wages and salaries component is more important than overall personal income; for the long-term, watch disposable personal income.

- Personal consumption expenditures (PCEs) give a broader view of household spending than retail sales but are not as timely.

- The Fed bases its interest rate decisions largely on the PCE price index numbers because the PCE price indexes are better measures of inflation than are the consumer price indexes.

Chapter 9

Consumer Sentiment and Confidence

In This Chapter

◆ The Consumer Sentiment Index

◆ The Consumer Confidence Index

◆ Differences between the two surveys

Nervous about the layoffs you're hearing about on the news? Upset over the price of gasoline? Or is the company you work for having a banner year? The answers to those questions can affect how consumers feel about the economy and whether they are up for making major purchases such as a house, a car, or even a new washing machine. There are two major surveys on consumer attitudes; we look at how they keep tabs on the consumer mood.

The Two Consumer Attitude Surveys

There are two major surveys about consumer attitudes that are tracked by financial markets and policymakers. These surveys are produced by the University of Michigan in collaboration with Reuters, and by the Conference Board, a nonprofit research organization for business. The Reuters/University of Michigan measure is called the *Consumer Sentiment Index* and the Conference Board's headline index is called the *Consumer Confidence Index*. Although the general news media (but not business news reporters) may use "consumer confidence" interchangeably for the two, the indexes do differ. For those in the know, "sentiment" is always associated with Reuters/University of Michigan and "confidence" is tied to the Conference Board. It's like matching names and faces at a cocktail party—don't mix them up or it's egg-on-your-face time!

def•i•ni•tion

The **Consumer Sentiment Index** is a measure of consumers' attitudes toward the economy. Likewise, the **Consumer Confidence Index** is a measure of consumers' attitudes toward the economy. They simply are measured by different organizations.

The Consumer Sentiment Index

The Consumer Sentiment Index comes from the Surveys of Consumers, which started back in 1946. The surveys are conducted by the Survey Research Center at the University of Michigan. Originally conducted only annually, the surveys were taken two or three times each year from 1953 through 1959. They were done quarterly from 1960 through 1977 and have been conducted monthly since 1978. Each month, a minimum of 500 interviews are conducted by telephone from the University of Michigan campus at Ann Arbor. The sample is designed to be representative of households in the contiguous 48 states, excluding Alaska and Hawaii.

The main questions in the surveys cover three broad areas of consumer sentiment: personal finances, business conditions, and buying conditions. There are additional questions concerning expected changes in inflation, unemployment, and interest rates, among others. (We'll talk about inflation in detail in the next chapter.) Finally, respondents are asked their views of present market conditions for buying large household durables, vehicles, and houses.

I mentioned that these surveys are done in collaboration with Reuters. Oh, yes—who's Reuters? Thomson Reuters is an information company headquartered in New York City. Although a diverse company, Reuters is best known to many as a news distribution company. Starting in 2007, Reuters established a relationship with the Survey

Research Center as the initial distributor of the monthly results of the Surveys of Consumers. Hence the name Reuters/University of Michigan Consumer Sentiment Index. We call it the Consumer Sentiment Index for short, as many do.

Key Facts About the Consumer Sentiment Index

Here's what's in the official report for the Consumer Sentiment Index:

◆ Official name: Reuters/University of Michigan Surveys of Consumers

◆ Release date: Twice monthly. Preliminary estimates for a month are released mid-month. Final estimates for a month are released near the end of the month. The reference month is the same as the month released (June data are released in June).

◆ Produced by: Thomson Reuters and the Institute for Social Research (ISR) of the University of Michigan

◆ Form of data: Indexes for sentiment indexes and percent for inflation expectations. Some series are seasonally adjusted.

◆ Market watchers focus on: The headline index level and the inflation expectations number (view reports at www.about.reuters.com/productinfo/university-michigan)

In the following table, you can see the key series in the Consumer Sentiment Index.

Consumer Sentiment Index, Key Series

The following table shows the part of the Consumer Sentiment Index report that markets focus on. At the time of news release, financial markets key in on the overall Consumer Sentiment Index, followed by the two component indexes plus two inflation outlook indexes.

	Feb 08	Nov 08	Dec 08	Jan 09	Feb 09
Consumer Sentiment Index	70.8	55.3	60.1	61.2	56.3
Current Conditions Index	83.8	57.5	69.5	66.5	65.5
Expectations Index	62.4	53.9	54.0	57.8	50.5
Inflation Expectations, 1 Year Out	3.6	2.9	1.7	2.2	1.9
Inflation Expectations, 5 Years Out	3.0	2.9	2.6	2.9	3.1

Behind the Consumer Sentiment Index

There are three key series on how consumers view the status of the economy in the Reuters/Michigan report:

♦ The Consumer Sentiment Index (the headline or overall index)

♦ The Index of Current Economic Conditions

♦ The Index of Consumer Expectations

The current conditions and expectations indexes essentially are components of the overall index. The Consumer Sentiment Index is based on answers to the following five questions:

♦ We are interested in how people are getting along financially these days. Would you say that you (and your family living there) are better off or worse off financially than you were a year ago?

♦ Now looking ahead—do you think that a year from now you (and your family living there) will be better off financially, or worse off, or just about the same as now?

♦ Now turning to business conditions in the country as a whole—do you think that during the next 12 months we'll have good times financially, or bad times, or what?

♦ Looking ahead, which would you say is more likely—that in the country as a whole we'll have continuous good times during the next five years or so, or that we will have periods of widespread unemployment or depression, or what?

♦ About the big things people buy for their homes—such as furniture, a refrigerator, stove, television, and things like that—generally speaking, do you think now is a good or bad time for people to buy major household items?

To calculate the Consumer Sentiment Index (CSI), the scores for each question are calculated. What is called the relative score for each question is the percent giving favorable replies minus the percent giving unfavorable replies plus 100. The scores are added up and then divided by the base period value for 1966 to put the number in index form.

The CSI has two components based on two groupings of the previous five questions. The Index of Current Economic Conditions is based on questions 1 and 5. Meanwhile, the Index of Consumer Expectations uses questions 2, 3, and 4.

Other Questions in the Surveys of Consumers

There actually are about 50 questions in this telephone survey. But in addition to the main questions, the ones getting the most attention from the media are related to inflation. These are for one-year-ahead inflation and long-term inflation.

◆ By about what percent do you expect prices to go up/down, on the average, during the next 12 months?

◆ By about what percent per year do you expect prices to go up/down, on the average, during the next 5 to 10 years?

There also are similar questions on expected unemployment, interest rates, and family income. Finally, respondents are asked about current conditions for buying and selling. These cover current conditions for buying and for selling a house (separate questions), buying furniture and appliances, and buying a car.

In the expectations versus real GDP chart that follows, you can see that the Consumer Expectations Index has frequently turned down well ahead of real GDP in recession.

> ### Only from an Economist
>
> You may remember from Chapter 2 that the Index of Consumer Expectations is one of the 10 components of the Conference Board's index of leading indicators. Apparently, consumers are psychic when it comes to the economy!

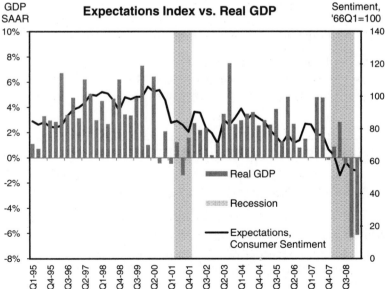

Expectations Index vs. Real GDP.

(Source for Expectations Index: 2009 The Regents of the University of Michigan. Surveys of Consumers: Survey Research Center, University of Michigan. Source for Real GDP: U.S. Bureau of Economic Analysis.)

The Consumer Confidence Index

The Consumer Confidence Index is published monthly by the Conference Board in the Consumer Confidence Survey. It began in 1967 as an every-other-month publication and became monthly in 1977. The Consumer Confidence Survey is based on a representative sample of 5,000 U.S. households. The survey is conducted by TNS and, according to the Conference Board, it's the world's largest custom research company with a focus on marketing research.

The survey has two main sections. The first covers consumers' assessment of current and expected conditions. This section results in the data for the headline indexes: the Consumer Confidence Index, the Present Situation Index, and the Expectations Index. Expectations questions also touch on consumer views on inflation in a year as well as interest rates and the stock market. The second focuses on buying plans for autos, homes, and major appliances, as well as on vacation plans.

Key Facts About the Consumer Confidence Index

Here's what's in the official report for the Consumer Confidence Index:

 ◆ Official name: The Conference Board Consumer Confidence Index

 ◆ Release date: Monthly, the last week of the month. The reference month is the same as the month released (June data are released in June).

 ◆ Produced by: The Conference Board

 ◆ Form of data: Indexes for confidence indexes and percent for inflation expectations. Some series are seasonally adjusted

 ◆ Market watchers focus on: The headline index level and the inflation expectations results (view reports at http://www.conference-board.org/)

The Major Components of the Consumer Confidence Index

The Consumer Confidence Index has two components: the Present Situation Index and the Expectations Index. The Present Situation Index focuses on consumer views on how good or bad business conditions are and employment conditions. The Expectations Index takes into account what conditions consumers believe will exist in six months from the time of the survey for business conditions, employment, and income. Here's a recap of the components and the range of possible answers to each key question:

- The Consumer Confidence Index has two components: present situation and expectations.

- The Present Situation Index focuses on: business conditions (are they "good," "bad," or "normal"?) and employment (are "jobs plentiful," "jobs not so plentiful," or "jobs hard to get"?)

- The Expectations Index (six months out) focus on: business conditions (is it "better," "worse," or "same"?), employment (are there "more jobs," "fewer jobs," or "same"?), and income (will it "increase," "decrease," or "remain the same"?).

Each of the indexes is based on netting the three answers—positive from negative, such as "good" less "bad." There are also special questions for "12 months hence" for the inflation rate, interest rates, and stock prices. For inflation, consumers are asked their opinion of the "average" inflation rate. For interest rates, the possible answers are "higher," "same," and "lower." For the 12-month-out stock prices question, respondents can reply with "increase," "same," or "decrease."

Take a look at the Consumer Confidence Index in the following.

Consumer Confidence Index

Composite indexes:	Feb 08	Nov 08	Dec 08	Jan 09	Feb 09
Consumer Confidence Index	76.4	44.7	38.6	37.4	25.0
Present Situation	104.0	42.3	30.2	29.7	21.2
Expectations	58.0	46.2	44.2	42.5	27.5
Appraisal of Present Situation:					
Business Conditions					
Good	19.1	10.1	7.7	6.5	6.8
Bad	21.3	40.6	45.8	47.9	51.1
Normal	59.6	49.3	46.5	45.6	42.1

continues

Consumer Confidence Index   (continued)

Appraisal of Present Situation	Feb 08	Nov 08	Dec 08	Jan 09	Feb 09
Employment					
Jobs plentiful	21.5	8.7	6.5	7.1	4.4
Not so plentiful	55.1	54.2	52.0	51.8	47.8
Jobs hard to get	23.4	37.1	41.5	41.1	47.8
Expectations for Six Months Hence:					
Business Conditions					
Better	9.7	11.5	13.4	12.8	8.7
Worse	21.6	28.3	32.9	31.1	40.5
Same	68.7	60.2	53.7	56.1	50.8
Employment					
More Jobs	8.9	9.2	9.8	9.1	7.1
Fewer Jobs	28.0	33.7	40.6	36.9	47.3
Same	63.1	57.1	49.6	54.0	45.6
Income					
Increase	18.0	13.1	12.7	10.3	7.6
Decrease	10.6	18.0	18.8	18.4	23.8
Same	71.4	68.9	68.5	71.3	68.6
Inflation Expectations, 12-Month Percent Change	5.4	5.9	5.8	5.6	5.9

Differences Between the Two Surveys

Let's take a minute to look at the differences between the Consumer Confidence Index and Consumer Sentiment Index.

Over the business cycle, the Consumer Confidence Index tends to have larger swings than the Consumer Sentiment Index. There are two likely reasons for this. First, the Conference Board's measure focuses more on labor markets, and the Reuters/ Michigan index gives more weight to financial conditions and income. Unemployment tends to be more volatile than overall financial conditions and income. Second, the expectations component in the Consumer Confidence Index has a shorter time horizon than in the Consumer Sentiment Index (six months out versus 12 months out for one question and five years out for another). The longer time horizon tends to smooth consumers' views on the outlook. You can see a graphical representation of the differences between the two surveys in the chart that follows.

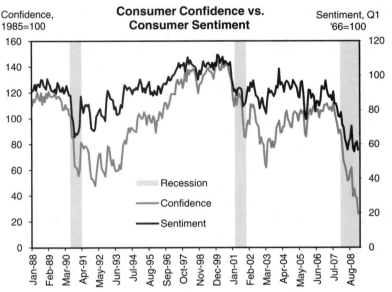

Confidence, 1985=100

Consumer Confidence vs. Consumer Sentiment

Sentiment, Q1 '66=100

Consumer Confidence vs. Consumer Sentiment.

(Source of Consumer Confidence Index: Reproduced with permission from The Conference Board, Inc. Consumer Confidence Index (2009). © 2009, The Conference Board, Inc. Source for Consumer Sentiment Index: 2009 The Regents of the University of Michigan, Surveys of Consumers, Survey Research Center, University of Michigan.)

The Consumer Sentiment Index is released twice during the month while the Consumer Confidence Index is released just once. The Consumer Sentiment Index is made public at mid-month and during the last week of the month. The initial release is based on about 60 percent of the survey sample while the end-of-the-month release is based on the full sample. The initial release gives the Reuters/Michigan survey a two-week advantage over the Conference Board's survey in terms of timeliness. For the same reference month as that covered by Reuters/Michigan, the Conference Board publishes near the end of the month.

The Consumer Confidence Index changes samples completely each month, whereas the Consumer Sentiment Index gradually changes the monthly sample. The monthly changeover in samples by the Conference Board creates some volatility in the monthly numbers.

Only from an Economist

Can you guess the point in U.S. history when consumer confidence hit an all-time high? After the big victories of World War II? During the go-go and space exploration era of the 1960s? Or during the yuppie boom of the 1980s? Well, I'll give you some hints.

Talking economics first, the unemployment rate was 4.0 percent and the federal deficit was actually a surplus of $255 billion for the calendar year! CPI inflation was 3.8 percent. For the year, the top musical hit according to Billboard was "Breathe" by Faith Hill. The world had just successfully survived Y2K. And Bill Clinton was starting the last year of his eight-year presidency. The all-time high in consumer sentiment was January 2000, which followed about 10 years of continuous economic expansion. But the plateau in consumer sentiment was short-lived. Recession began in April 2001 after the dot-com crash of 2000. The 2001 recession was caused largely by an asset bubble, which is not easily picked up by consumer attitude surveys.

The Conference Board survey is primarily a subscription service, whereas the Reuters/University of Michigan survey is more publicly available. The Conference Board sells detailed information from its Consumer Confidence Survey on a subscription basis. So nonsubscribers generally see only basic information in news releases. The basic numbers in news coverage usually include the overall index and its two components and likely the inflation expectations number. The Reuters/University of Michigan survey is made fully public without charge, but the full report comes out with a modest lag of several days.

Starting in 2007, Reuters obtained full rights for the initial distribution of the University of Michigan report and it immediately releases full results only to subscribers. But again, the full report is available for free within days. Key numbers are available immediately through various financial news services and websites.

How Markets Move on Release of Sentiment and Confidence

Both the Consumer Sentiment Index and the Consumer Confidence Indexes are evaluated in essentially the same manner by financial markets. A rise in the index is seen as a positive for the stock market—consumers are more likely to spend more—and the rise also tends to bump up interest rates. A rise in inflation expectations leads to higher interest rates, especially for medium-term and long-term notes and bonds since short-term rates are held hostage to whatever the current Federal Reserve interest rate target is.

In contrast to most economic indicators, the Consumer Sentiment Index and Consumer Confidence Index are seen as more general measures of consumer health rather than a measure of some specific facet of the consumer sector. For example, monthly changes in sentiment or confidence are not a good predictor of monthly changes in retail sales. We already know that retail sales can jump around due to "off and on" discounts by auto dealers and swings in gasoline prices. In the chart below, we take out those effects and compare consumer confidence with retail sales. In fact, the retail sales numbers in this chart are three-month-moving averages and there are still swings not explained by the Consumer Confidence Index.

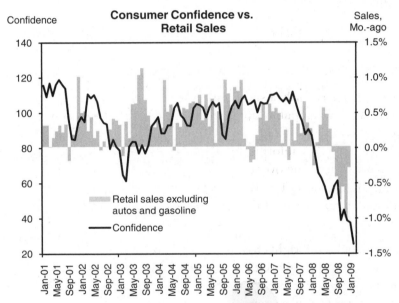

Consumer Confidence vs. retail sales.

(Source of Consumer Confidence Index: Reproduced with permission from The Conference Board, Inc. Consumer Confidence Index (2009). © 2009, The Conference Board, Inc. Source for retail sales: U.S. Bureau of the Census.)

However, it is clear that the two do move in common trends throughout the business cycle. You can predict any given month's retail sales well with the Consumer Confidence Index, and this holds true also for the Consumer Sentiment Index. The bottom line is that both indexes are good overall measures of the health of the consumer sector, but don't look to them to do a specific month's forecast.

Trader Tip _____

While markets usually just focus on the headline numbers for both surveys, the expectations components do a better job of forecasting future growth for the economy. So when either survey shows a sharp change in the expectations component, markets can move! If expectations go down, so may the stock market.

Finally, both surveys' inflation expectations numbers get market attention, especially in the bond markets because inflation numbers can have a large impact on longer-term interest rates. However, it's generally recognized that the Conference Board's inflation expectations numbers typically run higher than those from the Reuters/Michigan survey, and in fact, even higher than actual inflation. There hasn't been a good explanation for this. But market watchers focus on the change in expected inflation rather than the actual inflation numbers in the reports. That is, if expected inflation goes from 4 to 5 percent in the Conference Board survey, analysts focus on the fact that expected inflation has risen 1 percentage point rather than on the average response expecting a 5 percent inflation rate.

The Least You Need to Know

- The Consumer Sentiment Index and the Consumer Confidence Index give good summary measures of the health of the consumer sector.

- Indexes of consumer expectations are leading indicators for the economy.

- Remember which organization does which index on consumer attitudes. The University of Michigan does the "sentiment" index while The Conference Board does the "confidence" index.

Part 3

Inflation Numbers

If you buy gasoline for your car or buy fresh meat at the grocery store, you already know what inflation is about. But the government and financial markets want to know more than just that it cost more to fill the gas tank this week than last month. The nitty-gritty details on what consumers pay at the store also affect what the financial markets think that interest rates should be. Plus, the official inflation numbers can tip the balance on whether the Federal Reserve raises or lowers interest rates. And don't forget, when you retire, the inflation numbers will affect the next year's Social Security payment.

But there's more to inflation than what consumers have to pay. Key inflation numbers cover the labor markets, what manufacturers get for their products, and reflect the high-flying commodities markets that include oil and gold, among others.

Chapter 10

Consumer and Producer Price Inflation

In This Chapter

- ◆ Inflation, deflation, and other cool price definitions
- ◆ The Consumer Price Index report
- ◆ The Producer Price Index report
- ◆ How inflation affects the markets

No consumer likes higher prices. Paying more for an item really cuts into how far your paycheck goes, doesn't it? But high prices don't sneak up on you like a silent thief in the night, either. It's hard to ignore high prices when they practically scream out at you from gas station road signs or from the aisles in your local grocery store.

Inflation is on all our minds these days. So it's a great time to empower yourself with knowledge, right? There are two major reports on inflation: one at the consumer level and one at the producer level.

So, What Is Inflation?

We've briefly mentioned *inflation* in earlier chapters on GDP and personal income. But now is a good time to be more explicit about what inflation means.

Inflation is a trend of rising prices for goods and services in the economy. It is not a jump in prices for one or two things but a rise in the price level in general. The inflation rate is the pace at which the general price level rises. For example, if the inflation rate is 3 percent annually, an item costing $1.00 today will cost $1.03 in a year.

There are two related terms that are sometimes confused with each other. *Deflation* is when overall prices are falling. For example, if the rate of deflation is 3 percent per year, an item costing $1.00 today will cost $0.97 in a year.

def•i•ni•tion

Inflation is a trend of rising prices for goods and services in general in the economy. **Deflation** is a downtrend for the general level of prices. Overall prices are falling. **Disinflation** is a slowdown in the rate of inflation; prices still go up, but at a slower rate.

However, *disinflation* is often confused with deflation. Disinflation is merely a slowing in the rate that prices rise. With disinflation, prices still go up, but at a slower rate. Here's an example: If the inflation rate this year is 4 percent and next year it's 3 percent, this is a period of disinflation. Disinflation is not declining prices—just slower inflation!

Now that we understand the broad picture, let's take a look at the world's most important inflation report—the Consumer Price Index Report.

The Consumer Price Index Report

The Consumer Price Index (CPI) report is one of the most important economic indicators released by the government. It's probably number three in importance behind the employment and GDP reports. Bond traders—who are particularly sensitive to inflation—might rank it number two! Overall, inflation numbers matter to the financial markets, to businesses, and to consumers. This monthly index is published by the Bureau of Labor Statistics (BLS) which is a part of the U.S. Department of Labor. According to the BLS, the CPI is a measure of the average change in prices over time of goods and services purchased by households. The CPI is an index measuring a fixed basket of goods and services (it assumes the same items are purchased over extended periods of time), which currently includes over 200 categories of items. The CPI data are based on prices of food, clothing, shelter, fuels, transportation fares, charges for doctors' and dentists' services, drugs, and other goods and services that people buy for day-to-day living.

Only from an Economist

You know the CPI is an index, but what does that mean? First, the base period is January 1982 through January 1984 with the index equal to 100 for that three-year average. The CPI indicates how much higher or lower the general price level for consumers is relative to the base year. For example, the CPI for December 2008 was 210.228 (not seasonally adjusted). This means that consumer prices on average in December 2008 were 110.228 percent higher than in the 1982–1984 base period (210.228 minus 100 since 100 would match the level and be no change).

Prices are collected in 87 urban areas, from about 50,000 housing units, and from approximately 23,000 retail establishments, including department stores, supermarkets, hospitals, filling stations, and other types of stores. The CPI includes taxes (such as sales and excise taxes) that are directly associated with the prices of specific goods and services. However, the CPI does not include taxes (such as income and Social Security taxes) not directly associated with the purchase of consumer goods and services. Prices of most goods and services are collected by personal visits or telephone calls by BLS representatives. CPI prices are typically collected throughout the first 18 working days of each month.

There are two basic versions: the CPI for All Urban Consumers (CPI-U) and the CPI for Urban Wage Earners and Clerical Workers (CPI-W). Both the CPI-U and the CPI-W are based on data just from metropolitan areas. That is, the CPI-U and CPI-W are based on the same price data collected, but the components are weighted slightly differently to reflect the different spending habits of broad-based urban consumers (CPI-U) versus just wage and clerical workers (CPI-W). The CPI-W covers about 32 percent of the U.S. population while the CPI-U covers approximately 87 percent and includes the wage and clerical workers' portion. The All Urban version is tracked by the financial markets while many government programs that have inflation adjustment features often use the CPI-W. Generally, if there is no mention of "U" or "W" in the CPI, it means the CPI-U—the broader measure.

Key Facts About the Consumer Price Index Report

Here's what's in the official Consumer Price Index report:

◆ Official name: Consumer Price Index

◆ Release date: Monthly, mid-month for the prior month's data (July release has June data)

- Produced by: U.S. Bureau of Labor Statistics, U.S. Department of Labor

- Form of data: Index with base period of 1982–1984 = 100. Data are available seasonally adjusted and not seasonally adjusted.

- Market watchers focus on: Monthly percent changes in the overall index and in the index, excluding food and energy. (View reports at www.stats.bls.gov/news. release/cpi.toc.htm.)

Let's Talk About the Key Components of the CPI

To best understand the CPI, it is important to see what the major components are, what's in them, and if there are any major quirks. The organizational structure of CPI data is based on that of the Consumer Expenditure Survey conducted by the U.S. Bureau of the Census. This survey of consumers is conducted annually on consumer spending habits provides the basis for how much weight each component in the CPI gets.

On a technical note, there is a difference between the weights of each component and what the BLS calls "relative importance." The component weights are the shares of the components in the base period for the index (1982–1984 is the base period). The relative importance numbers are the component share weights for each year, taking into account both the base year weights and the change in relative prices between components from the base period to that particular year. That is, relative importance is the inflation-updated component shares each year. Components with higher inflation rates have rising relative importance numbers.

In the following table, you can see that there are eight major expenditure categories in the CPI: food & beverages, housing, apparel, transportation, medical care, recreation, education & communication, and other goods & services.

Relative Importance, December 2008

CPI Total	**100.000**
Food & Beverages	**15.757**
Food at home	8.156
Food away from home	6.474
Alcoholic beverages	1.127

Housing	**43.421**
Shelter	33.200
Rent of primary residence	5.957
Lodging away from home	2.478
Owners' equivalent rent	24.433
Tenants' & household insurance	0.333
Fuels & utilities	4.460
Household furnishings & operations	4.790
Apparel	**3.691**
Transportation	**15.314**
Private transportation	14.189
New & used motor vehicles	6.931
Motor fuel	3.164
Public transportation	1.125
Medical Care	**6.390**
Recreation	**5.741**
Education & Communication	**6.301**
Education	3.107
Communication	3.194
Other goods & services	**3.386**
Tobacco & smoking products	0.776
Personal care	2.610
Addendum	
CPI less food & energy	77.746
Food	14.629
Energy	7.624
Commodities	39.556
Services	60.444

Let's take a brief look at what's included in each of the major components:

◆ Food & Beverages

This expenditure category includes food at home, food away from home, and alcoholic beverages. Examples are breakfast cereal, milk, coffee, chicken, wine, full-service meals, and snacks.

◆ Housing

Housing includes the cost of shelter, operational expenses, and furnishings. Some key subcomponents are rent of primary residence (for those not buying their home), owners' equivalent rent, lodging while out of town, fuel oil, water and sewer fees, and bedroom furniture. The CPI specifically avoids treating owner-occupied housing as the cost of an investment. The CPI subcomponent for the cost of shelter in owner-occupied housing is the owners' equivalent rent. Basically, this cost is what one would pay to rent an equivalent house and the BLS uses a large housing sample to determine what those rents would be on the open market. A notably volatile component is "lodging away from home." Hotel rates are sensitive to the ups and downs of the business cycle. There are few discounts during good times and heavy discounting when the occupancy rate drops.

◆ Apparel

This category is pretty straightforward. It includes men's and boys' apparel, women's and girls' apparel, infants' and toddlers' apparel, and footwear.

◆ Transportation

This category has some of the biggest month-to-month volatility. This expenditure group includes new and used motor vehicles, motor fuel, parts and maintenance, and public transportation. The obvious cause of monthly swings can be changes in gasoline prices. But just as important are auto dealers' "off-and-on" discounts. Also, the public transportation component includes airline fares, and these can swing significantly in some months.

◆ Medical Care

This is broken down between medical commodities and medical services. The first group includes prescription drugs, nonprescription drugs, and medical supplies, among others. The second group includes physicians' services and hospital services, among others.

◆ Recreation

Recreation covers a wide range of goods and services such as televisions, toys, pets and pet products, sports equipment, and admissions to entertainment events (sports, movies, theater).

◆ Education & Communication

The education portion of this group includes tuition, other school fees, and educational books. For the communication part, you'll find personal computers, computer peripherals, software, and telephone services.

◆ Other Goods & Services

The two major categories are tobacco and smoking products and personal care. The first group can be a source of monthly volatility, but not on a regular basis. Price changes for tobacco products may happen once or twice a year by a given manufacturer, which then shows up at the store or gas station. Personal care is for products and services. The services portion includes wide-ranging services from haircuts to personal legal services, and even funerals (this is one personal service you'll be happy to forgo for a while!).

Trader Tip _____

The BLS has a really detailed database for consumer prices. If you think you need a price index for something really narrowly focused, don't rule it out. Check with the BLS website for data downloads. Here are a few examples of how detailed consumer price indexes can get. Under the food & beverages expenditure category, you can find detail for "frankfurters" as well as for "apples" and "peanut butter." Under housing, you can find a series for "garbage and trash collection." Under recreation, you not only will see "televisions," but also "pet food." So if you need a little excitement in your life, you can always go to the BLS data download site, www.stats.bls.gov/cpi/#data, and see what kind of CPI detail they have available.

Quality Adjustments: Understating Real Costs

Yes, you pay more for a car than the CPI says. How is that possible? The CPI is intended as a measure of the change in prices for a basket of goods and services. If it is to measure just changes in prices, then the goods and services have to be the same over time. The BLS calls this a constant-quality set of goods and services. So if the quality of a good or service improves, the BLS takes that into account. For example, over past decades, car safety has improved dramatically. The BLS therefore adjusted downward the price of a car for the portion of a price increase related to the quality improvement. The same applies to a number of CPI components. Another prime example is medical services. Many medical procedures are less invasive, less painful, and less time-consuming than in the past. These are quality changes, so the BLS interviews doctors to estimate the quality change and adjusts prices for those changes. Because you can't buy a quality-adjusted car, the amount that car prices have gone up in real life is greater than what's indicated by the CPI.

A related issue is that there are standards for each product being measured. When the BLS representative shows up at the grocery store, there is a standard weight for apples. And if the apple being priced is bigger or smaller than the standard, then the price is adjusted. Yes, the BLS is very meticulous with price measuring!

Uses of the CPI

Next, let's take a look at the different ways the CPI is used to make economic decisions.

◆ Measure of inflation

The CPI is used by government, business, labor, and private citizens as a guide to making economic decisions. In addition, the president, Congress, and the Federal Reserve Board use trends in the CPI to aid in determining fiscal and monetary policies.

The CPI and its components are also used to adjust other economic series for price changes and to translate these series into inflation-free dollars. The CPI is heavily used for calculating the PCE price indexes. Another example is that the components of the CPI are used to put personal consumption expenditures into inflation-adjusted dollars.

◆ Adjusting income payments

The CPI is often used to adjust consumers' income payments (for example, Social Security), to index income eligibility levels for government assistance, and to automatically provide cost-of-living wage adjustments to millions of American workers. Over 50 million Social Security beneficiaries—as well as military and Federal Civil Service retirees—have cost-of-living adjustments tied to the CPI. Eligibility criteria for a number of federal social programs are adjusted each year based on changes in the CPI. Such programs include food stamps and school lunch subsidies. Many collective bargaining agreements also tie wage increases to the CPI.

While the CPI is not a measure of the "cost of living," the CPI often is used in what are commonly called "cost of living adjustments" (COLAs). The CPI measures changes in the prices for a particular basket of goods and services. Measuring changes in the standard of living is more complex. The BLS prefers to use the term "escalation clauses" instead of COLAs. Escalation clauses often use the CPI to adjust payments for changes in prices. CPI escalation clauses are often used in private sector collective bargaining agreements, rental contracts, insurance policies with automatic inflation protection, and alimony and child support payments. The BLS does not offer legal advice on such issues, but does give general principles for developing escalation clauses at www.stats.bls.gov/cpi/cpi1998d.htm.

◆ Adjusting income tax structure

The CPI is used to adjust the federal income tax structure, including tax brackets, dependency exemptions, and standard deductions. These adjustments prevent inflation-induced increases in tax rates, an effect called "bracket creep."

Headline vs. Core CPI

In market watcher parlance, the headline number for a report is the overall figure—for the CPI, it is the overall All Urban Index. But market watchers look for any signs of unusual movement in the headline series and try to find a series that is adjusted for common sources of monthly "noise" in the underlying trend. For price indexes, the most typical source of monthly volatility is the energy component, which includes gasoline, heating oil, piped (natural) gas, and electricity. The first two provide the most volatility. Additionally, food has sharp swings on a frequent basis due to unexpected changes in supply, such as when a freeze occurs in a particular crop-growing region.

So the CPI, excluding food and energy, is seen by many to represent the underlying inflation trend. This is also called the "core" CPI.

While food and energy can have significant "noise" in some months, that does not mean one should ignore food and energy. If changes in these components become persistent, then they eventually do affect core prices, especially when production costs change because of higher or lower energy prices.

Take a look at the following CPI chart. During 2008, the energy component sharply diverged from the core rate as oil prices surged during the first half of the year and then fell in the second half.

Consumer Price Index, monthly change.

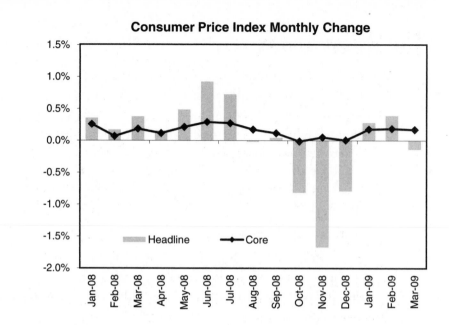

Consumer Price Index Monthly Change

Next, take a look at the following CPI chart that shows year-ago changes. Persistently higher energy costs in 2000 and from 2004 through 2006 led to boosts in the core CPI inflation rate. Over the longer run, the headline inflation trend may be more important than the core trend.

Consumer Price Index, year-ago change.

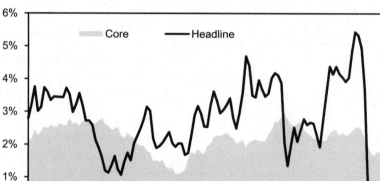

Consumer Price Index, Year-Ago Change

The Misery Index

What's the misery index? How much your taxes went up this year? Well, that would be a form of misery, but that's not what I'm referring to. Years ago, economists decided that consumer pain was not measured by the unemployment rate alone, nor just by the inflation rate. Before the 1970s, many economists believed inflation wouldn't rise if unemployment was going up and vice versa. So depending on where you were in the business cycle, economists focused on either unemployment or inflation but not both. That changed during the "stagflation" era of the 1970s, when the economy was stagnant (in recession or flat) and experiencing high inflation. To take this into account, the misery index came into vogue. The misery index is the unemployment rate plus the inflation rate.

As you can see in the following misery index chart, the misery index peaked in 1980. It also spiked in 2008 as the recession really got underway and a run up in oil prices caused inflation to temporarily spike. Stagflation was back—at least until oil prices plummeted during the latter months of 2008.

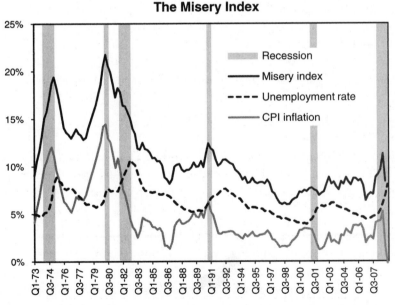

The Misery Index

The Misery Index.

Key Facts About the Producer Price Index

The Producer Price Index (PPI) is likely the second most important price measure for the United States after the CPI. There clearly are differences between the PPI and the

CPI. The PPI is based on revenues received by a producer while the CPI is based on prices paid from the purchaser's perspective. The BLS, which produces the Producer Price Index report, defines the PPI. The Producer Price Index measures average changes in prices received by domestic producers for their output. The focus is on the first commercial transaction by the producer within the United States.

There are PPIs for the products of virtually every industry in the mining and manufacturing sectors of the U.S. economy. The BLS, which produces the producer price index report, is also gradually phasing in PPIs for products of industries in the construction, trade, finance, and service sectors of the economy. More than 8,000 PPIs for individual products and groups of products are released each month. Most prices refer to one particular day of the month, namely, the Tuesday of the week containing the 13th of the month; this pricing date can range between the 9th and the 15th. As with the CPI, items in the PPI are standardized and some items—such as motor vehicles—have significant quality adjustments over time.

Only from an Economist

The PPI had been known as the Wholesale Price Index, or WPI, until 1978. The PPI in its original incarnation as the WPI began in 1902 and is one of the oldest economic indicators collected by the federal government. When the WPI report began, the word "wholesale" was used in reference to goods sold in large quantities and not, as understood today, in reference to distributors. Essentially, even though the general news media sometimes still calls the PPI the Wholesale Price Index, it has never been a measure of prices received by wholesalers, that is, distributors. It measures prices received by manufacturers and other producers.

What are some reasons for differences between the CPI and PPI? Sellers' and purchasers' prices can differ because of distribution costs, retailer markups, government subsidies, and sales and excise taxes. In addition, coverage differs between the CPI and PPI.

Changes in excise taxes—revenue collected on behalf of the government—are not reflected in the PPI because the intent is to measure net revenues retained by the producer. However, changes in rebate programs, low-interest financing plans, and other sales promotions are included when they affect the net revenues ultimately realized by the producer. For example, if an auto manufacturer offers retail customers a rebate of $500, the manufacturer's net proceeds are reduced by $500 and the PPI for new cars would reflect a lower price. In contrast, if an automobile dealer offers its customers an additional rebate with the cost being absorbed by the dealer rather than the manufacturer, the rebate would not affect the PPI for auto manufacturing. Of course, the CPI would reflect a customer rebate whether it was made by the manufacturer or the dealer.

The BLS created three broad sets of PPIs: stage-of-processing indexes, commodity indexes, and indexes for the net output of industries and their products. The stage-of-processing structure organizes products by class of buyer and degree of fabrication. This first group—the PPI stage-of-processing indexes—is what financial markets focus on, so this is what we'll focus on in the next section. But first, let's look at the PPI in general.

Here's what's in the official Producer Price Index report:

◆ Official name: Producer Price Index

◆ Release date: Monthly, mid-month—usually one or two business days after the CPI release—for the prior month's data (July release has June data)

◆ Produced by: U.S. Bureau of Labor Statistics, U.S. Department of Labor

◆ Form of data: Index with base period of 1982 = 100. Market watchers focus primarily on simple monthly percent changes with additional attention to year-on-year percent changes and on annualized monthly percent changes. Data are available seasonally adjusted and not seasonally adjusted.

◆ Market watchers focus on: Overall index for finished goods and also for excluding foods and energy, monthly percent changes www.stats.bls.gov/news.release/ppi.toc.htm

The Stage-of-Processing Indexes

The three stages of processing include finished goods; intermediate materials, supplies, and components; and crude materials for further processing. Let's go over each stage.

◆ Finished goods

These are commodities that will not undergo further processing and are ready for sale to the final-demand user, which is either an individual consumer or business firm. This stage consists of components for consumer goods and for capital equipment. Consumer goods are split into finished consumer foods and finished consumer goods excluding foods. Consumer foods include unprocessed foods, such as eggs and fresh vegetables, as well as processed foods such as bakery products and meats. Other finished consumer goods include durable goods such as automobiles, household furniture, and appliances, as well as nondurable goods, such as apparel and home heating oil. Capital equipment includes durable goods such as heavy motor trucks, tractors, and machine tools.

◆ Intermediate materials, supplies, and components

These consist partly of commodities that have been processed, but require further processing. Examples of such semifinished goods include flour, cotton yarn, steel mill products, and lumber. The intermediate goods category also encompasses nondurable, physically complete items purchased by business firms as inputs for their operations. Examples include diesel fuel, belts and belting, paper boxes, and fertilizers.

◆ Crude materials for further processing

These are products entering the market for the first time that have not been manufactured or fabricated and that are not sold directly to consumers. Crude foodstuffs and feedstuffs include items such as grains and livestock. Examples of crude nonfood materials include raw cotton, crude petroleum, coal, hides and skins, and iron and steel scrap.

The following table shows each stage and its components:

Producer Price Index Relative Importance, December 2008

Finished goods	**100.000**
Finished consumer goods	73.502
Finished consumer foods	18.710
Finished consumer goods, excluding foods	54.793
Capital equipment	26.498
Manufacturing industries	5.927
Non-manufacturing industries	20.571
Special grouping:	
Finished energy goods	17.777

Finished goods less foods and energy	63.513
Intermediate materials, supplies & components	**100.000**
Materials and components for manufacturing	44.001
Materials and components for construction	10.183
Processed fuels and lubricants	17.746
Containers	2.762
Supplies	25.308
Special grouping:	
Intermediate materials less foods and energy	74.072
Crude materials for further processing	**100.000**
Foodstuffs and feedstuffs	40.785
Nonfood materials	59.215
Special grouping:	
Crude nonfood materials less energy	18.254

Inflation Information from Stage-of-Processing PPIs

Some believe the stage-of-processing PPIs provide "pass through" information on inflation trends, where costs move along the production process to the consumer. From this perspective, a key feature of stage-of-processing PPIs is that they can provide earlier warning on price pressures, from crude materials to intermediate materials to finished goods of producers to consumer prices. For many specific goods, you can track input prices, intermediate production costs, and prices received by manufacturers. However, a big caveat is that the further you go "upstream" in the manufacturing process, the more sensitive prices are to shifts in either supply or demand. Crude material prices in particular have large ups and downs even without recession. This means that producer prices—notably for crude materials—can give false signals on changes in consumer inflation trends.

There is another huge caveat about pass through of costs from one stage of production to the next and to the consumer. Some assume that a price change recorded in a particular component of the PPI will eventually be seen in the same or most similar component of the CPI. But in reality, it is difficult to project whether, and to what extent, an increase in the PPI will end up in the CPI. For example, a producer may impose increased costs on the prices paid by a retailer. But conditions in the retail

Trader Tip _____

For those of you who are statistically inclined, using the monthly PPI numbers to forecast the upcoming CPI for trading purposes by comparing monthly changes in the overall finished goods PPI to those for the CPI is not the best way to do it. The PPI has goods only while the CPI also has services components. The CPI actually has special indexes for services, and for commodities (goods) excluding food and energy. Likewise, the finished goods PPI has special indexes for consumer goods excluding foods and energy. And the CPI and PPI have relatively equivalent food and energy components. So you can more specifically compare changes in the PPI and CPI versions of consumer goods excluding food(s) and energy as well as the food and energy components separately. (Note: for some reason the PPI uses the plural for foods while the CPI does not.) Then you can just look at the recent trends for CPI services, and add up what the different components tell you for the upcoming CPI. You can weight the component information by the relative importance figures of the CPI components you use.

market may preclude those costs being passed on to the consumer, or perhaps they will only be partially passed on.

Alternatively, there are times that consumer prices can lead producer prices. If there is unexpectedly strong demand for a consumer product, the retailer may jack up the price (or offer less discounting) before the manufacturer is able to take advantage of the situation. That is, the retailer sees the higher price opportunity before the manufacturer does. Examples include unexpectedly hot-in-demand Christmas toys or newly released consumer electronics—leading-edge cell phones, music devices, or game players.

Core PPIs by Stage of Production.

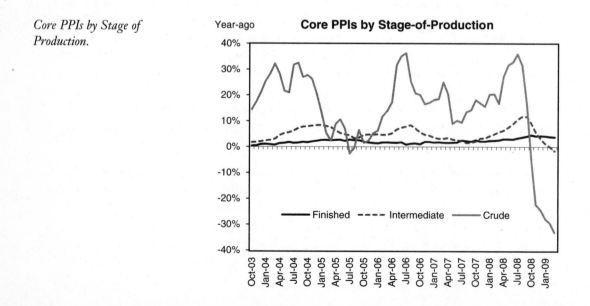

The farther one is upstream in stages of production, the more volatile the PPI. The following chart compares PPIs by stages of production for core series. If food and energy are included, the indexes are even more volatile.

Comparison of Price Indexes

We've covered several price indexes in the GDP and personal income chapters. And now you've learned about the CPI/PPI in this chapter. What you need now is a handy summary of the differences. Here's a recap as well as bullets on import and export prices, which will be discussed further in Chapter 18.

Producer Price Index for Finished Goods:

- Includes consumer goods and capital equipment
- Covers only domestically produced goods
- Monthly periodicity

Consumer Price Index:

- Includes consumer goods and services
- Covers prices of imported goods as well as domestically produced goods
- Monthly periodicity

GDP Price Index:

- Includes indexes for finished goods, services, and structures (residential, nonresidential, and public) across consumer, business, government, and foreign trade sectors
- Quarterly periodicity

Import and Export Prices Indexes:

- Include consumer goods, capital goods, and a wide range of commodities, supplies, and materials
- Cover only imported items for imports and domestically produced items for export prices
- Monthly periodicity

Market Reaction to the CPI and PPI News Releases

The importance of the CPI and PPI reports to financial markets can't be overemphasized. Inflation numbers play a key role in determining longer-run interest rates, so you can count on bond traders paying close attention. In turn, if interest rates rise, that isn't good for economic growth, either. Finally, the Fed watches, too. The CPI and PPI are the first comprehensive inflation measures each month. If there are sharp increases in these indexes, they could trigger the Fed to raise short-term interest rates to cool the economy. The Fed closely monitors the CPI report on whether inflation is too hot or even too weak. If the Fed fears deflation and either the CPI or PPI are showing declining prices, the Fed will cut interest rates. So moderation is what markets hope for when it comes to inflation numbers.

For both the PPI and CPI, financial markets focus on both the headline and core numbers, paying attention to monthly percentage changes as well as year-ago percentage changes. For the PPIs, almost all of the attention is on the finished goods numbers.

For both the CPI and PPI, analysts look for any special quirks in the monthly changes for components. At the top of the list are gasoline and heating oil. After that, the core rate can be affected by "off-and-on" discounts by auto dealers. For the CPI, these discounts (or not) show up in the transportation component. For the PPI, the impact will be in "passenger cars" in consumer goods and in "light trucks" in capital goods. Before the release, analysts note what auto dealers and manufacturers were doing in terms of discounts and rebates.

Food prices can also be affected by temporary factors, such as when there's a freeze in one area, but the price hike likely will be tempered if there is another region likely to fill in the missing supply. Food distributors have come to rely on shifting geographic locations for many foods as warm weather shifts locations. As for housing, there can be significant seasonal swings in rates for hotels in the lodging while out-of-town component. Such swings are difficult to seasonally adjust.

The Least You Need to Know

- The Consumer Price Index is the most important inflation measure in the United States.
- When the CPI or PPI are released, market watchers focus on the overall number and the core figures.
- Inflation rates play a key role in determining interest rates, especially long-term interest rates.

What About Inflation from Labor Costs?

In This Chapter

- ◆ How labor costs fit in with price inflation
- ◆ The productivity and unit labor costs report
- ◆ The employment cost report
- ◆ Market reaction to the reports

Everybody loves a big pay raise. And everybody hates inflation. But there's really a connection between the two. And here it is: labor-cost inflation.

Wondering how the economy balances low inflation with solid growth for workers? It's all about wages and salaries being based on workers being paid based on doing a good job. That is, it's okay if workers are paid for producing more. We are talking about worker productivity—that is, producing more each hour of work. Productivity links healthy economic growth with low inflation. While we get an early peek at wage pressures with the average hourly earnings numbers in the employment situation report, the best-known broad measures of labor costs can be found in the Productivity and Costs Report and the Employment Cost Index Report.

The Importance of Productivity for the Economy

Productivity is a measure of the efficiency of labor in producing the economy's goods and services. Productivity is output per unit of input. Productivity can reference any particular input of production, but the most common reference is to *labor productivity* (another could be capital productivity). Output is simply what is being produced, and a common unit of labor input is a work hour. So labor productivity can be thought of in terms of how much stuff gets produced when a worker puts in an hour's worth of labor. Unless stated otherwise, when we talk about productivity, we are talking about labor productivity.

def•i•ni•tion

Labor productivity is the ratio of the output of goods and services to the labor hours used in the production of that output; basically, higher output per hour means labor is more productive.

So who cares about productivity? Well, actually both workers and management do. High labor productivity tends to lead to higher profits. Higher profits mean the workers are more valuable to management, which tends to result in higher salaries and wages for workers. Higher productivity means that costs per unit produced are lower—meaning lower inflation pressures. So everyone benefits from higher productivity—company owners (stockholders), management, workers, and the rest of the economy.

High productivity means the economy can grow faster without wage-based inflation, even if labor markets are tight (at least up to a point). Basically, strong growth in productivity is good! Economists believe the long-term rate of growth in productivity sets the "speed limit" on economic growth that is sustainable without rising inflation.

What affects labor productivity? The most common factors that boost productivity are education, training, additions of capital (equipment and structures), and technological advances. Better-trained workers work smarter and get more done. If a factory adds more equipment to an assembly line, then the worker may be able to produce more. Better technology leads to higher output from labor, and this can mean anything from improved capital equipment to better software to new production procedures. Over the long run, all of these factors create a trend for rising labor productivity.

Factors that boost long-term productivity include:

◆ Higher capital-to-labor ratios

◆ Improvements in worker skills

◆ Technological improvements in the production process

♦ Shifts in the economy to high-productivity sectors (such as moving from services to manufacturing).

Since the Industrial Revolution began, some economists argue that every 50 to 75 years there has been a major shift in technology that boosts labor productivity and the economy. During the early 1900s, one such development was the invention of the assembly line. In the mid-1900s, it was cheap gasoline and affordable cars. In the late 1900s, many say the development of microchips and the personal computer led to a surge in productivity and economic growth.

A related measure is *unit labor costs*. Unit labor costs are the labor costs of producing each unit of output. This is the same as dividing hourly compensation by productivity. Thus, increases in productivity lower unit labor costs while increases in hourly compensation raise them. So we see that both productivity and unit labor costs are indicators of inflation pressures—or lack of inflation pressures—from labor costs.

In the following national income chart, notice that labor costs, consisting of wage and salary accruals and supplements (such as benefits) add up to about 65 percent of national income. So labor costs play a big role in the economy.

def•i•ni•tion

> **Unit labor costs** are total labor compensation divided by real output.

National Income, 2008

National Income, 2008.

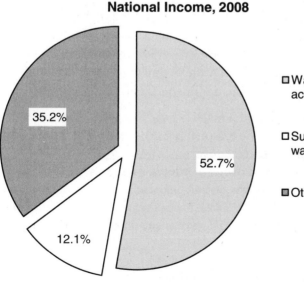

□ Wage & salary accruals

□ Supplements to wages & salaries

■ Other

35.2%

52.7%

12.1%

Key Facts About the Productivity and Costs Report

Here's what's in the official report for productivity and costs:

◆ Official name: Productivity and Costs

◆ Release date: Quarterly, with the first estimate ("preliminary") released the first week in the second month after the quarter and the final estimate ("revised") released the first week in the third month after the quarter. (The preliminary estimate for the first quarter is released in early May and the revised estimate is released in early June.)

◆ Produced by: U.S. Bureau of Labor Statistics, U.S. Department of Labor

◆ Form of data: Indexes with base period 1992 = 100. The official report has data in quarterly annualized percentage changes and year-ago percentage changes. Data are available seasonally adjusted.

◆ Market watchers focus on: Nonfarm productivity and unit labor costs, quarterly annualized and year-ago numbers (view reports at www.bls.gov/lpc/)

The Productivity and Costs Report

The Bureau of Labor Statistics (BLS) puts out the Productivity and Costs Report. It's largely based on much of the same data that go into measuring the expenditure side of gross domestic product (GDP).

The Productivity and Costs Report has data for several layers of the economy. These are the business sector, the nonfarm business sector, the manufacturing sector (with breakouts for durables and nondurables), and the nonfinancial corporate sector.

One of the key series in productivity is output. The BLS only has productivity measures for the sectors where productivity can be reasonably measured. So in using GDP source data, the BLS removes output for general government, private households, nonprofit institutions, and the rental value of owner-occupied dwellings. This leaves business sector output. Nonfarm business sector output also excludes farm output, and the news media focuses on this sector the most. The output measures for manufacturing are primarily based on data from the Federal Reserve instead of on GDP source data.

The compensation measure in unit labor costs is a very broad measure of labor costs and is based on the income components of GDP. Compensation is a measure of the cost to the employer of securing the services of labor. It includes wages and salaries, supplements (like shift differentials, all kinds of paid leave, bonus and incentive payments, and employee discounts), and employer contributions to employee-benefit plans (like medical and life insurance, workers' compensation, and unemployment insurance). It also includes an estimate for the earnings of the self-employed. This is because the output of proprietorships is included in the output measures for these sectors and industries.

The hours data for the labor productivity and unit labor cost measures include hours for all persons working in the sector. These include wage and salary workers, the self-employed, and unpaid family workers. The primary source for hours data is the BLS Current Employment Statistics (CES) program, which provides monthly survey data on the number of jobs held by wage and salary workers in nonfarm establishments.

Only from an Economist

So how does your short-term disability pay stack up? Short-term disability is a form of insurance that replaces an employee's income up to a specified amount and period of time when an employee is unable to work due to a nonoccupational illness or disability. The Society for Human Resource Management (SHRM), a nonprofit organization, provides some insight on who gets the best deal. According to its website, SHRM.com: "Generally, short-term disability as a percentage of salary is between 60 percent to 70 percent for all organizations. SHRM's 2008 Human Capital Benchmarking Database found that while the median short-term disability amount of salary is 60 percent for the health care, finance, and service industries, it is 70 percent for government industries. This finding supports the reputation of government agencies offering richer benefits plans than private sector employers, often as a way to compete for talent because salaries and bonuses are higher in the private sector."

Series in the Report

The data in the Productivity and Costs Report start out as indexes but are primarily evaluated in either quarterly annualized percent changes or year-ago percent changes. While the financial markets focus on productivity and unit labor costs, the official report has a number of series generally not tracked by financial markets. We have already discussed the compensation series, but there is also a real compensation series. This is compensation deflated by the CPI. Unit nonlabor costs include profits, consumption of fixed capital, taxes on production and imports less subsidies, net interest and miscellaneous payments, business current transfer payments, rental income of persons, and the current surplus of government enterprises. The implicit price deflator is current dollar output divided by the output index.

Productivity Report Indicators

	Produc-tivity	Output	Hours worked	Compen-sation	Real Compen-sation	Unit Labor Costs	Unit Nonlabor Costs	Implicit Price Deflator
Percent Change from Previous Quarter at Annual Rate								
07 4Q	-0.5	-0.7	-0.2	4.4	-0.5	5.0	-2.3	2.1
08 1Q	2.6	0.9	-1.7	3.7	-0.6	1.1	3.8	2.1
08 2Q	4.7	2.8	-1.7	1.7	-3.2	-2.8	6.9	0.9
08 3Q	2.2	-1.9	-3.9	5.7	-0.9	3.5	6.4	4.7
08 4Q	-0.4	-8.7	-8.3	5.3	15.9	5.7	-7.1	0.5
Year–Ago Percent Change								
07 4Q	2.6	2.4	-0.3	3.6	-0.4	0.9	3.6	2.0
08 1Q	3.5	2.8	-0.6	3.5	-0.7	0.0	4.3	1.6
08 2Q	3.4	2.1	-1.3	3.6	-0.7	0.1	3.6	1.5
08 3Q	2.2	0.3	-1.9	3.9	-1.3	1.6	3.6	2.4
08 4Q	2.2	-1.8	-4.0	4.1	2.5	1.8	2.3	2.0

Productivity and Labor Cost Trends

Over the long run, high inflation and high growth rates in unit labor costs have run together, as seen in the following productivity, labor costs, and inflation chart. There was an especially large spike in labor costs and inflation in the late 1970s and early 1980s. Inflation was more moderate during the late 1990s and during the 2000s as productivity growth strengthened.

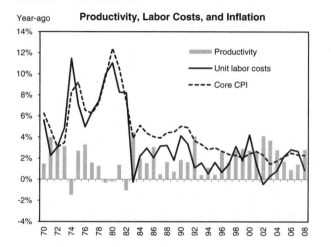

Productivity, Labor Costs, and Inflation.

The good news for workers from productivity gains is the opportunity for better income. Take a look at the productivity and real compensation chart below. Productivity growth was relatively strong from about 1996 through 2003. This also was a time when real compensation was strong. Once again, productivity is good not just for businesses but for workers, too!

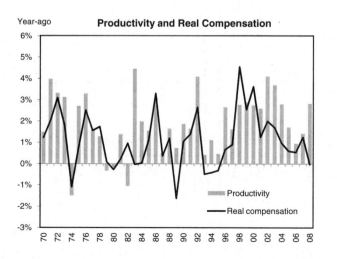

Productivity and Real Compensation.

Productivity in the Short Term

We already talked about factors such as training and the buildup of capital affecting long-term trends in productivity. These are quality-of-labor and capital-to-labor-ratio issues that are clearly long-run considerations. That is, there are not significant swings in these factors over any one business cycle. But in the short-term, output and hours worked can shift sharply due to cyclical swings in the economy.

Trader Tip _____

During the onset of recession, output typically falls before hours worked, resulting in a temporary drop in productivity and a spike in unit labor costs. So it is important to remember that long-term productivity determines the "speed limit" for long-term economic growth. Don't be misled by short-term cyclical gyrations in productivity numbers. They do not reflect the true, underlying trend.

Take a look at the following nonfarm productivity versus unit labor costs chart. Note how the quarterly swings in productivity and unit labor costs can be quite volatile due to quarterly changes in output, hours worked, and compensation. These quarterly changes have little or no meaning for long-term productivity trends.

Nonfarm Productivity vs. Unit Labor Costs.

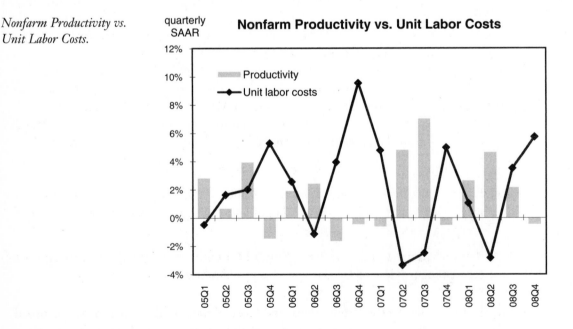

But over the business cycle, the Fed watches to see if unit labor costs are growing too fast compared to productivity. If labor costs heat up too much, then the Fed will raise interest rates to cool the economy and inflation pressures.

If productivity gains are strong, the Fed sees that and allows for faster GDP growth than otherwise, and is not as trigger happy about raising short-term interest rates.

Key Facts About the Employment Cost Index Report

The *Employment Cost Index* (ECI) is another measure of labor cost inflation pressures. It measures total employee compensation costs, including wages and salaries as well as benefits. The ECI is the broadest measure of labor costs. The Fed closely tracks this index when it feels labor-based inflation is becoming a problem. Compensation costs tend to heat up when economic activity is booming and the demand for labor is rising rapidly and labor supply is tight (few unemployed workers). During economic downturns, wage pressures tend to be subdued because labor demand is down and lots of unemployed workers are available. If wage inflation is picking up, businesses are likely to feel they need to boost prices to keep profits up.

def•i•ni•tion

The **Employment Cost Index** (ECI) is a measure of the change in the cost of labor, free from the influence of employment shifts among occupations and industries.

Here's what's in the official report:

- ◆ Official name: Employment Cost Index

- ◆ Release date: Quarterly, for the months of March, June, September, and December. Published at the end of the month after the reference month (March data are published at the end of April).

- ◆ Produced by: U.S. Bureau of Labor Statistics, U.S. Department of Labor

- ◆ Form of data: Indexes with base period 2005 = 100. The official report has data in quarterly simple percentage changes and year-ago percentage changes. Data are available seasonally adjusted.

- ◆ Market watchers focus on: The overall ECI number, quarterly and year-ago percent changes (view reports at www.bls.gov/ncs/ect/)

The ECI is similar to the Productivity and Costs Report in the way it provides broad information on labor costs. But there are significant differences. Rather than being based on adjusted GDP information, as with unit labor costs, the ECI is based on a specific survey for the purpose of measuring employment compensation costs. It's a fixed-weighted index, but the components are not for a fixed pool of benefits for workers; instead, it's a fixed pool of labor for employers. Basically, the ECI indicates what it costs employers to retain their workforce. The component weights are at the occupational level. Changes in wages or changes in benefits only affect the ECI as they actually are paid by employers to retain their workers.

As of 2008, the ECI survey was based on data from 13,600 business establishments in private industry and about 1,900 establishments in state and local governments. The ECI covers only civilian workers and not federal civilian workers; it specifically excludes the federal government as well as farms, households, the self-employed, owner-managers, and unpaid family workers.

The Key ECI Series

The two broad components of the ECI are:

- ◆ Wages and salaries
- ◆ Benefits

Wages and salaries are defined as the hourly straight-time wage rate or, for workers not paid on an hourly basis, straight-time earnings divided by the corresponding hours. This is before payroll deductions, but excluding premium pay for overtime and for work on weekends and holidays, shift differentials, and nonproduction bonuses. However, production bonuses, incentive earnings, commission payments, and cost-of-living adjustments are included with straight-time wage and salary rates. Straight-time merely refers to non-overtime rates for hourly workers and non-bonus income for salaried workers.

Benefits covered by the ECI are:

- ◆ Paid leave—This includes vacations, holidays, sick leave, and personal leave.

- ◆ Supplemental pay—This includes premium pay for work in addition to the regular work schedule (such as overtime, weekends, and holidays), shift differentials, and nonproduction bonuses (such as year-end, referral, and attendance bonuses).

- ◆ Insurance benefits—These include insurance benefits for life, health, short-term disability, and long-term disability.

- ◆ Retirement and savings benefits—These are for defined benefit and contribution plans.

◆ Legally required benefits—These include the usual suspects you regularly see on your pay stub—Social Security, Medicare, federal and state unemployment insurance, and workers' compensation.

Check out the following employment cost table. You can see the quarterly percent changes compared to a year ago.

Employment Cost Index

	Quarterly Percent Changes				Year-Ago Percent Changes		
	Mar 08	**Jun 08**	**Sep 08**	**Dec 08**	**Dec 07**	**Sep 08**	**Dec 08**
Civilian workers:							
Compensation	0.7	0.7	0.7	0.5	3.3	2.9	2.6
Wages and salaries	0.8	0.7	0.7	0.5	3.4	3.1	2.7
Benefits	0.6	0.6	0.6	0.4	3.1	2.6	2.2
Private industry:							
Compensation	0.8	0.6	0.6	0.5	3.0	2.8	2.4
Wages and salaries	0.8	0.7	0.6	0.6	3.3	2.9	2.6
Benefits	0.6	0.5	0.6	0.4	2.4	2.4	2.0

Only from an Economist

One of the uses of the Employment Cost Index is as a cost of living adjustment (COLA), especially for some labor contracts. But for some occupations, commissions can have a big impact on index changes. Therefore, for "sales and related workers," the BLS offers index versions with and without incentive pay.

When labor markets are tight, employers often cannot pass along to employees the cost of benefits such as health insurance. Employers also have to compete with other companies by offering better leave packages (like vacation and sick pay). In the following employment costs chart, you can see that these trends show up in a surge in benefit cost inflation.

Employment Costs.

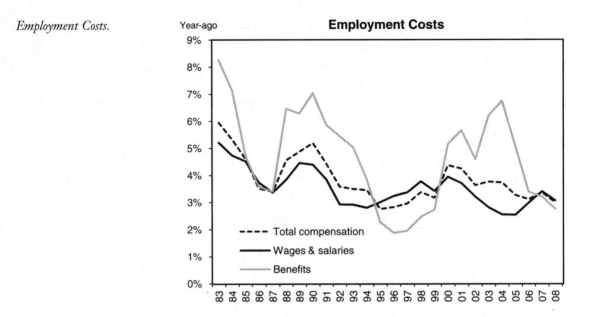

Year-ago

Employment Costs

But when the economy slows or profits are tight, companies can quickly cut back on many benefits previously offered. In recent years, many companies have cut benefit costs by raising workers' health insurance deductibles and by otherwise reducing the quality of health insurance coverage.

Productivity and Costs Report vs. the ECI

Both series present their data as index numbers, one-quarter or three-month percent change, and four-quarter or twelve-month percent change. The index numbers and year-over-year comparisons are consistent; however, the one-quarter and three-month percent changes are presented differently. ECI presents these data as the actual change over the three-month period while the hourly compensation measures are presented at a compound annual rate of change (that is, as if the same percent change were to continue for four quarters).

The ECI covers private industry and state and local government. Hourly compensation has series for private industry and also federal, state, and local government enterprises.

The ECI covers most private employees but excludes persons working for token wages as well as business owners and others who set their own wage (for example, corporate CEOs). The ECI also excludes family workers who do not earn a market wage.

The hourly compensation measure excludes employees of nonprofit institutions serving individuals (about 10 percent of private workers, mostly in education and medical care). However, the hourly compensation measure does include an estimate for the unincorporated self-employed because they are assumed to earn the same hourly compensation as other employees in their sector. Implicitly, unpaid family workers are also included in the hourly compensation measure with the assumption that their hourly compensation is zero.

◆ Compensation coverage

   The ECI includes wages and benefits that employers provide. The hourly compensation measures include wages and benefits that employees receive. Therefore, some types of compensation (such as tips received by employees) are included in the hourly compensation measures but not in the ECI. Also, the ECI does not include stock options as an employer-provided benefit. For the hourly compensation measures, the accrued employee income from stock options is incorporated into wages and salaries when the option is exercised.

◆ Weights

   The ECI uses a fixed set of industry and occupational weights to obtain a measure of the change in labor cost that is not influenced by changes in the industrial and occupational structure of the economy. The hourly compensation measures are influenced by changes in employment distribution. That is, even if the wages for all jobs in the economy were unchanged, hourly compensation could change if the distribution of jobs in the economy changed. In addition, the ECI holds hours worked constant, unless there is a plan change. Hourly compensation measures will show changes due to changes in hours at work and overtime.

Market Reaction to Productivity and ECI Reports

Both reports provide information on wage inflation pressures to the financial markets. High unit labor cost and ECI growth rates boost inflation expectations and are a negative for bond prices (boosting yields) and weigh on stock prices. Labor cost growth that is too strong cuts into company profits. Higher productivity numbers are a plus for stock prices and help interest rates to ease.

For the Productivity and Costs report, markets look at the nonfarm business sector numbers for overall productivity and unit labor costs, taking into account both quarterly changes and year-ago percent changes. For the ECI report, financial markets mainly look at the overall ECI for civilian workers, focusing on both quarterly and year-ago percent changes.

The Least You Need to Know

- ◆ Growth in productivity basically determines how fast the economy can grow without risking a rise in inflation.

- ◆ The Fed closely watches productivity, unit labor costs, and the Employment Cost Index for signs of "too strong" labor-cost inflation.

- ◆ When labor-cost inflation runs too high, the Fed will raise interest rates to slow the economy.

- ◆ High productivity growth typically results not just in higher profits for businesses, but also in higher real earnings for employees.

Oil, Gold, and Other Commodities Prices

In This Chapter

- ◆ Commodities explained
- ◆ Why oil is a special commodity
- ◆ How oil futures hint at where prices are headed
- ◆ The EIA Petroleum Status Report
- ◆ Commodity price indexes
- ◆ Why gold doesn't always glisten

We've talked about the major indicators of inflation, such as the Consumer Price Index, the Producer Price Index, and the Productivity and Costs Report, among others. But what is the part of the economy that is most sensitive to changes in inflation pressures? Commodities—that's what!

Tracking commodities can provide early inflation warnings. In this chapter, we take a close look at two special commodities: oil and gold.

Basics on Commodities and Inflation

First, just what is a *commodity*? Generally, a commodity is any good in a market for which the producer is indiscernible by any differences in the product, because the products are essentially identical. For a specific commodity, any producer's product is completely interchangeable with another producer's product of that commodity. Examples of commodities are wheat and copper.

def•i•ni•tion

A **commodity** is a good, such as gold, that isn't characterized by individual differences; that is, one ounce of gold is the same as the next one-ounce piece of gold.

In contrast to commodities, there are goods that are highly differentiated and so it matters who the producer is. Examples include consumer electronic goods whose features and quality can vary significantly from one manufacturer to another. Here, you can't blindly substitute one manufacturer's product for another. A more specific definition of a commodity is that it is a good that is traded on a specific commodity exchange. This chapter focuses on the second definition, but for more basic applications for tracking their impact on the economy than for trading purposes.

Speaking of commodity exchanges, when a commodity is traded on one of these, the commodity must meet specific minimum standards and be sold in specific quantities. There are two basic types of commodity transactions and prices: spot and futures. A *spot transaction* is for immediate delivery upon purchase, so a spot price is the price paid for immediate delivery of a commodity on a specific commodity exchange.

A *futures transaction* is the purchase of a commodity on a specific commodity exchange for delivery in a specific month in the future. Commodity exchanges have specific contract terms both for spot and futures transactions, but we aren't going to worry about those details now. We are focusing on the basic data and how they help us interpret inflation trends.

def•i•ni•tion

A **spot transaction** is for a commodity that's available for immediate delivery. A **futures transaction** is purchasing a commodity at a specific price and with a specific month in the future for delivery.

Commodities are generally used as inputs in the production of other goods. Many are raw materials that are very sensitive to changes in the strength of the economy. Examples include cotton, rubber, tin, corn, and lumber. So from our perspective, we care about commodities because they give us early warnings on changes in demand due to changes in economic growth. We are going to start our review of commodities with probably the most important commodity for the industrial economy—oil.

Oil—The Commodity That Makes or Breaks Inflation

Almost certainly, the commodity that plays the biggest role in inflation trends is oil. Oil prices have both a direct and an indirect impact on inflation. Goods that use oil as a major raw material input are directly impacted. Oil is the major material cost for energy goods, such as gasoline and heating oil, as well as for goods such as tires and fertilizer.

Oil has a big indirect impact on the cost of many consumer goods and business equipment because of its effects on transportation and production costs. For example, oil is not a raw material in food, but it significantly impacts food prices. This is because of its use in making fertilizer and because fuel costs are major expenses for farmers when running tractors and other field equipment.

> **Only from an Economist**
>
> Oil is priced in dollars per barrel. But what is a barrel? According to the U.S. Energy Information Administration, a barrel is a unit of volume equal to 42 U.S. gallons.

Overall CPI inflation and changes in prices for crude oil track closely, although changes in oil prices are much sharper than the CPI. This makes sense, though, because energy goods (gasoline and heating oil) are moderate percentages of the CPI rather than being the entire index. The bottom line is that if you want to track inflation trends, you have to know what's going on with oil. But what do you track? The following chart, showing crude oil and CPI inflation, headlines "West Texas Intermediate"—and that's a hint!

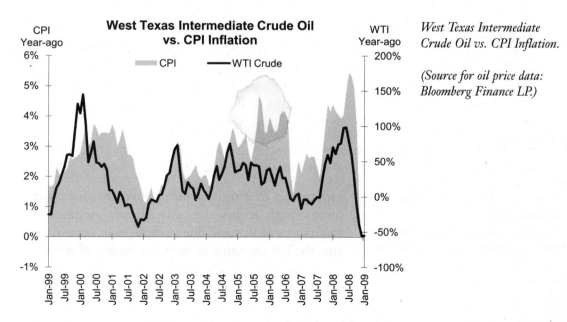

West Texas Intermediate Crude Oil vs. CPI Inflation.

(Source for oil price data: Bloomberg Finance LP.)

Only from an Economist
West Texas Intermediate spot prices set a record daily closing price of $145.29 per barrel on July 3, 2008.

The Big Names for Oil

No, we aren't talking about oil companies, but names for oil itself. Let's start with the question of where you go to "pick up" some crude oil if you want to buy some. Oil is a rather special commodity and because it largely travels by pipeline, you can only get delivery at specific locations, which are established by the oil industry.

While there are a number of delivery points around the world, for pricing purposes the most important location in the United States is Cushing, Oklahoma. This is where much of the crude oil in the United States is delivered for refining. While refineries are scattered throughout the U.S. oil-producing regions, Cushing is the primary pricing point and uses the traditional name of West Texas Intermediate (WTI) for the product delivered. WTI is a high-quality, low-sulfur-content crude oil that is highly valued for refining into gasoline and similar distillates. Because of its low sulfur content, WTI is known as "sweet" crude.

Another characteristic of oil is its wax content. Low-wax-content oils are known as "light" and are easier to pump and transport than those with high wax content. WTI is both light and sweet and priced higher than most other crude oils. So in the media and on various websites you will see WTI, Cushing, and "light, sweet crude" used interchangeably.

The primary competing crude oil for WTI is Brent. Brent refers to light, sweet oil produced in the North Sea of Great Britain. Its quality is slightly lower than WTI, but is still very high quality for refining into gasoline and similar products. While Cushing is a key price point for the United States, Brent is the pricing benchmark for about two-thirds of the internationally traded crude oil. The shipping terminal for Brent is at Sullom Voe in the Shetland Islands of Scotland.

So if you want to track oil prices, you want to track West Texas Intermediate—and maybe also Brent. Now when you hear the words "West Texas Intermediate," "WTI," "Cushing," or "Brent," you know they are talking about oil!

Tracking Oil Prices

Where can you find oil prices?

There are quite a few websites that offer price quotes for WTI, Brent, and other crudes. (WTI and Brent are quoted the most often.) Bloomberg.com carries price updates every 20 minutes during the trading day at www.bloomberg.com/markets/commodities/energyprices.html.

Brent is primarily traded electronically on the Intercontinental Exchange trading platform, which is also known as the ICE. Oil price data can be found on its website at www.theice.com.

You should note that websites often carry both spot prices and futures prices for oil. Don't confuse the two—pay attention to whether the quote is for spot or futures!

If you don't want to take the time to pull oil prices on a daily basis, you can get daily or monthly data from the U.S. Energy Information Administration in Excel and other formats for free. Go to www.eia.doe.gov and click the "Energy" section link. Click the link for the "Weekly Petroleum Status Report" and you'll see a page that has many links for free data.

Factors Affecting the Price of Oil

What factors affect the price of oil? The biggest factor is economic growth. The demand for oil is stronger and its price higher when economic growth is fast. But the world has changed a lot over the last 20 years or so. The United States or U.S. and European economic growth no longer affects the price of oil alone. China and India are now big players in the world economy. In fact, while the United States was already in recession in early 2008, rapid growth in those countries boosted oil prices well into mid-2008.

Markets are continually making their own evaluations of supply and demand for oil. But there are official forecasts for production and demand from various government agencies in the United States and other countries. For the United States, the agency with oil demand forecasts is the U.S. Energy Information Administration (EIA). The EIA puts out its forecasts on its website at www.eia.doe.gov/oiaf/forecasting.html.

Oil reserves (oil known to be in the ground) are not found just anywhere. A few countries provide the vast majority of the world's oil supplies. In 1960, a number of oil exporters formed the *Organization of Petroleum Exporting Countries (OPEC)*. It is a cartel of 12 countries made up of Algeria, Angola, Ecuador, Iran, Iraq, Kuwait, Libya, Nigeria, Qatar, Saudi Arabia, the United Arab Emirates, and Venezuela. OPEC sets production quotas for its members in order to try to stabilize oil prices in its members' favor. Any announcements by OPEC officials about price targets, production quotas, or changes in demand can lead to significant changes in oil prices.

Incidentally, Russia has become a major producer and exporter of oil (thanks to Western capitalists investing in Russian oil fields!). While Russia is not a member of OPEC, it has obtained "observer" status for official OPEC meetings and may end up coordinating its production with OPEC.

def•i•ni•tion

OPEC, according to the U.S. EIA, is an intergovernmental organization whose stated objective is to coordinate and unify petroleum policies among member countries. That is, OPEC attempts to coordinate oil production and prices among its members. It was created at the Baghdad Conference on September 10–14, 1960, by Iran, Iraq, Kuwait, Saudi Arabia, and Venezuela. Current additional members include Qatar, United Arab Emirates, Algeria, Nigeria, and Angola. Three other countries held membership but left the organization after becoming net importers of oil—Gabon, Indonesia, and Ecuador.

Oil is almost entirely priced in U.S. dollars, even when traded at exchanges overseas. This goes back to the birth of the oil industry, when most oil fields were owned by U.S. companies. After many oil-producing countries took over many oil fields, the policy of pricing in U.S. dollars continued because of tradition and also because of the safety of U.S. dollars. In the following oil prices chart, we see that the price of oil generally moves in the opposite direction of the dollar.

Oil Prices vs. the Trade-Weighted Dollar.

(Source for oil price data: Bloomberg Finance LP.)

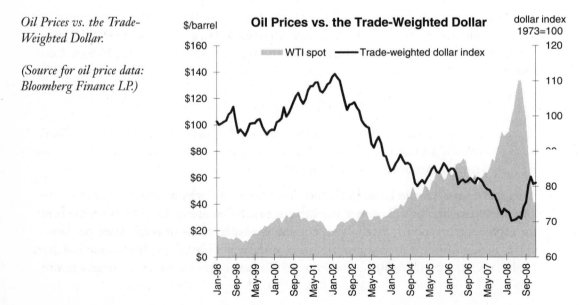

The result of pricing oil in U.S. dollars, though, means that the price of oil is affected by the exchange value of the dollar in currency markets. If the exchange value of the dollar falls, this puts upward pressure on the price of oil because oil producers want to maintain the purchasing power of oil sold. Of course, if the value of the dollar rises, that puts downward pressure on oil prices.

Oil, at times, can be perceived as a safe haven from inflation and from potential losses in other financial markets. From time to time, such as during the financial turmoil in 2007 and 2008, investors took money out of equities and bought oil. Stocks were seen as risky by the investors, and they believed oil would hold its value or rise in price. So when other financial markets lose value, you can see oil prices spike as investors run there for safety.

Political instability in oil-producing developing nations can also cause oil prices to surge. Nigeria's oil fields are near areas controlled by militants and production can be disrupted occasionally. Saber-rattling comments by Iranian officials have also rattled oil markets in the past.

Finally, any news about oil inventories or inventories of distilled products (such as gasoline) can move the price of oil sharply. That is, if oil inventories are lower than expected, that generally means demand is stronger than believed, and the price of oil goes up. We'll talk about oil inventories more in the section on the EIA's Weekly Petroleum Status Report. But first, let's have a little fun looking at oil futures prices.

Tracking Oil Futures

Oil futures are traded on a number of exchanges around the world, but the best-known exchange for this is the New York Mercantile Exchange—or the NYMEX. (Just so you know, the NYMEX is now owned by the CME Group in Chicago, but the floor trading still takes place at the traditional New York floor exchange.) While we aren't going to talk about actually trading oil futures, we can quickly learn how to get oil futures prices to see what they tell us about oil prices and inflation trends.

The most user-friendly website for oil futures prices is the one run by the NYMEX/CME Group. Oil futures can be found at www.nymex.com/lsco_fut_cso.aspx. In case this page has been moved, just look on the site for "crude oil."

This main page has the latest day's "Session Overview," which includes a column for "Most Recent Settle." These are the futures prices you are looking for with the price for each contract month listed. This column is easy to read—it is the price per barrel in U.S. dollars for delivery in the months shown. This table's shortcoming is that it only shows a few months into the future. To get additional future contract-month price data, you have to click the link for "Current Expanded Table" or "Previous Expanded Table." This website prepares for the next day's trading by moving "today's" numbers into "previous" sometime around 6:00 P.M. Eastern Time. So check the "previous" table if the "current" table looks empty.

The expanded table provides prices for oil futures contracts several years into the future. But after the first two years out, only contracts for June and December are traded. While it is nice to have futures data going out for many months, there is an important caveat. Beyond the first 6 to 9 months into the future, the trading is very thin. That is, there are not many trades taking place for those long-term delivery contracts. So those prices further out may not be that meaningful.

In the sweet crude oil chart that follows, we compare three different days that oil futures were trading. The key day is July 3, 2008, when oil prices hit a record high for that time; July 2, 2007, a year prior to the record high; and December 30, 2008 when the U.S. economy had been in recession for a year.

Light Sweet Crude Oil, Futures Prices.

(Source: Data courtesy of CME Group.)

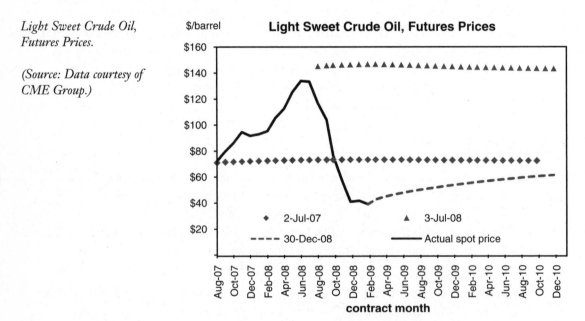

In July 2007, did futures market traders do a good job of forecasting the spot price for July 2008? No, they did a terrible job. In July 2007, traders believed that a price of about $70 per barrel would be stable and continue well into the future. Traders botched it again on July 3, 2008, when the spot price and futures prices for WTI topped $145 per barrel. They were narrowly focused, thinking that high oil prices would not impact economic growth and that demand would remain high, keeping

WTI over $140 per barrel well into the future. But by late 2008, recession had set in worldwide and oil prices plummeted to below $40 per barrel. Were any lessons learned? Traders at the end of 2008 believed the low prices would not last as economies improved around the world during the later part of 2009. This was likely more rational than the futures trades made in mid-2007 and mid-2008.

While the futures market has a mixed record for forecasting, it does indicate at what price levels some companies are locking in deliveries for oil. This can have an impact on company costs and profits.

Key Facts About EIA's Weekly Petroleum Status Report

If you care about oil markets, Wednesday mornings are important to you! Every Wednesday (except when moved back on weeks with holidays on Wednesday or earlier), the U.S. Energy Information Administration puts out a report on the prior week's inventory numbers for crude oil and for products refined from crude oil (such as gasoline and jet fuel). The inventory numbers indicate whether refineries are keeping up with demand or not. And oil prices can be impacted in a big way when the report comes out late Wednesday morning.

The Petroleum Status Report has a wealth of data on petroleum stocks (inventories), production, imports, and prices. The price data are already known by the markets, so the key information is the inventory numbers—at least for those trading in the oil markets.

Here's what's in the official report:

> **Only from an Economist**
>
> The record high for oil prices for the first-month-out futures contract for West Texas Intermediate is $145.29 per barrel, set on July 3, 2008. The last two days' of price spurts (on July 2 and July 3) to reach this record high were set off by a drop in crude oil inventories, which was reported in the mid-morning Weekly Petroleum Status Report of July 2.

- ◆ Official name: Weekly Petroleum Status Report

- ◆ Release date: Weekly, Wednesday mornings for the prior week ending on Friday. If there is a federal holiday on Monday, Tuesday, or Wednesday, the report typically is on Thursday for that week.

- ◆ Produced by: The U.S. Energy Information Administration of the U.S. Department of Energy

- ◆ Market watchers focus on: Petroleum stocks for crude oil, specifically focusing on the weekly change in stocks in millions of barrels (www.eia.doe.gov; go to the EIA home page and click on the "Energy" section)

Only from an Economist

The Strategic Petroleum Reserve (SPR) is the U.S. equivalent of a "rainy day fund" for oil. The SPR is an emergency store of oil maintained by the United States Department of Energy. It's the largest emergency supply in the world and has the capacity to hold up to 727 million barrels of oil. The United States started the SPR in 1975 after oil supplies were cut off during the 1973–1974 oil embargo. Storage is in multiple underground salt domes along the U.S. coast on the Gulf of Mexico.

Take a look at the following balance sheet for the Weekly Petroleum Status Report.

From the U.S. Petroleum Balance Sheet of the Weekly Petroleum Status Report: 4 Weeks Ending 03/06/2009

Petroleum Stocks (Million Barrels)	Week 06-Mar-09	Week 27-Feb-09	06-Mar-08	Level Change Weekly	% Change Weekly	% Change Yr/Yr
Crude Oil (Excluding SPR)	351.3	350.6	303.4	0.7	0.2	15.8
Total Motor Gasoline	212.5	215.5	231.7	–3.0	–1.4	–8.3
Kerosene-Type Jet Fuel	41.6	41.7	39.7	–0.1	–0.2	4.8
Distillate Fuel Oil	145.4	143.3	115.4	2.1	1.5	26.0
Residual Fuel Oil	38.1	36.6	38.9	1.5	4.1	-2.1
Propane/Propylene	37.7	38.3	28.4	–0.6	–1.6	32.7
Unfinished Oils	85.4	84.7	90.4	0.7	0.8	–5.5
Other Oils	127.1	125.9	113.5	1.2	1.0	12.0
Total Stocks (Excluding SPR)	1039.2	1036.6	961.4	2.6	0.3	8.1
Crude Oil in SPR	705.7	704.9	699.1	0.8	0.1	0.9
Total Stocks (Including SPR)	1744.9	1741.5	1660.5	3.4	0.2	5.1

Market Reaction to the Weekly Petroleum Status News Release

Markets primarily react to the "weekly change" figure for overall crude oil stocks, excluding Strategic Petroleum Reserves. Lower-than-expected stocks indicate that demand is running high and this typically boosts oil prices on release of the report. Higher-than-expected inventories tend to result in lower oil prices when the news is released.

Sometimes crude stocks and refined product inventories do not move in the same direction—perhaps crude stocks fall and gasoline stocks rise the same week. Traders may have to put on their thinking caps to figure out what's going on with overall demand for crude oil and petroleum products. In this situation, crude stocks may have fallen due to either crude production or due to refiners using up crude stocks at an unexpected pace. Meanwhile, gasoline stocks could have risen due to a fall in the pace of refining or gasoline demand could have risen.

The main markets that watch the numbers from the Weekly Petroleum Status Report are the oil markets and, to a lesser degree, currency markets. Currency markets care because oil is priced in U.S. dollars. Bond and equity markets start paying attention to the oil inventory numbers when oil prices have experienced strong upward or downward trends and are starting to impact inflation and/or overall economic activity.

> **Trader Tip**
>
> The U.S. EIA also produces a weekly report on natural gas storage levels. This is the Weekly Natural Gas Storage Report and is generally released mid-morning each Thursday for the week ending the previous Friday. This report is not followed as closely as the Weekly Petroleum Status Report.

Commodity Price Indexes

Oil is just one of the many commodities traded on exchanges around the world. Some commodities are more sensitive to changes in economic growth than others. However, government officials and private researchers have spent a good deal of time identifying which commodities are more sensitive to economic growth. Those who study trends in commodity prices quickly conclude this: No one commodity should be relied upon to determine what the commodity price trend is because special factors can affect one commodity and lead to an incorrect conclusion about building or easing inflation pressures. Therefore, a variety of commodity price indexes have been constructed so no one commodity dominates. This presents a clearer picture of price pressures overall. And while there are many commodities that are traded, we're going to focus on those most sensitive to changes in economic growth.

The Commodity Research Bureau Spot Index

One of the most tracked commodity price indexes is the Commodity Research Bureau (CRB) spot index. It began in 1934 as a series produced by the U.S. Bureau of Labor Statistics (BLS) as a daily index of spot prices. Today, the CRB, a private firm, carries on the BLS work on commodity price indexes. The daily spot index produced by the BLS was discontinued in 1969 and was replaced by a weekly index. In May 1981, the CRB began calculating the index on a daily basis.

The Spot Market Price Index is a measure of price movements of 23 sensitive basic commodities (as of March 2009) whose markets are presumed to be among the first to be influenced by changes in economic activity. Essentially, it acts as one early indicator of impending changes in business activity. The commodities used are, in most cases, either raw materials or products close to the initial production stage. The 23 commodities are combined into an "All Commodities" grouping, with two major subdivisions:

◆ Raw Industrials—Includes burlap, copper scrap, cotton, hides, lead scrap, print cloth, rosin, rubber, steel scrap, tallow, tin, wool tops, and zinc.

◆ Foodstuffs—Includes butter, cocoa beans, corn, hogs, lard, soybean oil, steers, sugar, Minneapolis wheat, and Kansas City wheat.

The items upon which the index is based are classified further into four smaller groups: Metals, Textiles, Fats and Oils, and Livestock Indexes. However, some of the 23 commodities do not fall into one of these four groupings. For example, sugar is not included in any of the subgroups. Also, the groupings are not mutually exclusive. Lard, for instance, is in both the Livestock Index and in the Fats and Oils Index. Note that the components listed are as of March 2009.

Differences Between Futures and Spot Indexes for CRB

The CRB Spot Index is based on spot prices. A key feature of the CRB Spot Index is that it does not include any petroleum-related components. So it gives you information about commodity demand separate from the oil markets. Many commodity price indexes have very large oil components, mostly tracking only oil prices. In fact, one of the most popular commodity price indexes based on futures prices is the

Reuters/Jefferies-CRB Index. About one third of its components are either crude oil or petroleum products. So be careful and know whether you're getting data for the Spot Index or the futures-based Reuters/Jefferies-CRB Index.

The CRB Spot Price Index can be obtained from CRB's website at www.crbtrader. com. The futures-based indexes can be found on some financial news websites, such as Bloomberg.com and WSJ.com.

How the CRB Spot Index Relates to Overall Inflation

As shown in the following WTI crude oil and CRB price index chart, the CRB Spot Index does not always move together with oil prices. The CRB Spot Index provides additional information about price pressures separate from the oil markets.

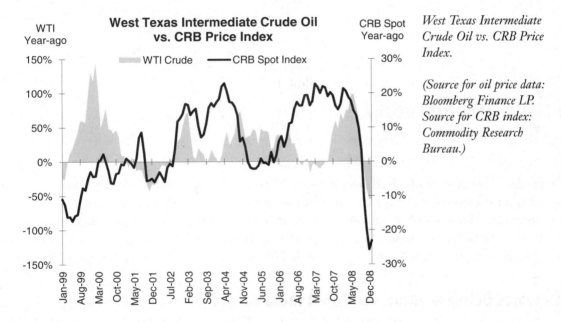

West Texas Intermediate Crude Oil vs. CRB Price Index.

(Source for oil price data: Bloomberg Finance LP. Source for CRB index: Commodity Research Bureau.)

Take a look at the next spot commodities and inflation chart. Generally, the CRB Spot Index does provide insight into pending changes in consumer price inflation. But there can be false signals in direction changes because commodity prices are more sensitive to changes in economic conditions than the CPI (consumer price index).

CRB Spot Commodities vs.
CPI Inflation.

(Source for CRB index:
Commodity Research
Bureau.)

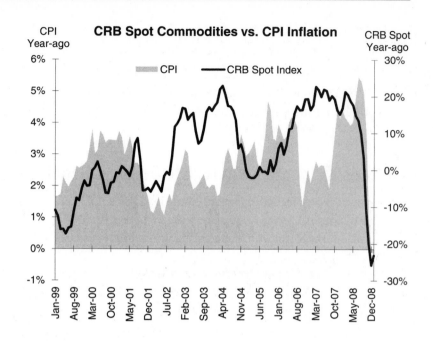

Gold as a Commodity

Yes, gold is pretty cool as jewelry. But we are going to briefly look at it as a commodity that some see as an inflation hedge as well as an investment.

Gold is traded in many exchanges around the world. A key exchange in the United States for gold futures is the NYMEX. As with oil futures prices, you can get gold futures prices on the NYMEX website. From an investor's long-term perspective, here's the bottom line question: Is gold a good investment? For economists and others who are keeping up with overall economic conditions, how well do gold prices indicate the direction of overall inflation?

The following gold prices chart shows the current-dollar price of gold (what you actually paid for it at the time) and the price of gold adjusted for consumer price inflation. Inflation-adjusted gold prices are in terms of January 1980 dollars when gold hit a record high, for a monthly average of $675.31 per ounce. In current dollars, the price of gold averaged $858.69 for the month of January 2009. This sounds good to many of us, but in January 1980 dollars, gold was only worth $315.67, reflecting a sharp decline in real value. An investment in gold in early 1980 would have been a lousy decision! For those buying gold in early 1980, the glitter did not last long.

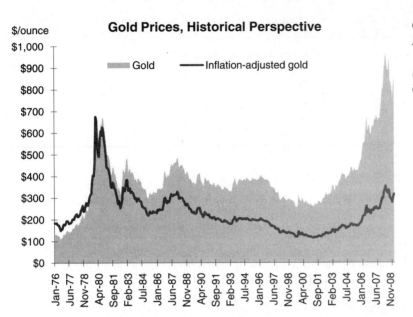

Timing, however, is everything with investments. Buying gold in May 2001 would have cost you just over $275 an ounce. So buying in 2001 would have been a good idea. The bottom line is that gold has a very volatile price. It hardly provides a steady return, so it's not a good long-term investment. Sure, day traders can try their hand at making a short-term buck, but it's probably a good idea to keep your retirement funds out of gold investments.

Gold prices tend to run up when the stock market falls sharply, such as in 1987 and then again in 2008–2009. This is primarily due to flight-to-safety actions by investors based on the belief that gold will hold its value. But often gold prices dip after the stock market regains its strength.

Do gold prices predict changes in inflation? The following gold prices and CPI chart shows how much more volatile gold prices are than consumer price inflation. But the main point from the chart is that there can be long periods in which gold price inflation has no relationship to CPI inflation. Gold price inflation was actually negative during much of the 1980s and 1990s while CPI inflation was notably positive.

Not only is gold a risky investment, it does not have much of the inflation-forecasting information that many other commodities have. This is because gold is more related to speculative trading activity than to real economic activity. Yes, gold does have some industrial uses, but those are minor compared to gold as an asset that's used for speculation by financial traders.

> ### Only from an Economist
>
> Until 2008, the daily record closing price of gold had been $850 per ounce set on January 21, 1980. Another peak was set on March 18, 2008, at $1,004 per ounce. Over this period, the CPI increased a cumulative 173 percent. This means that for the March 18, 2008, price to top the earlier record high in real terms, the price would have to have been over $2,321 per ounce!

The Least You Need to Know

- Oil is a key commodity in the world economy, affecting consumer prices directly for gasoline and heating oil, but also for many goods and services through oil's impact on costs of production.

- The primary oil contracts traded on exchanges are for West Texas Intermediate (WTI) and for Brent (a product of the United Kingdom).

- The biggest economic news for traders in oil markets is each Wednesday's Weekly Petroleum Status Report, which focuses on the latest oil inventory numbers.

- Commodity price indexes can provide additional information on building inflation pressures because of their sensitivity to changes in economic growth.

- Gold is traded on futures exchanges just like oil; however, gold has not been a good hedge against inflation over the long run.

Part 4

Housing and Construction

Housing always gets a lot of play in the media, whether it's down in the dumps or soaring into the stratosphere, because this sector has a key role in the economy. You might be surprised to learn that existing home sales are just as important for the economy as newly constructed homes!

Now that problems with mortgage markets and foreclosures have moved to the front burner of the economic stove, you will see how home sales and house prices fit in. A sharp decline in housing prices was the straw on the camel's back that caused Wall Street and economies around the world to come crashing down. Now you'll know why!

Chapter **13**

Housing Starts: Keeping Homebuilders Busy

In This Chapter

◆ Housing starts boost many related industries

◆ What you'll find in the Census report

◆ Why housing starts cause excitement in the financial markets

◆ Other indicators give a sneak peek at where starts are headed

Investors want to know where the economy is headed. Housing is an industry that typically leads the economy into recession and into recovery. Being able to track this sector is critical to understanding the direction of the economy.

In this chapter, we learn the definitions of housing starts and housing permits. We review why housing is so cyclical and leads the rest of the economy. Changes in homebuilding affect the fortunes of a number of industries, and knowing about them can be valuable to investors who track housing. Finally, housing is a leading indicator for the economy, and there are indicators that preview where housing starts are headed. These are introduced in this chapter.

Housing Starts: The Rock Star of Housing Data

The *housing starts* report is the most recognized economic news on the housing sector. The stock and bond markets can surge or plummet based on the monthly swings in housing starts. Not only do investors pay close attention to these numbers, but so do homebuilders, local governments, and even manufacturers of home appliances, among others.

Basically, a housing start takes place when that first shovelful of dirt is turned over to begin construction. The Census Bureau defines a housing start as "when excavation begins for the footings or foundation of a building." Housing starts include both single-family and multifamily buildings. Multifamily starts cover buildings such as apartments and condominiums. But group homes such as dormitories, nursing homes, and hotels are not included. Also, publicly owned housing is not included. Data are for privately owned *housing units*.

def•i•ni•tion

Housing starts refer to the number of residential units on which construction has actually begun.

A **housing unit** refers to a house, an apartment, a group of rooms, or a single room intended for occupancy as separate living quarters. Each unit must have its own entrance to the outside of the building or to a common hall.

Who Cares About Housing Starts?

A bump up in housing starts revs up the number of jobs for carpenters, bricklayers, electricians, and even landscapers. Construction workers tend to have relatively high wages, so store owners like having lots of construction workers around to spend their paychecks on everything from CDs to restaurant meals to clothes to new wheels. Also, sales pick up for concrete and brick makers, lumber yards, carpet makers, and appliance manufacturers when housing starts increase.

After the house is finished, homeowners buy furniture and home furnishings. When housing starts pick up, local governments get more revenue from building permits and sales taxes. Lots of businesses and local governments get a piece of the pie from housing construction.

Only from an Economist

Hourly wages for construction production workers are relatively high and indicate how important housing starts are for local economies. In 2008, the average wage for construction workers was $21.86, compared to the overall average worker's wage of $18.08. Construction wages are dramatically higher than retail trade wages, at $12.87 per hour, and even manufacturing wages, at $17.75 per hour in 2008.

Housing Starts Move the Financial Markets

Financial markets always try to figure out whether the economy is getting better or not. Those who trade or invest in company stocks look at housing markets to see if company revenues are going to rise or fall. A boost in housing starts is a good sign that the economy is improving and that company earnings will improve.

When housing starts pick up, traders in the stock market usually believe that they will see better profits for homebuilder companies, makers of construction supplies, and producers of home appliances, furniture, and home furnishings. Mortgage lenders and processors see a jump in revenues. However, a drop in starts does the opposite and is seen as dragging down the stock market.

A jump in starts also means that loan demand heads up, e.g., construction loans to finance homebuilder activity and mortgages for homebuyers. This boosts loans over-all and pushes up interest rates. Those trading in the bond markets see higher starts pushing down the price of bonds, which is the same thing as raising interest rates. A fall in starts eases the demand for loans and generally results in lower interest rates.

Key Facts About the Housing Starts Report

The housing starts report is the number-one indicator for housing. Market watchers eagerly jump on new numbers which come out each mid-month. The housing starts report also includes data on housing permits.

Here's what's in the housing starts report:

◆ Official name: New Residential Construction

◆ Release date: Monthly, just after mid-month for the prior month's data (July release has June data)

◆ Produced by: U.S. Census Bureau and U.S. Department of Housing and Urban Development, jointly

◆ Form of data: Starts as well as permits are counted as numbers of units and are not in dollars. The official report has data in thousands of units, annualized, although media analysts may convert numbers to millions. Being in annualized format, the monthly construction pace can be easily compared to yearly numbers. Market watchers focus both on levels and on simple monthly percent changes. Data are available seasonally adjusted and not seasonally adjusted.

◆ Market watchers focus on: Monthly percent changes and levels (view reports at www.census.gov/const/www/newresconstindex.html)

Both housing starts and permits are published with detail for total, for single units, for 2–4 units, and a final category of 5 units or more. The following table shows the commonly followed numbers in the starts and permits report.

Housing Starts and Permits

Housing Starts, United States, Thousands of Units

	Total	1 Unit	2–4 Units	5 or More Units
2006	1,800.90	1,465.40	42.7	292.8
2007	1,355.00	1,046.00	31.7	277.3
2008	904.30	622.40	17.2	264.7

Housing Permits, United States, Thousands of Units

	Total	1 Unit	2–4 Units	5 or More Units
2006	1,838.9	1,378.2	76.6	384.1
2007	1,398.4	979.9	59.6	359.0
2008	892.5	569.9	32.2	290.3

Housing Starts, Total, by Census Region, Thousands of Units

	Northeast	Midwest	South	West
2006	167.2	279.5	910.3	443.8
2007	142.9	210.1	681.1	320.9
2008	120.9	135.1	452.6	195.7

In addition to national totals, housing permits are published by Census regions: Northeast, Midwest, South, and West. Here's how the regions break down:

States in Census Regions

Northeast	Midwest	South	West
Connecticut	Illinois	Alabama	Alaska
Maine	Indiana	Arkansas	Arizona
Massachusetts	Iowa	Delaware	California
New Hampshire	Kansas	D.C.	Colorado
New Jersey	Michigan	Florida	Hawaii
New York	Minnesota	Georgia	Idaho
Pennsylvania	Missouri	Kentucky	Montana
Rhode Island	Nebraska	Louisiana	Nevada
Vermont	N. Dakota	Maryland	New Mexico
	Ohio	Mississippi	Oregon
	S. Dakota	N. Carolina	Utah
	Wisconsin	Oklahoma	Washington
		S. Carolina	Wyoming
		Tennessee	
		Texas	
		Virginia	
		West Virginia	

You can see in the following housing starts chart that the South Census region—stretching from Maryland to Florida to Texas—has the largest number of starts, followed by the West. But all regions suffered sharp declines in starts going into and during the recession that started in 2008.

Trader Tip

Multifamily starts and permits can be very "lumpy." For apartment and condominium complexes, each unit is counted separately as a permit or start. If weather is especially favorable for construction activity (dry and/or warm), multifamily permits and starts can surge. So to see the underlying trend in housing, the multifamily component should be viewed over several months. Bond and stock traders typically focus on the single-family component to see the underlying trend in housing.

Housing starts by region.

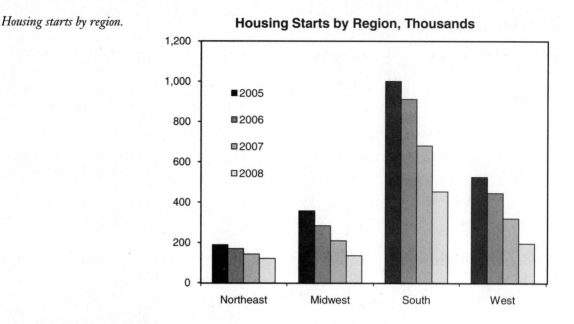

Housing Starts by Region, Thousands

- 2005
- 2006
- 2007
- 2008

Northeast   Midwest   South   West

Where Do Housing Permits Fit In?

Before actual construction of a house or apartment can begin, nearly all local governments require the builder to buy a building permit and file the appropriate paperwork to meet construction regulations.

A housing permit is authorization by the municipality or other local government for a builder to begin construction on one or more housing units. Not all jurisdictions require a permit before construction takes place. However, the Census Bureau estimates that less than 3 percent of all starts occur in areas that do not require permits.

While some think housing permits are leading indicators for housing starts, there is only a small grain of truth to that. Yes, building permits are issued first. But building permits cost money and builders generally wait until almost the last minute to buy a permit before actually starting construction. For single-family units, about 50 percent of housing starts take place the same month that permits are bought and about 30 percent start the very next month. From 2002 through 2008, the time from permit issuance to start in permit-issuing places averaged 0.8 months (less than a month!). For multifamily units, about 30 percent of the units start the same month as permit issuance and another 30 percent occur the month after issuance.

Behind the Numbers

The housing permit numbers are collected by the Census Bureau from about 20,000 permit-issuing jurisdictions. On a monthly basis, the bureau samples 9,000 of those jurisdictions. Monthly totals are estimated based on the long-term statistical comparison of the monthly numbers to annual numbers. Annual permit data are based on surveys sent to all 20,000 permit-issuing places.

Only from an Economist

Did you know that the housing permits series is part of the index of leading indicators? Economists' research has consistently found that housing starts and permits lead turning points in the economy—recovery and recession. As we saw in Chapter 2, the Conference Board—a private nonprofit group for business research—puts together the index of leading indicators, and it makes permits a key part of this index.

Starts estimates are based on the Census Bureau's Survey of Use of Permits (SUP). Field reps for the Census Bureau check on samples from 900 of the permit-issuing places and collect data on progress of the construction, including start date, completion, and date of sale if the single-family unit was built to be sold. Census has a separate survey for nonpermit areas, called the Nonpermit Survey (NP).

Housing Starts: A Roller Coaster Within the Economy

Housing starts statistics make large movements over the business cycle. Their ups and downs are bigger than for the overall economy. Starts are very sensitive to changes in mortgage rates and unemployment. When mortgage rates are high, most homebuyers put off buying a home until rates fall lower, making a mortgage more affordable. When unemployment rises, potential homebuyers worry about job security and delay home purchases until employment trends are brighter.

Check out the housing starts versus the unemployment rate chart that follows. Overall, starts tend to lead the economy into recession and into recovery. There are at least two reasons why housing starts decline prior to the peak of a business cycle. First, housing is more interest-rate sensitive than any other major part of the economy, except perhaps motor vehicle sales. The latter part of a business expansion typically includes higher interest rates, either due to strong demand or due to the Federal Reserve boosting rates to lower inflation pressures. This rise in rates makes housing less affordable. Housing purchases generally can be postponed until rates are lower and monthly mortgage payments are less.

Housing Starts vs.
Unemployment.

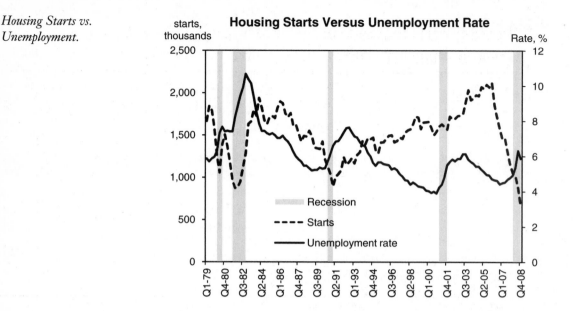

Housing Starts Versus Unemployment Rate

During recession, interest rates are lower because demand for loanable funds has soft-ened or because the Fed has cut rates to spur economic growth. In these interest rate cycles, housing starts typically lead changes in the business cycle because housing pur-chases are so interest-rate sensitive.

But housing starts can be affected by other factors. During 2007 and 2008, housing starts were depressed by an atypical credit crunch. Many mortgage lenders went out of business and others raised their lending standards. During the worst of the credit cri-sis, financial institutions became almost obsessed with raising capital and became very reluctant to lend even to very creditworthy customers.

Housing starts typically turn down many months ahead of the overall economy. From the 1969 recession onwards, starts turned down before the overall economy by a period of six months up to just over two years. The lead time has been a lot shorter coming out of recession, with the upturn in starts typically ranging from 2 to 10 months before the overall economy began recovery, but the lead has been as long as 16 months.

Housing Starts Compared to the Business Cycle in Recent Decades
Levels in Thousands, SAAR

Housing Starts Peak	Housing Starts Level	Business Cycle Peak	Housing Starts Trough	Housing Starts Level	Business Cycle Trough
Jan. 1969	1,466	Dec. 1969	Jan. 1970	1,085	Nov. 1970
Jan. 1972	2,494	Nov. 1973	Dec. 1974	975	Mar. 1975
Dec. 1977	2,142	Jan. 1980	May 1980	927	Jul. 1980
Jan. 1981	1,547	Jul. 1981	Jan. 1982	843	Nov. 1982
Jan. 1990	1,551	Jul. 1990	Jan. 1991	798	Mar. 1991
Feb. 2000	1,737	Mar. 2001	Jul. 2000	1,463	Nov. 2001
Jan. 2006	2.273	Dec. 2008	*	*	*

Trader Tip

During winter months, the seasonal factors for starts and permits are very large, and small movement in actual permits or starts can result in large seasonally adjusted changes. For example, in the northern states, a warm winter can lead to a modest jump in activity. In the southeastern states, winter is typically wet, so a drier than normal winter can lead to a modest gain in not seasonally adjusted starts, which translates into a large seasonally adjusted boost. Watch out for warmer or drier winters' effects on permits and starts data!

How Housing Starts Are Related to Other Economic Data

How do housing starts fit in with other economic data? There are a number of economic indicators that point to upcoming changes in housing starts. In turn, housing starts impact many indicators. For both situations, some series are related to the general economy, and some are specific to the housing industry.

For the overall economy, anything affecting the health of consumer finances impacts housing starts. Personal income determines whether consumers can afford to buy houses. The unemployment rate and job growth tell us how rapidly starts will rise or fall. Changes in mortgage rates probably have the fastest impact on housing starts because the interest rate directly affects the size of a monthly payment. Potential homebuyers typically put off buying a home when interest rates are high, leading to weakness in starts.

Housing starts impact other key areas of the economy. As starts rise, look for gains in consumer expenditures on household appliances and furnishings. In the retail sales report, starts eventually can impact specific components for furniture and home furnishings stores, electronics and appliance stores, building material dealers, and garden equipment and supplies dealers. These purchases by consumers then show up in data for personal consumption expenditures (PCEs) in the personal income report and in the GDP report.

When starts increase, industrial production for housing-related components gets a boost. The housing-related components in the industrial production report include appliances, furniture, carpeting, and construction supplies.

Finally, the starts data are key inputs into the monthly construction outlays series, which in turn go into the residential investment component of GDP.

How Markets Move on the News Release

When the starts and permits numbers are released, the financial markets primarily focus on the levels and the percentage change from the prior month. Typically, financial markets bake their expectations into the market values (stocks, bonds, currencies, oil, and other commodities). So how much starts and permits exceed or fall short of expectations affects how much markets react to the new release numbers.

What else do market participants watch for in the news release? The next big item is to sort out the single-family starts from the total. Multifamily starts are more volatile than the single-family component. And the single-family component is generally seen as more reflective of how strong the economy is. So pay more attention to the single-family component of starts.

Did atypical weather affect starts? Unusually wet weather can lead to a softening in starts while drier-than-normal winter and spring weather can lead to a surge in seasonally adjusted starts.

Is there a reason to believe that the recent trend in starts will change in the near future? Sometimes the latest release on starts is discounted because of other changes in the economy. If the latest release on starts is strong but the Federal Reserve just announced an interest rate increase and hinted at others to come, then markets may focus less on the current release and more on their expectations for the future.

Sneak Peek: Where Are Housing Starts Headed?

In this section, we'll take a look at the moderately long list of housing industry numbers. These tell us what direction housing starts are headed. They're important because investors and traders in the financial markets often use these series to estimate what starts will be in the next official report and in coming months.

NAR Pending Home Sales Index

The National Association of Realtors (NAR) compiles data on signed real estate contracts for existing single-family homes, condos, and co-ops. It usually takes four to six weeks for a contract to actually close. A boost in pending sales of existing homes typically reflects strength in the overall housing market, not just the existing component.

NAHB Housing Market Index

The National Association of Home Builders (NAHB) produces the Housing Market Index that rates the general economic and housing market conditions. It is based on a survey of the members of the NAHB. The Housing Market Index has three components: present sales of new homes, sales of new homes expected in the next six months, and traffic of prospective buyers in new homes. The last component is particularly useful for projecting housing trends.

MBA Mortgage Applications

The Mortgage Bankers' Association (MBA) compiles an index of mortgage applications at mortgage lenders. This index is a leading indicator for single-family home sales and, in turn, housing construction.

New Home Sales

The Census Bureau collects data on new home sales. This monthly report also includes data on inventories of unsold newly constructed houses on the market. Inventories are generally viewed in terms of the number of months' worth of unsold existing homes. When inventories rise too much, builders slow the pace of new construction and housing starts decline.

Take a look at the following chart of housing starts versus the supply of unsold homes. When the supply of houses on the market is high, homebuilders tend to ease back on new construction.

Housing Starts vs. Months' Supply Unsold Homes.

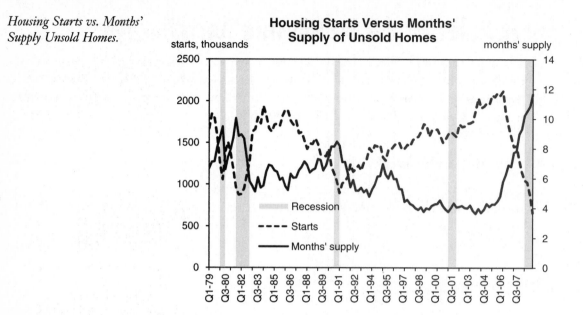

NAR Existing Home Sales

The National Association of Realtors each month compiles sales of previously constructed homes, condominiums, and co-ops. The trend in existing home sales leads the trend in starts. This report includes data on how many months' supply of unsold existing homes are for sale. This figure for unsold inventories affects housing starts since home buyers view existing homes as an alternative to newly constructed homes.

Effects of Changes in Building Codes

On rare occasions, changes in building codes can cause building permits and starts to spike. For example, New York City implemented a more restrictive building code, effective July 1, 2008. Developers rushed to obtain building permits in June to grandfather in the old building code for a large number of apartment and condominium projects.

When the June housing permits and starts data were first made public to the financial markets, traders were baffled that there was such a surge since housing had been at depressed levels for many months. The government press release explained the spike in a special memo not typically included in the report.

Key Facts About the Construction Spending Report

Housing starts and permits measure units of construction—not dollar value. But there is a monthly government report that puts construction activity in dollars. This is the Census Bureau's report on construction spending or construction expenditures. What is handy about this report is that it not only covers housing, but also nonresidential and public construction activity (by "public," we mean government construction spending).

This report does not get as much attention as the housing starts report, but it does paint a broader picture of the construction sector. Also, the numbers are not for planned spending as indicated by permits. Construction outlays have actually taken place, so the data are a measure of current production for construction. In fact, the spending numbers from this report are key source data for the residential and nonresidential structures investment components of GDP and for the structures portion of government expenditures in GDP.

If you think the value of construction is just the cost of materials, you'd be wrong—way wrong! The value of construction contains a lot more and includes these costs: materials installed or erected, labor and a proportionate share of the cost of construction equipment rental, contractor's profit, architectural and engineering work, miscellaneous overhead and office costs chargeable to the project on the owner's books, and interest and taxes paid during construction (except for state and locally owned projects).

This goes to show that there are a lot of pieces in the final value of construction. A big item not included is the price or value of the land for the construction project, though the cost of preparing the land is included. Also, these numbers primarily cover new structures, additions, renovations, and a few other related categories. Maintenance and minor repair of structures are not a part of construction expenditures in this report. Also not counted is mining activity such as drilling of gas and oil wells and building of mine shafts.

Here's what's in the construction spending report?

- Official name: Value of Construction Put in Place

- Release date: Monthly, first week of the month, two months after the reference month (July release has May data)

- ◆ Produced by: Bureau of the Census, U.S. Department of Commerce

- ◆ Form of data: Dollars, at an annualized rate. Data are available seasonally adjusted and not seasonally adjusted.

- ◆ Market watchers focus on: Monthly and year-ago percent changes (view the report at www.census.gov/const/www/c30index.html)

Key Numbers in the Report

The construction spending report has four main series that interest market watchers: total, private residential, private nonresidential, and public. The report does have a separate breakout table that shows residential and nonresidential outlays that are combined for the public and private sectors, but most analysts prefer to focus on the private sector numbers for those categories. A good feature of this report is that it has extensive detail on nonresidential construction.

Behind the Numbers

Major components of the construction spending data are estimated separately. First, outlays on single-family homes are based on spending patterns using the housing starts and new home sales data from the U.S. Census Bureau's Survey of Construction (SOC). So we see starts (an indicator of planned activity) and new home sales (an indicator of completion of activity) as numbers feeding into a measure of current production for construction.

Values for multifamily residential construction spending are also based on a sub-sample from the SOC. Once a project is selected, monthly construction progress reports are requested from the owner until the project is completed. About 2,500 projects are in the survey each month.

For nonresidential construction spending, the Census Bureau conducts a monthly Construction Progress Reporting Survey. This survey sample is based primarily on data from McGraw-Hill Construction.

For public construction outlays, the Census Bureau also creates separate survey samples from McGraw-Hill Construction data for state and local government and then for federal government. Progress reports are requested from the appropriate agency in charge of the project or its designated agent, such as the builder or architect responsible for the project.

Take a look at the following construction expenditures chart. Construction components have behaved differently over the last two recessions. In 2001, nonresidential construction was weaker than residential outlays. In 2008, the reverse was true. For both recession years, government construction spending merely slowed.

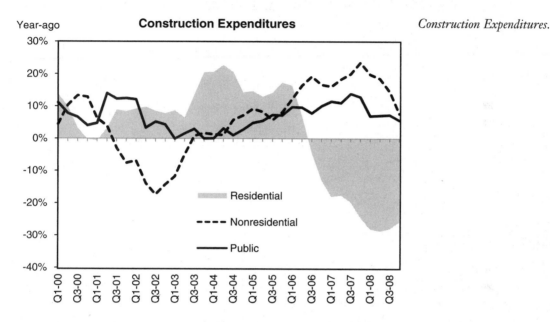

Construction Expenditures.

Construction Expenditures and Market Reaction

As with other construction sector indicators, stronger numbers tend to boost the stock market and lead to higher interest rates. Market watchers focus on the monthly percent changes and, to a lesser degree, year-ago percent changes. Although the overall figure is important, the private sector component gets more attention because it is more sensitive to recession and economic boom than the public component.

The latest construction outlays numbers can cause economists who forecast the economy to adjust their GDP forecasts, primarily in components for residential and non-residential structures investment, since construction outlays are their key source data.

The Least You Need to Know

 ◆ The housing starts series is the most important indicator for housing.

 ◆ Starts are strongly led by the overall economy, heavily affected by unemployment rates and interest rates, and lead the economy.

- Starts impact the following key manufacturing industries: construction materials and household appliances and furnishings.

- Financial markets focus on the single-family component.

- Financial markets see rising housing starts as a plus for the stock market and a negative for the bond market (because it boosts rates).

- Construction outlays provide valuable insight into nonresidential and public construction as well as housing.

Home Sales: Is Your Real Estate Broker Happy?

In This Chapter

- ◆ Why you should care about existing and new home sales
- ◆ Key numbers in two home sales reports
- ◆ How home sales move financial markets
- ◆ Why house prices are important for the economy

It might seem odd to you that the sale of a house built years ago is important. After all, with an existing home, it's just one homeowner turning the house keys over to the new owner. That doesn't seem quite as exciting as the thought of a brand-new home being sold.

The truth is, though, that existing home sales create a lot of excitement in financial markets. Want to know why? Because existing home sales are the backbone of the housing market. Read on and you'll understand why.

Why Existing Home Sales Are Important

There are two main reports on home sales: *existing home sales* and new home sales. The report on existing home sales is produced by the National Association of Realtors (NAR). The report on new home sales is produced by the Census Bureau.

The size of the existing home sales market is vastly larger than that for new homes. In 2008, the number of new homes sold in the United States was 482,000. The number of existing homes sold was 4.349 million! About 89 percent of home purchases were for used homes with the remainder for newly built houses. However, 2008 was a down year for home sales and new home sales typically fall off more than existing homes during economic downturns.

In the next chart, notice that since 1999 (when existing home sales data start), used homes typically have made up 83 to 85 percent of all home sales. In fact, typically more than 8 out of 10 *single-family home sales* are for used homes.

def•i•ni•tion

An **existing home sale** occurs when the attorneys have signed off on all of the paperwork, a new name is on the deed, and house keys are exchanged. It's not counted as part of the National Association of Realtors' statistics until it's a "done deal."

A new **single-family home sale** takes place when a deposit is taken or sales agreement is signed for the purchase of a newly constructed home.

Existing Share of Single-Family Home Sales.

(Source for existing home sales: National Association of Realtors®.)

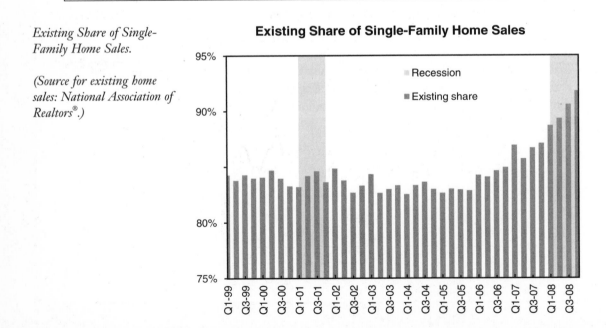

Existing Share of Single-Family Home Sales

Existing home sales include single-family houses, townhomes, condominiums, and co-ops. But the NAR has its own specific definition of an existing home sale. They say the sale is not counted until the actual closing. This contrasts with the Census Bureau's definition of a new home sale—when a homebuyer signs a contract or makes a deposit on a newly constructed home.

Used Home Sales—No Hammers, But Big Impact

Why is your real estate broker happy about used home sales? First, he or she just got a nice commission check. It's hard not to be happy about that! But existing home sales also boost the local economy where the agent operates. With an existing home sale, there's often quite a bit of construction-related activity. Many used homes get a face lift before going on the market. This might mean a new paint job, a new roof, or a renovated kitchen. So all this prepping for an existing home sale can result in big bucks going into the hands of local craftsmen and other workers.

After the sale of a used home, renovation activities often continue. And the new homeowner also spends money elsewhere. Who can resist adding a new refrigerator to your kitchen or buying new furniture for the family room? This spending after the sale of an existing home creates ripple effects on the economy.

Take a look at the following chart to see how existing home sales fare against the ups and downs of mortgage rates. As the mortgage rate decreases, the home sales increase.

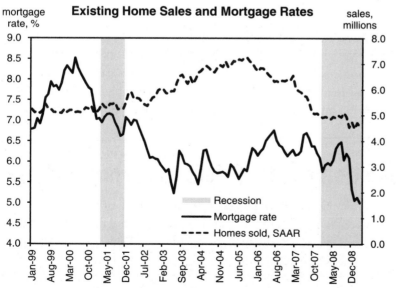

Existing Home Sales and Mortgage Rates.

(Source for existing home sales: National Association of Realtors®.)

Key Facts for Existing Home Sales

The monthly existing home sales report provides an important update on the health of the housing sector. The key series in the report are for existing home sales, housing inventory (homes for sale), months' supply (how many months it would take to sell the homes on the market at the current sales pace), and prices of homes sold. So what's in the NAR's Report on Existing Home Sales?

◆ Official name: Existing Home Sales

◆ Release date: Monthly, on or about the 25th for the previous month's data (July release has June data)

◆ Produced by: National Association of Realtors (NAR)

◆ Form of data: Existing home sales and inventories are counted in numbers of units, not in dollars. The official news release has sales and inventory data in millions of units, annualized, although various data tables may use thousands or single units. Sales data are available seasonally adjusted and not seasonally adjusted. Price data are in dollars, not seasonally adjusted. Months' supply is a ratio of homes for sale to sales made. Data are available for the United States and for Census regions.

◆ Market watchers focus on: Monthly and year-ago percent changes for sales and home prices; levels for months' supply of homes for sale (www.realtor.org/research/research/ehspage)

The series reported each month are existing home sales, inventory, months' supply, and sales price. The news release includes the latest monthly numbers and recent annual data. The existing home sales report is based on a monthly survey of a representative sample of 160 local Realtor associations/boards and multiple listing services (MLS). The NAR believes its sample captures 30–40 percent of all existing home sales monthly.

Why Prefer Median Home Sales Prices to Average Prices?

Most of the traders in the financial markets prefer to focus on median prices rather than average prices. The average price is more volatile than the median price. And a moderate change in the mix of homes sold—in terms of high-end share versus low-end share—can have a noticeable impact on changes in prices.

Here's an example: Suppose we have a market of five existing homes, which sold in June for the following: $180,000, $190,000, $200,000, $220,000, and $220,000. The median price is the price at the exact middle of the distribution, so the median price in June is $200,000. The average price, however, is $202,000 (add all five figures and divide that sum by five).

And let's say that in July, there is a five-house sample with the following prices: $185,000, $195,000, $205,000, $225,000, and $260,000. For July, the median price is $205,000 while the average price is $214,000. The average price has gone up much more than the median price. And there is a good chance that the average has gone up because of a shift in the distribution of the types of homes sold.

Now, the survey used for the existing homes sales report does not have the same sample each month, and this can affect price trends. Typically (though not always), when the economy is weak, the share of low-end homes sold falls faster than the share of high-end homes sold. This tends to add to sales prices even though sales are weakening overall. The median price is more likely to capture price weakness than the average price.

Developers' Delight: New Single-Family Home Sales

A surge in sales of new single-family houses is what developers and homebuilders count on for loading up the wheelbarrow with a pile of profits. New home sales reflect the purchase of newly constructed houses with no prior occupant. While existing home sales do give an important signal on the health of real estate, the new sales series is a direct measure of what homebuilders are facing in their market. That is, homebuilders can't keep building if new homes aren't selling. And suppliers of construction materials and manufacturers of household appliances and household furnishings lose business. On average, each new home sold reflects more impact on the economy than an existing home sold.

Key Facts for New Home Sales

Here's what's in the report for new home sales:

♦ Official name: New Residential Sales

♦ Release date: Monthly, near the end of the month following the month of the data (July release has June data)

♦ Produced by: U.S. Bureau of the Census and U.S. Department of Housing and Urban Development

◆ Form of data: New single-family home sales and inventories are counted in numbers of units and not in dollars. The official news release has sales and inventory data in thousands of units, annualized. Sales data are available seasonally adjusted and not seasonally adjusted. Price data are in dollars and are not seasonally adjusted. Months' supply is a ratio of homes for sale to sales made. Median months for sale is the median number of months for sale since completion. Sales data are available for the United States and for Census regions.

◆ Market watchers focus on: Monthly and year-ago percent changes for sales and home prices; levels for months supply of homes for sale (view reports at www.census.gov/const/www/newressalesindex.html)

The series reported each month are new single-family home sales, homes for sale (inventory), months' supply, and sales price. The news release includes the latest monthly numbers and recent annual data.

The Census Bureau/HUD Joint Report

The monthly new single-family home sales report is a joint news release produced by the U.S. Bureau of the Census and the U.S. Department of Housing and Urban Development. The key series in the report are for single-family home sales, housing inventory (home for sale), months' supply, and prices of homes sold.

Not all sales of newly built homes are included in the Census Bureau's definition. To be included in these sales numbers, the sale must include land in addition to the house. Excluded are houses built for rent and houses built on an owner's land (regardless of whether built by the owner or by a general contractor).

For new homes, the sale can take place in any stage of construction, but typically, about 25 percent take place at the time of completion. The remaining 75 percent are evenly split between those under construction and those not yet started. When is a new single-family home considered to be "for sale"? A house is "for sale" when a permit has been issued in a permit-issuing place or work has been started on the foundation or footings in nonpermit areas. In addition, neither a sales contract has been signed nor a deposit has been made.

Differences in the Home Sales Reports

There are some obvious and not-so-obvious differences between new and existing home sales reports. Both are released about the same time, late each month for the prior month's data. But how do they compare in terms of how the data reflect actual transaction times?

You now know that the NAR says that an existing home sale occurs at the time of closing. But a closing is almost always preceded by the arrangement of financing, which typically starts after the signing of the sales contract. Mortgages generally take 30 to 60 days to close, so there's a notable lag between the sales date for an existing home and when it is recorded as an actual sale in the data. Because of differences in the definition of "sale," new home sales typically lead existing home sales regarding changes in the single-family housing market. Starting in January 2005, the NAR created a pending home sales series to alleviate this lag problem. The pending home sales definition is roughly equivalent to that for new home sales.

Home Sales and Market Reaction

When the news releases come out for new and existing home sales reports, market trackers focus on essentially the same things for both. These are:

♦ Sales, monthly percent changes and levels

♦ Months' supply of unsold homes

♦ Median sales price of new homes sold, monthly percent change, and dollar level

♦ Year-ago percent changes for sales and prices for judging longer-term trends

When monthly percent changes for sales and home prices are strong, this is generally healthy for stock market prices. But it can also result in higher interest rates (lower bond prices). Strong housing sales and home prices reflect a robust economy. A drop in months' supply points to a pickup in future construction and generally boosts equities.

Trader Tip _____

Market watchers also look for news on whether atypically adverse or mild weather hurt or helped sales. Remember, the numbers are seasonally adjusted, and if the weather is unseasonable, then the seasonal adjustment assumptions cause swings in the data. You won't find this information in official reports, but news commentaries often carry such analysis, especially during winter and early spring if weather is unusual.

Check out the following new home sales and supply chart. Recession causes home sales to plummet and the supply of unsold homes on the market to spike. But a credit crunch led sales to fall in 2006 and 2007 well before the onset of recession in 2008.

New Home Sales and Supply.

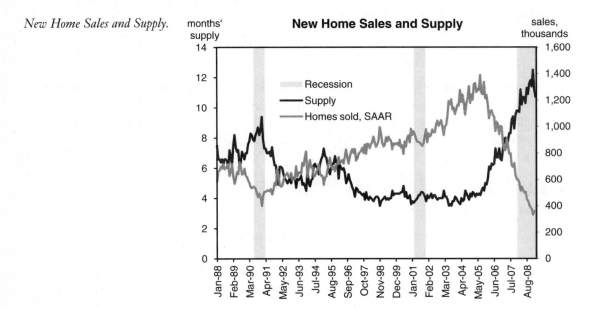

New Home Sales and Supply

months' supply — sales, thousands

Recession
Supply
Homes sold, SAAR

Home Values, Housing Activity, and the Economy

Just recently, the bursting of a housing bubble led to the start of the worst recession in the United States since the Great Depression. In the remainder of this chapter, we'll focus on how changes in home values filter through the economy. Yes, rising home values boost the economy, while falling home values cut into economic growth. Let's see how changes in home values fit in. Later, we'll look at various measures of home prices as an indicator of home values.

Home values really affect the economy, especially the housing and consumer sectors. Periods of rising home values encourage new construction, while periods of soft home prices can dampen housing starts. Changes in home values play key roles in consumer spending and in consumer financial health. During the first half of this decade, sharply rising home prices probably boosted the amount of home equity you have. Many homeowners who experienced this increase were able to draw upon expanding home equity lines of credit (HELOC). But in 2007 and later, home prices fell—with many economists blaming that as the start of the latest recession.

So does this mean falling house prices cause recession? Here's how it all works:

♦ Purchasing a home is an important contribution to wealth accumulation in the United States. Generally, house price appreciation leads to large capital gains for the homeowner when a house is sold.

♦ Rising home prices boost the consumer sector through homeowners' access to HELOC accounts, raising consumer spending.

♦ Rising home prices lift the construction industry because homebuilders accelerate construction. As home prices rise, so do profits.

♦ Rising home prices boost the local economy. Real estate brokers make more sales and new construction adds to the incomes of construction workers and craftsmen.

♦ Rising home prices boost other industries. As real estate sales and new construction increase, sales and production for items such as home appliances and construction materials increase.

♦ Rising home prices add to the value of bank assets and improve a bank's lending ability.

Now, if home prices decline, all of the above positives become negatives for economic growth. The negative effects of declining home prices played a key role in pushing the U.S. economy into recession in 2008.

How Home Values Affect Mortgage Financing

During the early and mid-part of this decade, there was an increased effort to boost home ownership among those with modest incomes. Without getting into the complex issue of whether it was appropriate, let's discuss some key facts about *subprime loans*.

def•i•ni•tion

> **Subprime loans** are offered to borrowers who do not meet prime underwriting guidelines. These borrowers might have low credit ratings or for some other reason have a higher perceived risk of default. They may have a history of loan delinquency or default, a recorded bankruptcy, or have limited debt experience. Subprime lending is found in a variety of credit types, including mortgages, auto loans, and credit cards, but in the media in recent years it has been used in reference to mortgages.

First, many of the subprime loans had little or no down payment, and many had adjustable rate mortgages with low teaser rates to help modest-income borrowers qualify. But lenders and borrowers operated on the assumption (whether fully understood or not is another issue) that when the initial teaser rate eventually reached the date for conversion to a higher fixed rate, the homeowner would have experienced enough appreciation (resulting in homeowner equity) to refinance the loan at a lower rate.

But apparently it wasn't understood (by many, it seems) that if the home didn't appreciate, the homeowner would not have the home equity to qualify for refinancing. By 2006, the housing market began to slow and was in full recession by 2007, remaining so through 2008 and at least into 2009. House prices declined in some local markets and stagnated in many others.

As a result, many subprime borrowers actually had negative equity in their home. That is, the amount owed on the mortgage was greater than the market value of the house. So for many subprime borrowers, when the teaser rate expired and refinancing was not an option, the mortgage payment became unaffordable. For these subprime borrowers, the economically rational choice was to walk away, leaving the house in foreclosure.

House Price Effects on Broader Credit Markets

The broader credit markets have been severely affected by the decline in house prices, largely due to recent "innovations" in mortgage finance. In years past, many lenders originated mortgages to retain them on their own balance sheets and for their own income. But the recent trend has been for most mortgage originators to resell bundles of mortgages to others for their own investment. These originators did not have the same incentives for maintaining mortgage quality as did originators who retained their own originations.

Most of the mortgages were bundled and purchased for Fannie Mae and Freddie Mac, who then would sell these bundled securities with various maturities. They sound like the names for an eccentric aunt and uncle, but Fannie Mae and Freddie Mac are actually government-sponsored enterprises (GSE) created to bolster housing by helping to create broader mortgage markets.

In the past, Moody's (a private bond rating company) has rated these mortgage-backed securities (MBS) with the highest investment grade and many financial institutions bought these MBS for safe and healthy returns. Many purchasers are overseas, and a number of mutual funds are also holders.

When house prices declined at the start of and during the latest recession, the value of these MBS unexpectedly fell as many subprime borrowers were unable to refinance and then became delinquent at higher interest rates. Because of how they were bundled, it became difficult to determine the value of these assets and institutions were unwilling to buy them. But some firms were able to determine that losses were so great that they were insolvent—or at least in need of massive amounts of new capital. That was the case for Bear Stearns, Fannie Mae, Freddie Mac, Lehman Brothers, and Merrill Lynch, among others. In fact, Bear Stearns and Merrill Lynch were bought out and Lehman Brothers closed their doors outright. This is the basic story behind how the decline in house prices led to much of the gridlock in credit markets in 2007, 2008, and 2009.

What Are the Traditional House Price Indexes?

The reports on new and existing single-family home sales both have numbers on home prices. But many economists complain that those home price series aren't an accurate reflection of how home prices really change. That is, the prices for existing home sales in the NAR report and in the Census report for new homes are affected by the share of sales according to price range. For example, if low-end home sales drop relative to high-end sales, that shift alone boosts the average and median home sales price. This would happen even if none of the individual homes in the samples had a price increase.

For years (and even currently), the house price measures that most market watchers read come from monthly economic reports on new home sales and on existing home sales. As you learned earlier, the Census Bureau and the Department of Housing and Urban Development produce the new home sales report, and the NAR produces the existing home sales report.

You can see a comparison in the following chart. The surveys used for the new and for the existing homes sales reports do not have the same sample each month and this plays some role in price trends.

You also already know that when the economy is weak, the share of low-end homes sold usually falls faster than the share of the high-end ones. This tends to add to sales prices even though sales are weakening overall.

Both reports include average and median sales price. The median price is less volatile than the average price but still suffers from shifts in sales between low- and high-end houses. There is no direct comparison of prices for the same house being purchased and then resold later.

House Price Indexes.

(Source for existing home sales: National Association of Realtors®.)

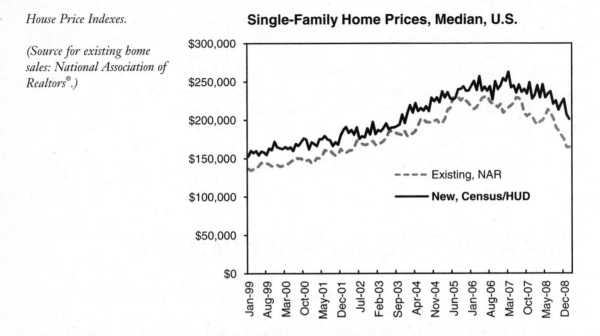

Single-Family Home Prices, Median, U.S.

Key Facts for the Case-Shiller Home Price Index

There are other home price measures that are newer than those in the new and existing home sales reports. These newer indicators provide somewhat different perspectives. Because of the depressed housing sector (starting in 2007) and the credit market woes tied to house prices, one particular price index has gained significant market attention. This is the Case-Shiller home price index.

Named for its developers, Karl E. Case and Robert J. Shiller, this monthly index is a measure of resale price changes for existing single-family homes that compares changes for same houses. This repeat sales methodology captures the true appreciated value of each specific home sold (or its depreciated value). The Case-Shiller home price index report is a joint product of Standard & Poor's and Fiserv, Inc. (S&P/Case-Shiller is a registered trademark of Standard & Poor's). There are 10-city and 20-city composites and data for each component city.

What's in the S&P/Case-Shiller Home Price Index:

◆ Official name: S&P/Case-Shiller Home Price Index

◆ Release date: Monthly, on the last Tuesday of each month for data two months prior (July release has May data)

- Produced by: Standard & Poor's in conjunction with Fiserv, Inc.

- Form of data: Index levels with January 2000 = 100. Monthly reports included monthly and year-ago percentage changes.

- Market watchers focus on: Monthly and year-ago percent changes (www. standardandpoors.com; type in "Case Shiller" in the search box to find the index home page)

Many market analysts believe the Case-Shiller index is the best measure of changes in house values. A useful feature of the Case-Shiller Home Price Index report is the detail for numerous metropolitan areas. The original 10-City Home Price Index covers these metropolitan areas: Boston, Chicago, Denver, Las Vegas, Los Angeles, Miami, New York, San Diego, San Francisco, and Washington, D.C. For the more recently developed 20-City Home Price Index, the additional 10 metropolitan areas are: Atlanta, Charlotte, Cleveland, Dallas, Detroit, Minneapolis, Phoenix, Portland, Seattle, and Tampa. Standard & Poor's also has data for other cities on a subscription basis.

Key Facts for the FHFA House Price Index

The Federal Housing Finance Agency (FHFA) House Price Index (HPI) is another series that has garnered market attention. This index covers single-family housing, using data provided by Fannie Mae and Freddie Mac. The House Price Index is derived from transactions that involve conventional mortgages purchased or securitized by Fannie Mae or Freddie Mac.

In contrast to other house price indexes, the sample is limited by the ceiling amount for loans purchased by these government-sponsored enterprises (GSE). The loan limit in 2007 was $417,000. The limit was raised temporarily in February 2008 to as much as $729,750 in high-cost areas of the country. The loan limit for 2009 was $417,000 for one-unit homes in most areas, but could be as much as $625,500 in certain high-cost areas in the continental United States. Mortgages insured by the FHA, VA, or other federal entities are excluded because they are not "conventional" loans.

The FHFA House Price Index is also a repeat transactions measure, which means it compares prices or appraised values for similar houses. In contrast to the Case-Shiller index, the FHFA HPI treats appraisals for refinancing as a transaction for the index. Hence, the FHFA HPI, using overall transactions, is not a pure sales price index. But this index is a broad measure of house prices and also provides "stress test" information on the capital adequacy of Fannie Mae and Freddie Mac. FHFA also has a set of transactions-only indexes.

The FHFA monthly index formerly had been called the Office of Federal Housing Enterprise Oversight (OFHEO) monthly house price index. OFHEO works to ensure the capital adequacy and financial safety and soundness of two housing GSEs—Fannie Mae and Freddie Mac. In 2008, the FHFA was created as an independent federal agency, resulting from the merger of the Federal Housing Finance Board and the Office of Federal Housing Enterprise Oversight. The House Price Index is part of FHFA's tracking of the health of mortgage-backed securities guaranteed by Fannie Mae and Freddie Mac. Because the FHFA's index tracks prices on homes purchased with conventional home loans backed by Fannie Mae and Freddie Mac, it excludes many homes bought with riskier financing. This likely explains why the FHFA index did not fall as much as the Case-Shiller index in 2007 and 2008.

Here's what's in the FHFA House Price Indexes:

◆ Official name: Federal Housing Finance Agency House Price Index

◆ Release date: Monthly, between the 22nd and 25th of the month for a reference month two months prior (July release has May data)

◆ Produced by: Federal Housing Finance Agency (FHFA), which is part of the OFHEO under the U.S. Department of Housing and Urban Development

◆ Form of data: Index levels with January 1991 = 100. Monthly reports include monthly and year-ago percentage changes.

◆ Market watchers focus on: Monthly and year-ago percent changes (view reports at http://www.fhfa.gov/)

And here are some key characteristics of the Case-Shiller and FHFA Home Price Indexes:

◆ Case-Shiller and FHFA are repeat transaction home price indexes that are not affected by shifts in the housing market between low-end and high-end sales.

◆ Case-Shiller is based purely on market sales of existing homes, while FHFA includes both market transactions and refinance appraisals as price changes. FHFA does have a "transactions only" set of indexes.

◆ FHFA's data are derived from conforming, conventional mortgages provided by Fannie Mae and Freddie Mac. The Case-Shiller indexes use information from county assessor and recorder offices, meaning the Case-Shiller indexes have broader coverage of types of home financing.

◆ FHFA data have broader geographic coverage, including all states being represented. The Case-Shiller indexes do not have coverage in 13 states.

What Do Markets Watch for in House Price Indexes?

When house price index reports are released, financial markets focus on monthly and year-ago percent changes. Those tracking conditions in local real estate markets also check on numbers for metropolitan areas. In the following house price indexes chart, notice that during the housing recession that began in 2006 (well before the start of the overall recession in January 2008), the Case-Shiller Home Price Index showed a greater decline for home prices than other major indexes.

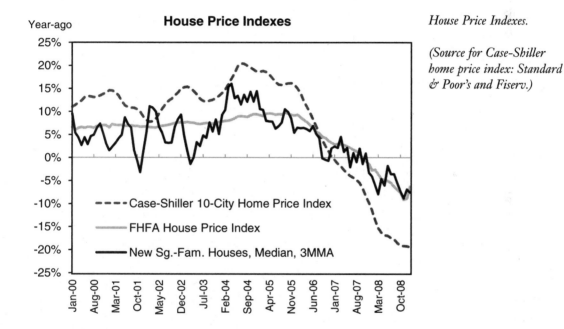

House Price Indexes.

(Source for Case-Shiller home price index: Standard & Poor's and Fiserv.)

The Least You Need to Know

◆ Existing home sales make up more than 80 percent of single-family home sales.

◆ Inventories of both existing and new homes on the market affect the rate of home construction.

◆ New home sales directly impact construction employment, but both new and existing home sales impact employment for craftsmen, such as roofers and cabinet makers.

◆ New and existing home sales both affect consumer spending on household appliances, furniture, and furnishings.

◆ Weak prices for homes can affect the ability of homeowners to refinance and, in turn, create a credit crunch.

◆ The most reliable house price index is the Case-Shiller house price index with the 10-city composite and 20-city composite providing similar information.

Chapter 15

Early Warnings on Housing

In This Chapter

- ◆ The Pending Home Sales Index leads existing home sales
- ◆ The Housing Market Index gives homebuilders' views on the housing market
- ◆ MBA mortgage applications are an early indicator of house purchases

Housing is an important sector of the economy. It leads the overall economy into and out of recession. Many manufacturing and service industries are affected by the fortunes of homebuilders and real estate brokers. These include everything from carpet manufacturers to bricklayers to landscapers, from appliance salespersons to mortgage lenders.

If housing affects your business, it pays to get any advance notice you can on where housing is headed. Yes, such early warnings do exist. In this chapter, we take a look at some of the early signs that indicate where housing might be headed.

Key Facts About the Pending Home Sales Index

Probably the most underrated broad measure of housing activity is the Pending Home Sales Index (PHSI). The lack of attention is likely due to its relatively recent history (data only go back through 2001). The National Association of Realtors (NAR) started this series partly because of one specific criticism of their existing home sales series: existing home sales are based on actual closings, while the Census Bureau's new home sales numbers are based on contract signings. That means the existing home sales data tend to lag the turning points in the new home sales data. The NAR Pending Home Sales Index is based on a definition similar to that for new home sales. Consequently, the PHSI typically precedes changes in existing home sales by one or two months.

Here's what's in the official report for the Pending Home Sales Index:

- ◆ Official name: Pending Home Sales Index

- ◆ Release date: First week of the month for two months prior data (June data are released the first week of August).

- ◆ Produced by: National Association of Realtors

- ◆ Form of data: Index with the base period reflecting the average level of contract activity during 2001 and equaling 100 for that year. Report also has monthly and year-ago percent changes.

- ◆ Market watchers focus on: Monthly and year-ago percent changes (view reports at www.realtor.org/research/research/phsdata)

The Pending Home Sales Index report includes data for the United States and the four major Census regions. This is seen in the following table.

Pending Home Sales Index Report for January 2009

	United States	Northeast	Midwest	South	West
Seasonally Adjusted Annualized Rates, 2001 = 100					
Jan 08	85.9	72.0	84.2	90.4	91.3
Oct 08	86.6	69.5	80.3	87.7	104.7
Nov 08	83.1	64.8	75.1	85.2	102.6
Dec 08	87.1	66.2	80.0	93.3	101.1
Jan 09	80.4	57.8	72.6	82.2	103.6

Month-Ago Percent Changes					
Oct 08	–4.7	–2.9	–3.8	–1.8	–9.9
Nov 08	–3.9	–6.7	–6.5	–2.8	–2.0
Dec 08	4.7	2.1	6.5	9.4	–1.4
Jan 09	–7.7	–12.7	–9.2	–11.9	2.4
Year-Ago Percent Change					
Jan 09	–6.4	–19.7	–13.8	–9.1	13.5

Source: National Association of Realtors

Behind the Numbers in the Pending Home Sales Index

The NAR collects pending home sales from Multiple Listing Services and large brokers. According to the NAR, their sample includes over 100 Multiple Listing Services and 60 large brokers, covering 50 percent of the existing home sales sample, which equals 20 percent of all transactions.

A pending home sale occurs when a seller accepts a sales contract on a property and it is recorded into a Multiple Listing Service (MLS) as a "pending home sale." Based on this definition, over 80 percent of all pending home sales go to settlement within a two-month time period, with a sizeable share of the rest closing within a three-month or four-month time frame. However, not all pending home sales go to "close" and those that don't end up being cancelled.

In contrast to existing home sales and new home sales, the Pending Homes Sales Index, obviously, is an index, which means the numbers are not in unit sales. Part of the reason for using an index is that while the NAR has data for unit sales, they are relative to the sample used and there is not a good benchmark for translating the sample's units into a national number for units.

So the useful comparison is with index values and percent changes in the index. Conceptually, percent changes in unit sales (if actually estimated) would match percent changes in the index. The PHSI base level of 100 is equal to the average level of contract activity during 2001, the first year of data.

Pending Home Sales Index Trends

As shown in the following pending and existing home sales levels chart, the Pending Home Sales Index and existing home sales have closely tracked each other since the PHSI data began in 2001. Looking at levels for the two series using a long-term view, it is hard to see the PHSI forecasting existing home sales.

Pending and Existing Home Sales, Levels.

(Source for pending home sales: National Association of Realtors®.)

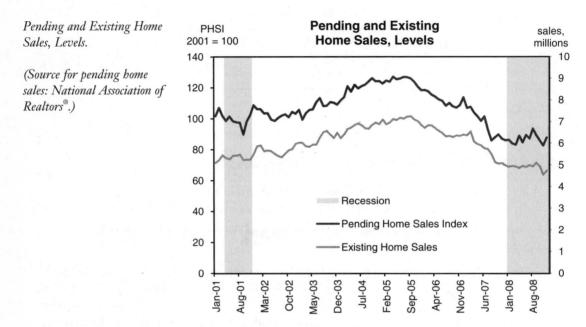

However, when you look at monthly percent changes in the pending and existing home sales chart, over a short period of time you see the pattern of changes in the PHSI are somewhat mirrored by changes in existing home sales one or two months later. It's not perfect, but the PHSI is indeed a leading indicator for existing home sales.

Trader Tip

If you want to try to beat the consensus forecast for this month's existing home sales number, your best bet may be to look at the latest Pending Home Sales Index report!

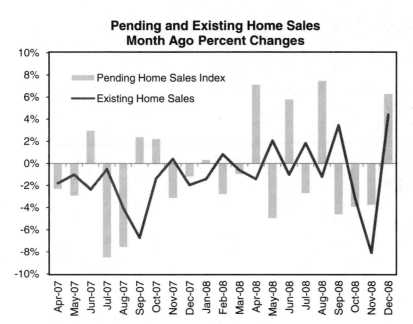

**Pending and Existing Home Sales
Month Ago Percent Changes**

Pending Home Sales Index
Existing Home Sales

Pending and Existing Home Sales, Month-Ago Percent Changes.

(Source for pending home sales: National Association of Realtors®.)

Key Facts About the Housing Market Index (HMI)

Another important leading indicator for housing sales and construction is the National Association of Homebuilders/Wells Fargo Housing Market Index (HMI). Many housing market indicators are from the viewpoint of Realtors, or sales. But the HMI takes a different tack by polling the views of homebuilders about conditions in the housing sector. The HMI also has a component that is further upstream than most housing indicators.

Here's what's in the official report for the Housing Market Index:

- ◆ Official name: NAHB/Wells Fargo Housing Market Index

- ◆ Release date: Monthly, mid-month, one day prior to the housing starts report. However, data are for the same month as the release (June data are released in mid-June).

- ◆ Produced by: The National Association of Homebuilders

◆ Form of data: Index that nets positive and negative responses to three questions about housing conditions. The index ranges from 0 to 100, with 100 reflecting all positive and 0 reflecting all negative responses.

◆ Market watchers focus on: Index levels (view reports at www.nahb.org/page.aspx/category/sectionID=1053)

National Association of Homebuilders/Wells Fargo Housing Market Index for March 2009

	2008										2009		
	Mar	Apr	May	Jun	Jul	Aug	Sep	Oct	Nov	Dec	Jan	Feb	Mar
Overall:	20	20	19	18	16	16	17	14	9	9	8	9	9
Components:													
One-family Sales													
Present Time	20	18	17	17	15	16	17	14	9	8	6	7	7
Next 6 Months	26	30	28	27	23	24	28	19	18	16	17	15	15
Prospective Buyer													
Traffic	19	19	18	16	12	13	14	11	7	7	8	11	9

What's in the HMI Survey?

The HMI is based on a survey that the NAHB sends to a panel of its homebuilder members. This monthly survey goes back to January 1985. Builders are asked to rate housing market conditions based on their experiences. About 400 responses are received each month. The bottom line? The HMI is based on firsthand knowledge of current housing market conditions. Also, the HMI is one of the most timely housing market indicators in the United States. The initial results are based on responses received in the first 10 days of the month with the news release at mid-month for that month. That is, June survey results are made public in mid-June. How's that for being up-to-date?

The survey sent to the panel of homebuilders has three questions, the answers to which form the basis for calculating the index. The survey questions ask builders to rate three aspects of their local market conditions, which include:

- Current sales of single-family detached new homes (homebuilder responses can be "good," "fair," or "poor").

- Expected sales of single-family detached new homes over the next six months (homebuilder responses can be "good," "fair," or "poor").

- Traffic of prospective buyers in new homes (homebuilder responses can be "high to very high," "average," or "low to very low").

How do answers to these questions help us understand housing market conditions? The first question obviously gives the homebuilders' take on current sales, which is timely information. The question about expected sales over the next six months is important. Homebuilders are not going to invest in much new construction unless they believe sales are going to be good. Unsold newly constructed homes require bank financing and payments even while waiting on buyers. Unsold homes and required payments on construction loans can quickly put a homebuilder out of business. So you can trust what homebuilders believe to be true about potential sales! Finally, the amount of traffic—actual walk-ins onto new home sites—helps builders gauge the strength of the market. The more walk-ins there are, the more confident builders become. Confident builders are more likely to ramp up construction.

Putting Together the HMI Indexes

So how are the index numbers calculated? Three indexes are first compiled for each of the questions, based on netting the "good" and "poor" responses and netting the "high to very high" and "low to very low" responses. The final index values range from 0 to 100 with 100 being "all good" responses. Sometimes you see the HMI label in charts or tables as "100 = All Good."

The overall HMI is a composite of the indexes for the three component questions. The NAHB did some statistical analysis between housing starts and the three component indexes, and decided that the following component weight combinations had the best predictive power for housing starts for the overall index: present time, 59.20 percent; next six months, 13.58 percent; and traffic, 27.22 percent.

In contrast to typical data series in index form, the index base level (for the overall index and the component indexes) is not tied to a particular time period. The index values for the HMI do not tell you directly how much higher or lower it is compared to a base period (like the Consumer Price Index does) because there is no base period time. The HMI is a special type of index called a *diffusion index*. It measures how similar the answers are. That is, for the HMI, are answers all good, all bad, or a mix in between? For the HMI, as noted, 100 means all answers are positive and 0 means all answers are negative. A level of 50 indicates that half of the responses were positive about housing activity and half were negative. Put simply, a number over 50 indicates that more builders believe sales conditions are good than poor. So, for the HMI diffusion index, 50 is a "break even" point.

def•i•ni•tion

A **diffusion index** measures how diffuse an indicator's components are—or how closely (or not) the components move together.

HMI Trends

The HMI composite index has been a good indicator for near-term changes in housing starts and new single-family home sales. Indeed, the HMI has generally tracked single-family housing starts quite well. When the HMI has not moved in tandem with starts, it has often preceded starts. The HMI did a good job of anticipating the housing recession that started in 2006, with the HMI peaking in November 2005 while single-family housing starts topped out in January 2006.

Take a look at the following HMI, traffic, and new home sales chart. The overall HMI and present sales component are good near-term indicators for starts. But if you want to focus on predicting home sales, the traffic component in the HMI is likely a better forecaster than the overall HMI index.

Housing Market Index, Traffic, and New Home Sales.

(Source: HousingEconomics.com, National Association of Home Builders.)

Key Facts About the MBA Weekly Mortgage Applications Survey

One final early warning for housing trends is from the Mortgage Bankers Association (MBA). The MBA publishes a weekly survey on lending activity—specifically, on mortgage applications—based on information from its members and others in mortgage lending. Although some mortgage applications are completed after signing a contract to purchase a home, many times applications are made in advance. Either way, changes in mortgage application numbers provide insight into how strong home sales are in coming weeks.

Additionally, mortgage applications are split into two major categories: new purchases and refinancing. Each provides better information on different aspects of the housing and consumer sectors than the overall applications index.

Here's what's in the official report for the MBA Weekly Applications Survey:

◆ Official name: MBA Weekly Applications Survey

◆ Release date: Weekly, on Wednesday for the week ending the prior Friday

◆ Produced by: Mortgage Bankers Association

◆ Form of data: Indexes with base period of March 16, 1990 = 100

◆ Market watchers focus on: Index levels and weekly percent changes. Focus is as much on the two components, the Refinance Index and the Purchase Index, as on the overall Market Composite Index (www.mortgagebankers.org; look for the link for "Weekly Application Survey").

The survey covers approximately 50 percent of all U.S. retail residential mortgage applications, and has been conducted weekly since 1990. Respondents include mortgage bankers, commercial banks, and thrifts (also known as savings & loans institutions). Thrifts have had special regulatory status in the United States and traditionally have been required to have the vast majority of loans in mortgages.

According to the MBA, this survey contains 15 indexes covering application activity for fixed rate, adjustable rate, conventional, and government loans for home purchases and refinancing. The report also includes percent changes in number and dollar volume of applications from a week, a month, and a year ago; average loan size; average contract interest rates and corresponding points for six popular mortgage products; the shares of applications that are refinance loans; and the shares of applications that are for adjustable rate mortgages.

The headline index is called the Market Composite Index and measures mortgage loan application volume. The baseline comparison for index levels is March 16, 1990, being set equal to 100 and other months' levels being relative to that period. The primary component indexes are the Refinance Index and the Purchase Index.

The components of the MBA applications index are probably more interesting than the composite. The Purchase Index provides a good indication as to where home sales are going. When consumers refinance, they free up income that had been spent on mortgage payments, and the Refinance Index indicates that. When refinancing is up, consumers feel richer.

Market Reaction to the Reports

For all of these early warning indicators, a more positive number is typically going to boost equities and firm bond yields, as stronger numbers indicate faster growth in housing and in the economy. For the Pending Home Sales Index, markets focus on the monthly percentage change. For the Housing Market Index, traders watch the overall index but frequently give more attention to the Traffic Index. Investors also notice when the future sales index is diverging from the present-time index for sales.

The Housing Affordability Index receives almost no market attention. However, it is an important measure of the health of the demand for housing and should be tracked by those who have a stake in the housing industry, directly or through investments.

The MBA Weekly Applications Survey does get moderate attention from the financial markets even though it is a high-frequency indicator. Generally, the Purchase Index is the focus of markets, but if there is a surge in the Refinance Index, that can be seen as a boost for the consumer sector, leading to a jump in stock prices, especially for consumer discretionary purchases.

The Least You Need to Know

- The Pending Home Sales Index (PHSI) is a leading indicator for existing home sales.

- The Housing Market Index (HMI) gives the homebuilders' perspective on housing activity.

- The HMI does a good job forecasting housing starts and the traffic index component, especially, points the way to where home sales are headed.

- The MBA Weekly Applications Survey provides valuable information on mortgage applications for refinancing and for purchases.

Part 5

Manufacturing and International Trade

The other sector of the economy (besides housing) that causes the biggest ups and downs is manufacturing. You'll see how manufacturing production is measured but also how it all flows. Factory orders tell you where manufacturing is headed while inventories give you a good hint at whether manufacturing has been running too hot or needs to pick up the pace. You'll see how inventories provide warning signals on the economy for retailers and manufacturers.

But it's also not the middle of the twentieth century anymore for manufacturing. The world economies have grown and become intertwined. We're talking about international trade—imports and exports have risen sharply worldwide. What's the United States importing and exporting and how do they impact U.S. economic growth?

Industrial Production: Keeping the Assembly Lines Running

In This Chapter

♦ The key measures of industrial output are explained

♦ Manufacturing capacity utilization portends inflation and investment

♦ The durable goods orders report tells us where manufacturing is headed

♦ The factory orders report is more comprehensive than the durables report

The industrial sector is important to the economy even though it is not the largest component. Industrial production is very sensitive to the business cycle since it's responsive to changes in interest rates as well as to consumer and business income.

Did you know that more discretionary purchases are produced in the industrial sector than in the services sector? These include notable durables purchases such as for automobiles and household appliances. Yes, you "need" them, but you have lots of discretion over when you buy them if the economy is not so good. Well, we're going to take a look at not only what's in industrial production, but also at how related indicators—factory orders, shipments, and inventories—tell us what direction industrial production is headed.

Key Facts About the Industrial Production and Capacity Utilization Report

The Federal Reserve Board produces this report—the "industrial production report" for short. It covers three major industrial sectors: manufacturing, mining, and utilities. Industrial production includes nearly everything that is physically produced in the United States, whether for buyers in the country or overseas. Industrial production covers a wide range of areas, including electricity, oil, cars, newspaper print, military tanks, and even canned peaches.

The industrial production index measures the real output of the manufacturing, mining, and electric and gas utilities industries in the United States. The industrial sector is one of the most cyclical parts of the economy—it can push the economy into recession or pull it out. Industrial production is also important because it's a source of high-wage jobs and high-value products. Manufacturing employment and wages closely track changes in industrial production.

Here's what's in the Industrial Production and Capacity Utilization Report:

- Official name: Industrial Production and Capacity Utilization

- Release date: Monthly, mid-month for the prior month's data (July release has June data)

- Produced by: Federal Reserve Board

- Form of data: Production in index format with base period of 2002 = 100. Capacity utilization in percent format. Data are available seasonally adjusted and not seasonally adjusted.

- Market watchers focus on: Overall industrial production and manufacturing component, monthly percent changes (view reports at www.federalreserve.gov/releases/G17/)

A key point about the production numbers is that they are in index form. Industrial production reflects physical quantities produced in each industry, which are combined for different levels of aggregation. The base year reflects the year of the most recent quinquennial (meaning once every five years) Census of Manufactures and Mineral Industries. The Census Bureau has a detailed accounting of what companies produced that year. The Federal Reserve ties its industrial production index to those numbers. The current base year is 2002 set equal to 100, but the 2007 Census of Manufactures and Mineral Industries will soon be published and then become the new base year for the industrial production index. Since 1997, the total IP index has been constructed from 312 individual series.

Industrial Production
Monthly Percent Changes, Seasonally Adjusted

	2008 Proportion	Dec 08	Jan 09	Feb 09	% chg
Total	100.00	–2.4	–1.9	–1.4	–11.2
Major Market Groups:					
Final products and industrial supplies	55.61	–1.0	–2.5	–1.1	–9.2
Consumer goods	29.48	–1.9	–1.9	–0.7	–8.5
Business equipment	8.93	2.6	–4.2	–1.3	–11.8
Defense and space equipment	1.76				
Construction supplies	3.99	–3.9	–4.2	–2.2	–18.2
Business supplies	10.59	–2.9	–0.1	–2.5	–10.9
Materials	44.39	–3.5	–1.7	–1.5	–12.4
Major Industry Groups:					
Manufacturing	77.42	–2.9	–2.7	–0.7	–13.1
Mining	12.91	–1.4	–1.0	–0.4	–1.9
Utilities	9.67	0.4	2.6	–7.7	–7.8
Electric	7.88	0.1	2.3	–6.5	–6.9
Gas	1.79	1.7	4.1	–12.5	–11.5

continues

Monthly Percent Changes, Seasonally Adjusted (continued)

	2008 Proportion	Dec 08	Jan 09	Feb 09	% chg
Special Aggregates:					
Total excluding motor vehicles and parts	95.98	–2.1	–1.0	–1.8	–9.8
Manufacturing excluding motor vehicles and parts	73.13	–2.6	–1.6	–1.2	–11.5
Motor vehicles and parts	4.28	–8.2	–24.7	10.2	–38.5

Capacity Utilization Rates, Seasonally Adjusted

	Nov 08	Dec 08	Jan 09	Feb 09	Capacity Growth Year-Ago
Total Industry	75.2	73.3	71.9	70.9	1.1
Manufacturing	71.9	69.7	67.9	67.4	1.2
Mining	90.9	89.6	88.7	88.2	0.7
Utilities	84.5	84.7	86.8	80.1	2.1

The Key Components of the Industrial Production Index

Industrial production is measured in two ways: from the supply side and from the demand side. That is, one set of data comes from the industry (producers) side, and the other comes from the market group (users) side. Financial markets primarily focus on the industry groups because they readily break out the more important manufacturing component.

Industry Groups

The three broad components of the industry groups are manufacturing, mining, and utilities. Their shares of total production in 2008 were manufacturing, 77.42 percent; mining, 12.91 percent; and utilities, 9.67 percent.

Manufacturing is further broken down into durables and nondurables manufacturing, with 2008 shares of 36.45 percent and 37.54 percent, respectively.

- ◆ Durables industries are (2008 component shares of total industrial production in parenthesis) wood products (0.99), nonmetallic mineral products (2.16), primary metal (2.67), fabricated metal products (5.50), machinery (4.64), computer and electronic products (6.55), electrical equipment, appliances and components (1.95), motor vehicles and parts (4.28), aerospace and miscellaneous transportation equipment (3.40), furniture and related products (1.25), and miscellaneous (3.06).

- ◆ Nondurables industries are food, beverage, and tobacco products (10.88), textile and product mills (0.83), apparel and leather (0.53), paper (2.47), printing and support (1.74), petroleum and coal products (6.55), chemical products (11.62), and plastics and rubber products (2.93).

Market Groups

The two main categories for market groups are final products and nonindustrial supplies, and materials. The first group includes consumer goods, business equipment, defense and space equipment, construction supplies, and business supplies. Detail for consumer goods can be found for automotive products, home electronics, appliances, furniture, carpeting, miscellaneous durable goods, foods and tobacco, clothing, chemical products, paper products, and energy. Business equipment covers transit, information processing, industrial, and other.

Auto Assemblies

The industrial production report has a special section on auto assembly rates. This table actually has the production counts in units of motor vehicles instead of in indexes. Many auto industry analysts track these numbers and compare them to unit new motor vehicle sales to see whether or not sales are running higher or lower than production.

Millions of Units, Seasonally Adjusted Annual Rate

Item	2008 Average	Sep	2008 Oct	Nov	Dec	2009 Jan	Feb
Total	8.67	8.41	8.02	7.56	6.61	3.83	4.73
Autos	3.78	3.99	3.84	3.42	2.86	1.31	1.65
Trucks	4.90	4.42	4.19	4.15	3.75	2.52	3.08
Light	4.67	4.22	3.98	3.95	3.54	2.38	2.92
Medium and Heavy	.22	.20	.21	.20	.21	.14	.16
Autos and light trucks	8.45	8.21	7.82	7.37	6.40	3.69	4.56

Durables manufacturing output is far more cyclically volatile than that for nondurables. Durables include discretionary items for both consumers and businesses. We've talked about how consumers can put off buying a new car during tough economic times and businesses can defer buying new equipment. Nondurables, on the other hand, include necessities such as food, clothing, and energy goods.

Trader Tip

When evaluating the monthly industrial production changes, be sure to see if utilities output was particularly strong or weak due to atypical weather. The manufacturing component gives a better picture of the underlying health of industrial production.

Capacity Utilization

The first part of this monthly report is for production. The second part covers capacity utilization, which is a simple but very important concept. Capacity is how much a plant can produce. The capacity utilization rate is the percentage of capacity that a plant or industry is using.

Here's an example: Let's say a manufacturing plant has the capacity to make 1,000 cars per month, but it's only producing 850 cars per month. Its capacity utilization rate is 85 percent (850/1,000 = .85, or 85 percent).

Essentially, capacity utilization is a measure of how much unused production capability is available to meet an increase in demand. High capacity utilization rates mean that if demand for the product rises, increased production might not be able to meet that demand. And then what? You guessed it—prices and inflation pick up because demand is outstripping capacity. So capacity utilization is an important warning signal for inflation. Also, when capacity utilization is high, that is when firms are more likely to buy new equipment or build bigger facilities. Capacity utilization helps to predict business investment in the industrial sector.

The Federal Reserve has a specific definition for capacity utilization. For a given industry, the capacity utilization rate is equal to an output index (seasonally adjusted) divided by a capacity index. The Fed has a realistic definition of capacity, using the concept of "sustainable maximum output." This is the greatest level of output a plant can maintain based on a realistic work schedule, taking into account normal downtime (such as for maintenance), and assuming that there is no shortage of input materials for operating existing machinery.

The following capacity utilization chart shows that CPI inflation often rises with capacity utilization rates. This relationship is not as tight as in years past. We did see both rise during the late 1980s and during the early part of this decade. However, inflation eased during the 1990s even though U.S. capacity utilization was high. This was a period of rising import penetration into U.S. markets and U.S. producers had to compete with low import prices. Capacity utilization is still important, but now it's worldwide capacity utilization that matters. During the middle of this decade, world capacity utilization was high, helping to keep inflation moderate even as capacity utilization in the United States was relatively high.

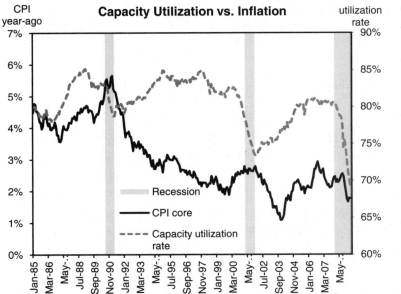

Capacity Utilization vs. Inflation.

Market Reaction to the Industrial Production News Releases

Industrial production is a major measure of economic activity. A strong headline number generally is good for stock prices, but also tends to cause interest rates to firm. While markets focus on the monthly percentage change for overall industrial production, most analysts look for special factors that might have caused unusual monthly changes.

The utilities output components experience sharp swings most frequently. Atypical temperatures in the winter and summer can cause dramatic moves in utilities output. A cold snap (more than usual) in the winter can boost electricity and natural gas demand. Warm weather in winter does the opposite. You can see similar effects during summer for electricity if weather is unusually hot or mild.

Trader Tip _____

Due to the volatility in the utilities component in overall industrial production, many traders focus as much on the manufacturing index as they do on the headline index.

Another component that has sizeable swings from time to time is the automotive industry component in manufacturing. Auto manufacturers adjust somewhat jerkily to swings in dealer inventories, which can jump around due to off-and-on sales incentives. Also, auto manufacturers may have atypical retooling downtime some years. Some economy watchers check out the auto component to see how it's doing and also look at special indexes that exclude autos. These special indexes are: total production excluding motor vehicles and manufacturing output excluding motor vehicles. Tracking overall production, autos alone, and production excluding autos gives you a well rounded view of what's causing monthly changes in industrial production.

Key Facts About the Durable Goods Orders Report

The industrial production report is the most important monthly news release on industrial production and manufacturing. The second most important is what is commonly called the "durable goods orders report," even though it also has information on factory shipments and inventories of durable goods. Also, the report is for orders to manufacturers or to factories, although that part of the indicator name is often assumed and left out in conversations among economists or financial traders. We are not talking about orders to retailers or to distributors.

Within manufacturing, the durables component has the higher value and is more cyclical than nondurables. Durable goods—especially for capital equipment—take longer to produce than nondurables and provide more momentum for manufacturing. That is, when an order for a tractor or airplane comes in, production is going to continue on that order for some time. This report is an important indicator for changes in the strength of business investment in equipment. We'll see that the durable goods report is part of other related (and later-released) reports for total factory orders and also for business inventories.

Here's what's in the durable goods orders report:

◆ Official name: Advance Report on Durable Goods Manufacturers' Shipments, Inventories, and Orders

◆ Release date: Monthly, last week of the month for the prior month's data (July release has June data)

◆ Produced by: U.S Bureau of the Census, U.S. Department of Commerce

◆ Form of data: In dollars. Data are available seasonally adjusted and not seasonally adjusted. Levels are not annualized.

◆ Market watchers focus on: Overall new orders for durable goods and overall new durables orders excluding transportation, monthly percent changes (view reports at www.census.gov/indicator/www/m3/index.htm)

The Advance Report on Durable Goods Manufacturers' Shipments, Inventories, and Orders is produced by the Bureau of the Census and is released the last week of the month for the prior month's data. Revised and more comprehensive data are published about a week later as part of total factory orders.

The M3 Survey

The durable goods data come from a survey produced by the Census Bureau—the Manufacturers' Shipments, Inventories, and Orders Survey. However, the survey covers not just durables but also nondurables. It's just that the Census Bureau processes the durables data first for the advance report. If you want to look like you are a real insider on economic data, you can call this survey the "M3" survey. This is the official Census designation for the report. Lots of Census reports are designated with a letter and a number, but only a few are recognized by such names outside of the Bureau. The monthly M3 estimates are based on information obtained from most manufacturing companies with $500 million or more in annual shipments. In order to strengthen the sample coverage in individual industry categories, the Census Bureau adds selected smaller companies to the survey. Selection of these additions is based on information from the quinquennial economic censuses and the Annual Survey of Manufactures

(ASM). The monthly M3 survey is based on about 4,300 reporting units. Later, the monthly data are benchmarked to the most recent Annual Survey of Manufactures or quinquennial economic census.

The M3 survey asks manufacturers for dollar amounts for new orders, shipments, unfilled orders, and inventories. New orders are net of order cancellations and include orders received and filled during the month as well as orders received for future delivery. Orders are those supported by binding legal documents such as signed contracts, letters of award, or letters of intent, although in some industries this may not be strictly applicable.

Shipments data represent net selling values after discounts and allowances, excluding freight charges and excise taxes. Unfilled orders are those that have not been shipped. Generally, unfilled orders at the end of the reporting period are equal to unfilled orders at the beginning of the period plus net new orders received less net shipments. Inventories in the M3 survey are collected on a current cost basis. The inventory data are organized stage of fabrication—that is, finished goods, work in process, and raw materials and supplies.

Although the M3 questionnaire asks for information for new orders, not all companies are able to report new orders; on the other hand, some are able to report new orders, but not unfilled orders. In fact, the M3 survey does not track unfilled orders for non-durable goods industries because most manufacturers fill the orders within the same month. In this case, the new orders are the same as shipments.

After all that work getting new orders numbers, guess what? Because of a lack of 100 percent reporting for new orders, the new orders data series are derived using a formula using shipments and unfilled orders. New orders for the current month are equal to current shipments plus current unfilled orders minus prior-month unfilled orders. Of course, for nondurables, new orders equal shipments.

Here's the formula for calculating new orders: New orders = shipments (current) + unfilled orders (current) – unfilled orders (prior).

The Key Components of Durable Goods Orders

Durable goods orders are broken down into industry categories. These are primary metals; fabricated metal products; machinery; computers and electronic products; electrical equipment, appliances, and components; transportation equipment; and all other durable goods.

However, market watchers focus more on specially calculated components in the report than on industry categories, with the exception of the transportation industry.

New Factory Orders for Durable Goods, 2008 Totals

	Millions of Dollars	Percent of Total
New Orders	2,464,050	100.0%
Less transportation	1,814,336	73.6%
Less defense	2,313,699	93.9%
Industry Groups		
Primary metals	247,047	10.0%
Fabricated metals	327,745	13.3%
Machinery	355,655	14.4%
Computers and Electronic Products	324,428	13.2%
Electrical equipment	123,713	5.0%
Transportation	649,714	26.4%
Other	435,748	17.7%

Capital goods include machinery, tools, and equipment used to produce other products, structures, or services for consumption. For example, cars are generally considered consumer goods (although for leasing companies they are capital goods) since they are typically bought for use by the consumer.

In contrast, dump trucks are considered to be capital goods since they are used by manufacturing and construction companies to help with production of other goods or structures by hauling various materials. Capital goods should not be confused with financial capital, which is money for investing in companies.

def•i•ni•tion

Capital goods are goods used to produce other goods, structures, or services.

Market Reaction to the Durable Goods Orders News Releases

The main focus is on new orders, although shipments and inventories are not ignored. But for new factory orders for durable goods, financial traders pay as much attention to special series as to the overall number. The bottom line is that traders and investors want to know the underlying trend based on the latest report. This means that it is usually a good idea to sort out the volatile components.

Trader Tip _____

Rule number one for reacting to the durable goods report—don't jump on the headline number for new orders for durable goods! Wait half a second and see what this new orders series does when the transportation component is excluded. This component includes the hugely volatile aircraft orders series and can give a misleading picture of the underlying strength or weakness in durables orders.

Two of the most volatile components are transportation and defense. So two special series that many look at immediately after checking out the headline number are new durables orders excluding transportation and also the new durables orders excluding defense. Unfortunately, you cannot come up with a series for durables orders excluding both transportation and defense because transportation and defense overlap.

Let's look closely at the transportation component to see what the big deal is. There are three components: motor vehicles, nondefense aircraft, and defense aircraft. For other economic indicators, motor vehicles are a problem child because of the sharp monthly swings either in sales data or production numbers. But for new orders, motor vehicle volatility pales in comparison to nondefense and defense aircraft subcomponents.

If you think about it, nondefense aircraft orders usually come from airlines, and the order contracts are generally for more than one or two aircraft. The deals are usually for significant upgrades or expansions of airline fleets, so each new order contract involves many aircraft. Each commercial jet purchased by an airline typically costs $150 million to $250 million (in 2008 dollars), while the cost per jet for defense aircraft can be even higher. You can see why new orders for aircraft swing so sharply from month to month.

Another important series is capital goods, especially for nondefense capital goods. This new orders series is a leading indicator for the equipment component in GDP for business fixed investment. In fact, the shipments data for nondefense capital equipment are the primary source data for this component of GDP (with the other two main source data being capital goods imports and capital goods exports—one is added to shipments and the other is subtracted from nondefense capital goods shipments).

Some more sophisticated analysts give attention to more than just new orders. Shipments—often known as sales—tend to be more stable than new orders. Customers may order many quantities of a product but only one can be produced at a time. Shipments are therefore more representative of production.

Only from an Economist

I'll bet you have always been curious about what goes into "defense capital goods." Well, according to the Census Bureau, the following are included in its durable goods report: small arms and ordnance manufacturing, communications equipment manufacturing, search and navigation equipment manufacturing, aircraft manufacturing, and ship and boat building. For most of these categories, you can find both civilian and defense components but only the defense portions are included in defense capital goods.

Inventories can warn us about whether production is getting out of line with demand. A continued rise in inventories without any gains in shipments likely means that production will have to be cut back soon. Yes, it's okay to have rising inventories if it is to keep up with demand, but it's not okay if demand is easing. Some analysts like to look at inventory-to-sales (I-S), or shipments, ratios. If inventories rise to keep up with higher shipments, this will show up in a stable I-S ratio. If inventories show sharp gains, check out the I-S ratio to see if the increase is to keep up with demand. If the I-S ratio is rising, then a production cut is likely down the road.

Finally, unfilled orders can suggest building or waning momentum for manufacturing. If unfilled orders (or backlogs) are rising, this means production is not keeping up with new orders. The good news is that backlogs can provide some buffer when demand slows. But if the economy turns really sour, don't count too much on unfilled orders—they often can be cancelled or the customer may have gone out of business!

Only from an Economist

The Census Bureau does not name any specific companies in its advance report on durable goods (or the full-blown factory orders report, which is discussed next). But when it comes to nondefense aircraft, the numbers are almost entirely from Boeing. The United States has only one major manufacturer of commercial jets, although there are a number of producers of small corporate jets. Boeing manufactures make up all but a fraction of commercial jets in the United States.

So what does it cost to buy a commercial jet? Boeing actually posts prices on its website. A smaller jet from the 737 family will cost you $51 million to $87 million (as of early 2009). If you want something from the bigger 787 family, that will set you back $150 million to $206 million per jet.

Advance Report on Durable Goods, January 2009

	Monthly Percent Changes		
	Jan 09	**Dec 08**	**Nov 08**
New Orders			
Total	−5.2	−4.6	−4.0
(previous)	−3.0	−4.0	
Excluding transportation	−2.5	−5.5	−2.0
Excluding defense	−2.3	−7.5	−4.2
Transportation Equipment	−13.5	−1.5	−9.9
Motor vehicles	−6.4	−6.4	−2.2
Nondefense aircraft	81.7	−59.1	−46.2
Defense aircraft	−28.3	14.1	−7.0
Capital Goods	−8.8	−3.4	−3.7
Nondefense capital goods	−2.7	−10.2	−5.3
Excluding aircraft	−5.4	−5.8	1.1
Defense capital goods	−35.3	44.8	8.6
Inventories			
Total	−0.8	0.4	0.3
Shipments			
Total	−3.7	−1.4	−4.2
Unfilled Orders			
Total	−1.9	−1.5	−0.9

As seen in the following new orders for durable goods chart, overall new factory orders for durable goods are more volatile on a monthly basis when the transportation component is taken out. Financial markets focus on total new orders excluding transportation.

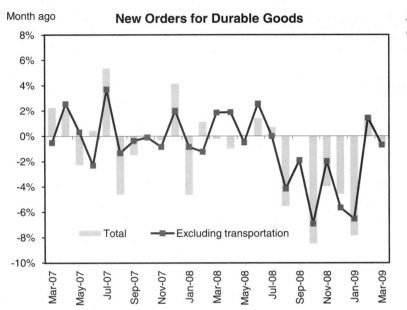

New Orders for Durable Goods.

Key Facts About the Factory Orders Report

The second report each month based on the Census Bureau's Manufacturers' Shipments, Inventories, and Orders Survey is what is commonly called the new factory orders report. It comes out a week after the advance report on manufacturers' durable goods. The official name of the survey is the Full Report on Manufacturers' Shipments, Inventories and Orders. It includes revisions to the durable goods portion based on more complete survey data and also includes information on nondurables. As with the advance report, there is information on new orders, unfilled orders, shipments, and inventories.

Here's what's in the new factory orders report:

- ◆ Official name: Full Report on Manufacturers' Shipments, Inventories and Orders

- ◆ Release date: Monthly, first week of the month for two months prior data (July release has May data)

- ◆ Produced by: U.S Bureau of the Census, U.S. Department of Commerce

- ◆ Form of data: In dollars. Data are available seasonally adjusted and not seasonally adjusted. Levels are not annualized.

- ◆ Market watchers focus on: Revisions to new factory orders for durable goods, monthly percent changes (view reports at www.census.gov/indicator/www/m3/index.htm)

The Key Components of Factory Orders

We've already talked about what industries are in the durables sector. The part we have not talked about in the full report on factory orders is for nondurables industries. These industries include: food products, beverage and tobacco products, textiles, textile products, apparel, leather and allied products, paper products, printing, petroleum and coal products, chemical products, and plastics and rubber products. In 2008, nondurables made up 52 percent of total new factory orders, leaving 48 percent for durables.

Earlier, we mentioned that nondurables industries essentially have no unfilled orders. Nearly all orders are shipped the same month. The Census Bureau treats new orders as being equal to shipments in this report. That is why you only see industry detail for shipments, but not for new orders. Industry numbers for new orders would be an identical table to that for shipments. So if you want new orders data for nondurables industries, you have to go to the shipments table; the Census Bureau only publishes nondurables new orders numbers in summary tables.

Market Reaction to the Factory Orders News Releases

Investors and traders have already seen much of what is in the factory orders report because they saw the durables report a week earlier. But sometimes the durables numbers do get notably revised. Therefore, the main thing market watchers look for is the size of the revisions to new factory orders for durables.

Factory Orders Report, January 2009

	Summary Numbers		
	Month-Ago Percent Change		
	Jan 09	Dec 08	Nov 08
New orders, total	−1.9	−4.9	−6.5
Durable goods orders	−4.5	−4.6	−4.0
(previous)	−5.2	−4.6	−4.0
Nondurable goods orders	0.5	−5.1	−8.7

The nondurables component is new information. But new nondurables orders have to be taken with a grain of salt. While demand for nondurables is relatively steady in terms of physical quantities, prices for nondurables are not.

In 2008, almost 60 percent of nondurables new orders were directly related to the price of oil (for the industries of petroleum and coal products, chemical products, and plastics and rubber products). When the price of oil moves sharply, so do nondurables new orders—but not by the same magnitude.

This is seen in the following new nondurables orders vs. oil prices chart. Markets realize that there is a lot of price-induced volatility in new orders for nondurables and that part of the report does not get much attention.

Once again, unless you are interested in industry-specific information on nondurables, all the financial markets care about in the factory orders report is whether new factory orders for durables were revised significantly.

Trader Tip

When the factory orders report is released, financial traders react to whether the advance number on new factory orders for durables was revised much or not. That's their key focus for this report.

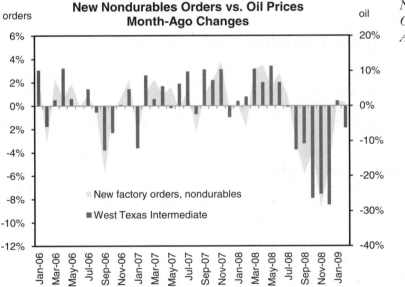

New Nondurables Orders vs. Oil Prices, first line; Month-Ago Changes, second line.

The Least You Need to Know

- The industrial production report is the most important monthly news on the manufacturing sector.

- The manufacturing component is the most important part of industrial production.

♦ Utilities output can swing sharply because of unseasonable weather.

♦ The durable goods report provides warning signs on the direction of manufacturing over the business cycle.

♦ The best measure in the durable goods report is new orders for durable goods excluding transportation since transportation includes volatile orders for aircraft.

♦ Watch the inventory-to-shipments ratio to see if any imbalances develop between demand and inventories.

Chapter 17

Manufacturing Surveys: An Early Glimpse

In This Chapter

- ◆ The Institute for Supply Management's manufacturing survey
- ◆ The Fed's District banks' manufacturing surveys
- ◆ Diffusion indexes
- ◆ Related nonmanufacturing surveys

The financial markets love advance warnings, and early signals for industrial production are no exception. An important early barometer for manufacturing at the national level is a private survey conducted by the Institute for Supply Management (or ISM). The ISM is a nonprofit organization that supports supply management professionals with research, promotional activities, and education. There are also similar surveys conducted by some District Federal Reserve Banks that grab the market's attention.

And because we are on the subject of surveys, there are two nonmanufacturing surveys that markets often react to. In this chapter, we'll touch on what those surveys cover plus a whole lot more.

The ISM Manufacturing Report

The *ISM manufacturing index* is the first major economic indicator released each month. It's released on the first business day of the month with data for the prior month. This report helps set the markets' mood for the rest of the month—at least for the manufacturing sector. The official name of the report is the "ISM Manufacturing Report on Business." ISM stands for "Institute for Supply Management." If you are an old-timer at tracking the economy, you may know ISM better under its old name: the National Association of Purchasing Management (NAPM). The NAPM became the Institute for Supply Management on January 2, 2002, as part of an effort to broaden the organization's reach beyond the purchasing function and into strategic supply management.

def•i•ni•tion

ISM manufacturing index is a national index released by the Institute of Supply Management, which reflects a survey of purchasing executives from about 300 industrial companies.

In order to publish this report, the ISM is responsible for conducting a monthly survey of its members. Each month, the ISM sends out a questionnaire on manufacturing conditions to about 300 members. The survey is sent out about mid-month of the reference month and results are tallied around the 21st of that month.

Key Facts About the ISM Manufacturing Index

Let's take a look at the basic information you'll find in the report. Here's what's in the ISM manufacturing index:

- Official name: The ISM Manufacturing Report on Business

- Release date: Monthly, first business day of the month for the prior month's data (July release has June data)

- Produced by: Institute for Supply Management

- Form of data: Diffusion indexes, reflecting net positive responses for composite index and other economic activity covered. Some indexes are seasonally adjusted.

- Market watchers focus on: The overall composite index (view reports at www. ism.ws)

The headliner for the ISM manufacturing report is the PMI. It originally meant Purchasing Managers' Index, which is what it was called under the original NAPM name. ISM simply uses PMI. It's a composite index that's comprised of five indicators that come from questions on the monthly survey. The PMI is based on seasonally adjusted, equally weighted diffusion indexes for the indicators in the table below.

Components of the Composite PMI

Index	Weight
New Orders	20 percent
Production	20 percent
Employment	20 percent
Supplier Deliveries	20 percent
Inventories	20 percent

Although not in the PMI composite index, the survey also asks questions about customer inventories, prices paid, backlogs of orders, new export orders, and imports. The answers are reported with diffusion indexes. Remember diffusion indexes from the Housing Market Index in Chapter 15? If not, don't worry. We'll talk more about them shortly.

For now, here's a summary of what each index is intended to cover, according to the ISM:

- ◆ New Orders: reflects the levels of new orders from customers.

- ◆ Production: measures the rate and direction of change, if any, in the level of production.

- ◆ Employment: reports the rate of increase or decrease in the level of employment.

- ◆ Supplier Deliveries: reveals if deliveries from suppliers are faster or slower.

- ◆ Inventories: reflects the increases and/or decreases in inventory levels.

- ◆ Customer Inventories: rates the level of inventories the organization's customers have.

- ◆ Prices: reports whether organizations are paying more or less for products/ services.

- ◆ Backlog of Orders: measures the amount of backlog of orders, whether growing or declining.

◆ New Export Orders: reports on the level of orders, requests for services, and other activities to be provided outside of the United States.

◆ Imports: measures the rate of change in materials imported.

Take a look at the ISM Manufacturing Indexes for February 2009:

ISM Manufacturing Indexes, February 2009 Report
Diffusion indexes, seasonally adjusted unless otherwise noted

	Feb 09	Jan 09	Dec 08	Nov 08	Year-ago Feb 08
PMI	35.8	35.6	32.9	36.6	48.8
New Orders	33.1	33.2	23.1	28.1	48.9
Production	36.3	32.1	26.3	32.0	51.3
Employment	26.1	29.9	29.9	34.3	47.0
Supplier Deliveries	46.7	45.3	45.7	48.6	51.2
Inventories	37.0	37.5	39.6	40.1	45.8
Customers' Inventories*	51.0	55.5	57.0	55.0	49.0
Prices*	29.0	29.0	18.0	25.5	75.5
Backlog of Orders*	31.0	29.5	23.0	27.0	45.0
New Export Orders*	37.5	37.5	35.5	41.0	56.0
Imports*	32.0	36.5	39.0	37.5	47.5

Not seasonally adjusted.

Reviewing Diffusion Indexes

In Chapter 15, you learned that a diffusion index measures how closely (or not) constituents of an indicator move together. Here's ISM's definition of a diffusion index, which is very similar to what we discussed earlier:

"A diffusion index measures the degree to which a change in something is dispersed, spread out, or "diffused" in a particular group. If all members of a group of people (sample population) are asked if something has changed and in which direction, they will answer in one of three ways: it has not changed, it has increased, or it has decreased." Essentially, respondents in the ISM survey are asked whether activity for each of the indicators compared to the previous month is "Better," "Same," or "Worse."

How are these answers put into an index? First, be warned—there is more than one way to calculate diffusion indexes. We'll see this in the next major section of this chapter. But for now, let's look at how the ISM calculates its diffusion indexes.

The ISM indexes are derived by taking the percentage of respondents that report that the activity has increased ("Better"), and then adding one half of the percentage reporting no change ("Same"). Using half of the "Same" percentage in the diffusion index essentially assumes that half of those in the "Same" category are leaning positive and half are leaning negative (on average).

Here's an example of calculating a diffusion index: If the response to the question on new orders is 20 percent "Better," 70 percent "Same," and 10 percent "Worse," then the diffusion index is 55 percent. This is based on adding half of the "Same" response percentage to the full 20 percent responding "Better": .70 ÷ 2 = .35, or 35 percent; 20 percent + 35 percent = 55 percent.

> **Only from an Economist**
>
> For the ISM manufacturing report, the break-even point for the diffusion indexes is 50. Values above 50 indicate that the manufacturing sector is growing while a reading below 50 represents contraction (negative growth) for this sector.

If the diffusion index were 100, all would be reporting "Better." If the diffusion index were 0, then all responses would be "Worse." But indexes fall in between those extremes. In fact, the break-even point where "Better" responses equal "Worse" responses is an index value of 50.

More Fun with Diffusion Indexes

The diffusion indexes are best interpreted as another form for growth rates for the economic activity covered. Although a diffusion index technically just measures how much in tandem the respondents move each month, statistical comparisons of diffusion indexes show that higher and higher index levels above the break-even level of 50 correspond to higher and higher positive growth rates. The same holds true for index levels below 50. Lower and lower levels below 50 indicate a more rapid pace of decline.

Here's a summary of how to interpret index levels and changes:

As seen in the following PMI and industrial production chart, the PMI level closely tracks monthly growth rates in the manufacturing component of industrial production. The PMI level of 50 is basically a borderline between positive growth in manufacturing and negative growth.

ISM's PMI vs. Industrial Production.

(Source for ISM data: Institute for Supply Management™ and Norbert J. Ore, CPSM, C.P.M., Chair, ISM Manufacturing Report on Business®.)

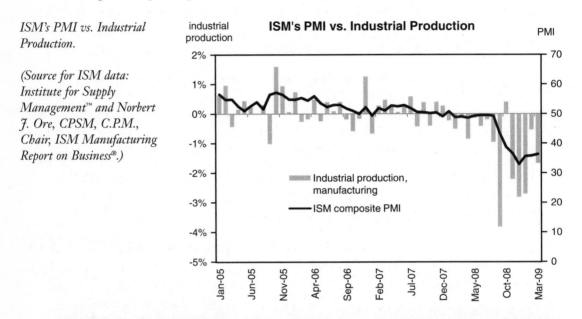

ISM's PMI vs. Industrial Production

Only from an Economist

The ISM not only has compared index levels to break-even points in manufacturing but has also done statistical analysis of the PMI to overall economic growth, or real GDP growth. The ISM discovered that a PMI in excess of 41.2 percent, over a period of time, indicates that the overall economy, or gross domestic product, is generally expanding; below 41.2 percent, it is generally declining. The below-50 break-even point for the overall economy is because the service sector is typically still growing when manufacturing first enters recession.

It takes more than just a slight decline in manufacturing to pull the overall economy down. Although other indicators will also point down, when the PMI drops below 41.2, look for many economy watchers to be screaming that the economy is in recession. This number changes slightly each year after GDP is revised.

Supplier Deliveries: A Leading Indicator

Two components in the PMI have leading indicator qualities for manufacturing and the overall economy. One you would likely guess—new orders. But the other you might not—supplier deliveries. This component is also known as "vendor performance." This series reflects how quickly the suppliers are making deliveries to manufacturers—that is, whether they are more timely or less timely. The question on supplier deliveries has answers that differ from the others. Answer choices are "Faster," "Same," and "Slower." Interestingly, the answer that suggests a stronger economy is "Slower."

When manufacturing is strong, demand for inputs and supplies is robust. This means that supplier inventories may be low or that the vendor is running short on delivery personnel. When manufacturing is strong, delivery times for supplies lengthen. If the economy is slack, filling an order quickly is not difficult. Therefore, the diffusion index for supplier deliveries is the percentage reporting "Slower" deliveries plus one half of the "Same" percentage.

Do you remember from Chapter 2 that the supplier deliveries index is part of the Conference Board's index of leading indicators? If you did, pat yourself on the back!

Trader Tip _____

Some financial traders like to use the ISM manufacturing report to predict upcoming releases for industrial production, new factory orders for durable goods, and manufacturing employment, among others. But when they do the statistical analysis, they compare ISM index levels (not percent changes or differences) with monthly growth rates for the government indicator. Because the ISM report comes out first, traders have the opportunity to use ISM numbers to statistically guess the government report's number.

Market Reaction to the ISM Manufacturing News Releases

The key focus of the ISM manufacturing report is the PMI composite index. A rise in the PMI is seen as reflecting strong growth in manufacturing (or at least less negative growth) and generally boosts stock prices. A rise in this index also tends to result in higher interest rates.

Financial markets also pay attention to the price index for signs of inflation heating up or cooling off. A rise in the price index tends to lead to a firming in interest rates. However, the price index generally does not directly impact stock prices unless the concern about building inflation pressures is such that a high price index number is seen as leading the Fed to raise its target interest rate. This, in turn, would weigh on stock prices.

Federal Reserve District Manufacturing Surveys

While the ISM manufacturing report gets a lot of attention because it covers the U.S. manufacturing sector and comes out so early in the month, some Federal Reserve manufacturing surveys produced by District Banks also get a good deal of market attention. The more closely followed of these are put out by the Federal Reserve Bank of Philadelphia (or Philly Fed, for short) and the Federal Reserve Bank of New York.

Just to give you a quick heads up, two things will stand out as different in both the Philly and New York Fed surveys from the ISM manufacturing report. These are:

- ◆ The Philly Fed and New York Fed headline indexes are not composites based on other indicator series. The headline for each is a general business conditions question.

- ◆ The diffusion indexes for the Fed surveys are calculated differently. The range of possible values for their indexes goes from minus 100 to plus 100. The break-even point is zero.

Key Facts About the Philadelphia Fed Manufacturing Survey

The Philly Fed's Business Outlook Survey (BOS) is the old-timer among District Fed manufacturing surveys. It was started in 1968 and has remained essentially unchanged. A survey questionnaire goes out to about 250 large manufacturers located in the Third Federal Reserve District. Typically, between 100 and 125 firms respond each month. The Philly Fed District geographically covers central and eastern Pennsylvania, southern New Jersey, and Delaware. The questionnaire asks respondents to indicate whether the value of each economic indicator (except capital expenditures) has increased, decreased, or stayed the same over the past month. Respondents are also asked about their expectations for each indicator over the next six months.

The surveys are sent out near the end of each month, and the Philly Fed asks that responses be returned by the end of the first full week of the following month. This results in the survey collection period spanning two calendar months. For example, the survey for July 2008 was sent out in late June with a return deadline in early July. So, most responses were based on activity in early July, although some were based on activity in late June.

Here's what's in the Philadelphia Fed Manufacturing Survey:

- ◆ Official name: Business Outlook Survey (BOS)
- ◆ Release date: Monthly, the third Thursday of each month for the same month's data (July release has July data)
- ◆ Produced by: Federal Reserve Bank of Philadelphia
- ◆ Form of data: Diffusion indexes, reflecting net positive responses for areas of economic activity covered
- ◆ Market watchers focus on: The General Activity Index (view reports at www. philadelphiafed.org)

The Business Outlook Survey has indexes covering many of the same manufacturing activities as found in the ISM manufacturing report. However, the BOS also covers prices received (in addition to prices paid), average employee workweek, and capital expenditures. The following BOS table shows the coverage of the main indexes. The Philly Fed report has a six-month outlook question for each of the types of manufacturing activities.

Business Outlook Survey for March 2009

	Current Conditions			Six-Month Outlook		
	Mar 09	Feb 09	Jan 09	Mar 09	Feb 09	Jan 09
General Activity	−35.0	−41.3	−24.3	14.5	15.9	7.4
Company Business Indicators						
New Orders	−40.7	−30.3	−22.3	10.6	22.2	11.4
Shipments	−26.5	−32.4	−16.7	7.9	19.6	3.9
Unfilled Orders	−22.8	−32.1	−31.1	−10.3	7.3	−12.0
Delivery Time	−30.8	−29.2	−26.5	−7.6	−6.0	−14.7
Inventories	−55.6	−24.3	−34.6	−24.1	−15.5	−23.6

continues

Business Outlook Survey for March 2009   (continued)

	Current Conditions			Six–Month Outlook		
	Mar 09	**Feb 09**	**Jan 09**	**Mar 09**	**Feb 09**	**Jan 09**
Prices Paid	–31.3	–13.7	–27.0	–3.0	2.9	3.7
Prices Received	–32.6	–27.8	–26.2	–20.6	–13.4	–9.7
Number of Employees	–52.0	–45.8	–39.0	–16.5	–16.9	–29.3
Average Employee Workweek	–31.6	–44.9	–30.3	–1.5	–4.0	–13.0
Capital Expenditures	—	—	—	–21.8	–17.8	–16.4

Philly Fed Diffusion Indexes

The BOS consists of questions about business activities such as new orders, shipments, employment, and workweek hours among manufacturing firms in the Third Federal Reserve District. Diffusion indexes are calculated for each question in the survey. Answers to questions can be "Increase" (in the level of activity), "No Change," or "Decrease." The diffusion index is calculated by subtracting the percentage "Decrease" from the percentage "Increase." The resulting diffusion index can vary from +100, when all firms report an increase, to –100, when all firms report a decrease. The answers have never been unanimous in actual surveys and the diffusion indexes range in value between –100 and +100. The midpoint is 0, when the percentage of firms reporting increases equals the percentage reporting decreases.

This calculation is different from the ISM diffusion indexes, which are calculated as one half of the percentage of firms reporting no change added to the percentage reporting an increase:

Philly Diffusion Index = Percent "Increase" – Percent "Decrease"

The fallout from the difference is that the break-even point for the Philly Fed manufacturing indexes is zero. Readings above zero indicate positive growth while readings below zero represent negative growth. When you compare ISM indexes to Philly Fed indexes, you have to remember the break-even point for ISM indexes is 50, while for Philly Fed indexes it's zero. In fact, all of the manufacturing surveys conducted by regional Fed banks use the same diffusion index calculation as that of the Philly Fed.

The Philly Fed Headline and Prices Indexes

Another difference between the Business Outlook Survey and the ISM report is that the overall index in the Philadelphia Fed's BOS is derived from a separate question that measures manufacturers' assessments of overall business conditions. The headline index is called General Activity. In the ISM survey, the overall index is a composite of the indexes calculated for specific questions. The Business Outlook Survey for the headline index asks respondents, "What is your evaluation of the level of general business activity?" The question is for their industry in general—not for their firm specifically, although their firm's activity can affect their views. Answers for the headline question can be "Increase," "No Change," or "Decrease."

The headline index question is the only question not directed toward firm-specific activity. Except for the first question on general business activity, all the questions refer specifically to a firm's own activity. The response to the first question is not necessarily based solely on information from the firm, but the high correlation of aggregate responses to this question. And the responses to the question on shipments indicate that a firm's answer to the first question is primarily based on its own activity.

The headline numbers for various regional Fed manufacturing surveys can give different perspectives on the strength of manufacturing. As seen in the following Philly Fed vs. NY Fed chart, the Philly Fed's index was more negative than the New York Fed's index during early stages of the recession starting in 2008.

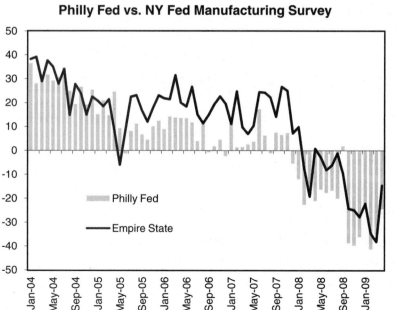

Philly Fed vs. NY Fed Manufacturing Survey.

Another notable difference between the BOS survey and the ISM survey is for prices. The BOS survey has questions for both prices paid and prices received, while the ISM manufacturing survey only asks about prices paid. The Philly survey gives a more complete prices picture and can indicate whether manufacturers are in a price squeeze. That is, it shows if prices paid are rising faster than prices received, or whether producers are passing along price increases. Look at the following prices received vs. prices paid chart. The gap between the two indexes can give insight into manufacturers' profits.

Philly Fed Manufacturing Survey, line one; Prices Received vs. Prices Paid, line two.

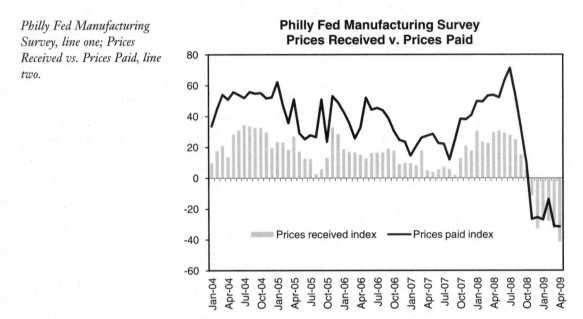

Key Facts About the New York Fed's Manufacturing Survey

The Fed manufacturing survey that receives the second highest amount of attention from financial markets is the New York Fed's Empire State Manufacturing Survey. Many believe the Philly Fed's survey has more coverage of "heavy manufacturing" than does New York's. But the Empire State survey covers many of the same types of activity as the Philly Fed survey.

Here's what's in the New York Fed manufacturing survey:

◆ Official name: Empire State Manufacturing Survey

◆ Release date: Monthly, the 15th of each month (next business day if the 15th is on a weekend) for the same month's data (July release has July data)

◆ Produced by: Federal Reserve Bank of New York

◆ Form of data: Diffusion indexes, reflecting net positive responses for areas of economic activity covered

◆ Market watchers focus on: The General Business Conditions Index (view reports at www.newyorkfed.org)

The New York Fed's survey is a relative newcomer. The first report was produced for April 2002, although survey data go back to July 2001. The survey questionnaire is sent on the first day of each month to about 200 manufacturing executives in New York State, and it asks for information for both month-ago changes and expectations six months out. About 100 responses are received each month.

Like the Philly Fed survey, the Empire State report's main index, the General Business Conditions Index, is not a weighted average of other indicators. It's based on a distinct question in the survey. Respondents are asked, "What is your evaluation of the level of general business activity?" Possible answers are "Increase," "No Change," or "Decrease."

Also like the Philly Fed survey, the diffusion indexes are calculated as the percent of positive responses minus the percent of negative responses. The break-even point for these indexes is zero. The indexes above zero reflect positive growth.

Take a look at the Empire State Manufacturing Survey for March 2009.

> **Only from an Economist**
>
> Although the Empire State Manufacturing Survey covers only the state of New York, the New York Fed as the Second District of the Federal Reserve System actually includes all of New York State, the 12 northern counties of New Jersey, and Fairfield County in Connecticut.

Empire State Manufacturing Survey, March 2009
Diffusion Indexes, Seasonally Adjusted

	Current Conditions			Six-Month Outlook		
	Mar 09	**Feb 09**	**Jan 09**	**Mar 09**	**Feb 09**	**Jan 09**
General Business Conditions	−38.23	−34.65	−22.20	3.14	−6.56	−3.95
New Orders	−44.76	−30.51	−22.81	4.41	−4.31	−8.30
Shipments	−26.66	−8.13	−13.12	5.33	1.86	−7.29

continues

Empire State Manufacturing Survey, March 2009
Diffusion Indexes, Seasonally Adjusted   (continued)

	Current Conditions			Six–Month Outlook		
	Mar 09	Feb 09	Jan 09	Mar 09	Feb 09	Jan 09
Unfilled Orders	−23.60	−24.14	−26.14	−11.81	−15.64	−22.12
Delivery Time	−12.36	−12.64	−18.18	−8.99	−10.34	−14.77
Inventories	−26.97	−8.05	−19.32	−20.22	−13.79	−11.36
Prices Paid	−14.61	−13.79	−18.18	0.00	−2.30	4.55
Prices Received	−23.60	−20.69	−3.41	−14.61	−9.20	5.68
Number of Employees	−38.20	−39.08	−26.14	−20.48	−29.35	−11.30
Average Employee Workweek	−23.60	−31.03	−23.86	−5.62	−13.79	−3.41
Capital Expenditures	—	—	—	−19.10	−11.49	−11.36
Technology Spending	—	—	—	23.60	−19.54	−15.91

Market Reaction to the Philly Fed and Empire State News Releases

Market watchers focus on the headline series for current conditions. This is the General Activity Index for Philadelphia's Business Outlook Survey and the General Business Conditions Index for the Empire State Survey. Stronger index numbers tend to boost stock prices and lead to higher interest rates. The "prices paid" and "prices received" indexes also receive market attention. Gains in price indexes can boost interest rates. Also, if "prices paid" indexes rise faster than "prices received" indexes, this can indicate a profit squeeze. This would weigh on stock prices for manufacturers.

Key Facts About Other Regional Federal Reserve Bank Manufacturing Surveys

Four other regional Fed banks also conduct monthly manufacturing surveys— the Federal Reserve Bank of Chicago, the Federal Reserve Bank of Dallas, the Federal

Reserve Bank of Kansas City, and the Federal Reserve Bank of Richmond. However, they do not get as much market attention as the Philadelphia and New York Fed reports. These other surveys have questionnaires very similar to those for the Philadelphia and New York Fed surveys.

Here are the other regional Federal Reserve Bank manufacturing surveys and how to find them on the Internet:

Federal Reserve Bank of Chicago:

- ◆ Official name: Chicago Fed Midwest Manufacturing Index
- ◆ Release date: Monthly, the last week of each month for the prior month's data; July release has June data (view reports at www.chicagofed.org)

Federal Reserve Bank of Dallas:

- ◆ Official name: Texas Manufacturing Outlook Survey
- ◆ Release date: Monthly, the last Monday of each month for the same month's data; July release has July data (view reports at www.dallasfed.org)

Federal Reserve Bank of Kansas City:

- ◆ Official name: Survey of Tenth District Manufacturers
- ◆ Release date: Monthly, the second Monday of each month for the prior month's data; July release has June data (view reports at http://www.kc.frb.org/)

Federal Reserve Bank of Richmond:

- ◆ Official name: Fifth District Survey of Manufacturing Activity
- ◆ Release date: Monthly, the fourth Tuesday of each month for the same month's data; July release has July data (www.richmondfed.org)

Non-Manufacturing Surveys

The two best known non-manufacturing surveys in the United States are the ISM Non-Manufacturing Report on Business and the ISM-Chicago Business Survey. Let's take a look at both of these surveys.

Key Facts About the ISM Non-Manufacturing Survey

The Institute for Supply Management also has a non-manufacturing survey. The questions on the monthly survey are similar to the manufacturing version. Each month the questionnaire goes out to about 400 ISM members. The non-manufacturing survey has two headline numbers, however. The survey historically focused on business activity and asked a question on the respondents' overall impression of the economy. But in 2008, the ISM began publishing a composite index that's made up of four equally weighted components: Business Activity, New Orders, Employment, and Supplier Deliveries. The composite index is called the Non-Manufacturing Index, or NMI. Market watchers focus on the two headline numbers plus "Prices Paid" to a lesser degree. The break-even point for the ISM non-manufacturing indexes is 50.

Here's what's in the ISM Non-Manufacturing Index:

- Official name: The ISM Non-Manufacturing Report on Business

- Release date: Monthly, third business day of the month for the prior month's data (July release has June data)

- Produced by: Institute for Supply Management

- Form of data: Diffusion indexes, reflecting net positive responses for the composite index and other economic activity covered. Some indexes seasonally adjusted.

- Market watchers focus on The overall composite index (view reports at www. ism.ws)

Key Facts About the ISM-Chicago Business Survey

Again, if you are an old-timer in the financial markets, you would likely recognize this survey by its old name: the NAPM-Chicago report. When the NAPM changed its name to ISM, the Chicago group held on to their old name. Others called it the Chicago PMI (and still do in many media reports), which is short for Chicago Purchasing Managers' Index. This report is now produced by Kingsbury International, LTD., in Highland Park, Illinois, for the Institute for Supply Management-Chicago, Inc. The survey covers both manufacturing and non-manufacturing for the Chicago area. So be careful not to make direct comparisons of this survey to surveys that cover just manufacturing.

Here's what's in the ISM–Chicago Business Survey:

- Official name: The ISM-Chicago Business Survey

- Release date: Monthly, last business day of the month for the reference month's data (July release has July data)

- Produced by: Kingsbury International, LTD, and Institute for Supply Management-Chicago, Inc.

- Form of data: Diffusion indexes, reflecting net positive responses for composite index and other economic activity covered. Some indexes are seasonally adjusted.

- Market watchers focus on The Chicago Business Barometer (www.kingbiz.com)

The headline index is the Chicago Business Barometer. It's calculated from five component indexes with the following weights.

Index	Weight
Production	25 percent
New Orders	35 percent
Order Backlog	15 percent
Employment	10 percent
Supplier Deliveries	15 percent

As with the national ISM diffusion indexes, the break-even point for the ISM-Chicago diffusion indexes is 50.

One issue you should be aware of is that the Business Barometer report is released to private subscribers three minutes before the public release of the report. This explains why you may see occasional market activity just before the official release.

The Least You Need to Know

- The ISM manufacturing report, which is released the first business day of the month, is the first major economic indicator published each month.

- The ISM manufacturing report and the regional Fed manufacturing indexes are good indicators for the upcoming industrial production index—at least for the manufacturing portion.

◆ The diffusion indexes are similar to growth rates; changes in the indexes reflect acceleration or deceleration in growth.

◆ The break-even point for ISM diffusion indexes is 50, while those for the regional Fed surveys are zero.

International Trade: How Our Dollars Come and Go Overseas

In This Chapter

- ◆ The monthly international trade report

- ◆ End-use categories

- ◆ Import and export price report

- ◆ Treasury international capital report

Over the last several decades, international trade has expanded dramatically. International trade touches everyone's daily life more and more. That shirt hanging in your closet may have come from Southeast Asia or even Central America. And the dump truck your neighbor helped build may have gotten shipped to the Middle East.

How does international trade affect prices? International trade makes that shirt made in Southeast Asia cheaper for you. And it also makes the dump truck cheaper for the buyer in the Middle East. As you can see, lots of money flows back and forth in trade between countries. And financial markets pay close attention to what money is going where.

Key Facts About the International Trade Report

The international trade report provides valuable information regarding demand for goods and services in the United States and overseas. In this context, demand is how much consumers and business want to purchase. In this report, category detail can indicate what industries are doing well here and abroad. While the trade deficit is not large relative to overall GDP in the United States, changes in the trade deficit can have a significant impact on economic growth. Exports are a key source of demand for U.S. manufacturers.

Also, one cannot ignore the importance of international trade on financial markets. Certainly, stock prices for specific companies are directly affected by whether or not exports for various industries are growing. But trade also affects overall financial markets, especially currency and bond markets. A rising deficit puts downward pressure on the exchange value of the dollar. This, in turn, puts upward pressure on U.S. bond rates as higher yields are needed to offset the declining currency value.

International trade is complex, and the federal government actually has two reports to cover this facet of the economy. The first report, which provides information on exports and imports, is monthly and it is our focus here. The second report is quarterly and has more detailed information on financial flows between the United States and other countries, in addition to exports and imports. The second report is generally referred to as "balance of payments" and includes information on changes in financial capital positions. But markets focus almost entirely on the timelier first report, named "U.S. International Trade in Goods and Services."

Here's what's in the international trade report:

- Official name: U.S. International Trade in Goods and Services

- Release date: Monthly, mid-month for two months prior data (July release has May data)

- Produced by: Census Bureau and Bureau of Economic Analysis, U.S. Department of Commerce

- Form of data: In dollars. Data are available seasonally adjusted and not seasonally adjusted.

◆ Market watchers focus on: The overall trade gap and the nonpetroleum deficit as well as monthly percent changes for exports and imports (view reports at www. bea.gov/international/index.htm#trade)

Take a look at the following trade deficit and import/export growth chart. You can see how the deficit compares to import and export growth.

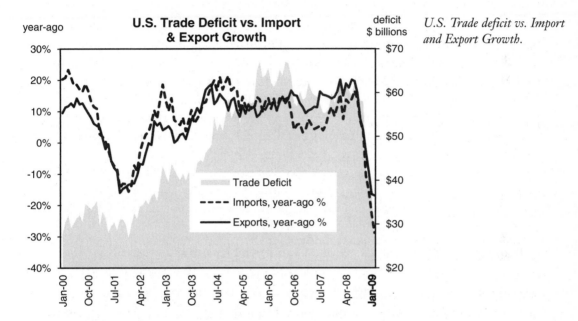

U.S. Trade deficit vs. Import and Export Growth.

More Facts About the International Trade Report

What are the basics about this report? It covers exports, imports, and the *trade balance*. The trade balance is the difference between dollar values of exports and imports. When exports are greater than imports, there is a trade surplus. When imports are greater than exports, there is a trade deficit. Overall, the United States is in a trade deficit, but a number of components are in surplus. You might not have thought about it, but international trade is composed of both merchandise (goods) and also services.

def•i•ni•tion

Trade balance is the difference between dollar values of exports and imports. For the United States, this is the dollar value of what other countries purchase of goods and services from the United States minus the dollar value of goods and services purchased from other countries for use in the United States.

Merchandise trade data are available by export, import, and trade balance for six principal end-use commodity categories and for more than 100 principal Standard International Trade Classification (SITC) system commodity categories. Data are also available for over three dozen countries and geographic regions. There are also special series for oil and motor vehicle imports. The services portion of the report provides data on exports, imports, and trade balance for seven principal end-use categories. We talk about these shortly.

How are the numbers collected? The merchandise or goods data that are on a Census basis are compiled by the U.S. Customs and Border Protection Agency. Exports and imports reflect the movement of goods between foreign countries and the 50 states, the District of Columbia, Puerto Rico, the U.S. Virgin Islands, and U.S. Foreign Trade Zones. There are a number of exclusions, the key ones being shipments between the United States and its territories and possessions and transactions with the U.S. military, diplomatic, and consular installations abroad. However, data for exports to Canada are based on a more detailed source—Canada. The Census Bureau believes Canada documents imports from the United States better than the United States calculates exports to Canada. Every country is more meticulous about imports because tax levies are usually involved! So the data for U.S. goods exported to Canada are derived from import data compiled by Canada.

For the various services categories, the Commerce Department primarily relies upon private trade association data to estimate overall services exports and imports.

The monthly international trade numbers are used as source data for exports and imports in the quarterly gross domestic product estimates. Among other adjustments to the monthly data, the Commerce Department adjusts the export and import figures for U.S. national borders by excluding U.S. territories.

End-Use Categories

The Census merchandise exports and imports are divided into end-use categories, according to their primary end use. The major end-use categories are:

- ◆ Food, feeds, and beverages
- ◆ Industrial supplies and materials
- ◆ Capital goods except autos

- Automotive vehicles, parts, and engines
- Consumer goods except autos
- Other goods

Most of these categories tend to be in deficit for the United States. The two end-use categories that typically are in surplus are food, feeds, and beverages, and capital goods. Let's see what's in each end-use category.

The foods, feeds, and beverages category typically is in surplus because of the United States' large volume of agricultural exports. For instance, grain crops are a source of export strength. The United States heavily exports foods and feeds that use wide expanses of farmland and high-productivity farm equipment extensively. Such crops include grains such as corn and wheat. Food imports are mostly for crops that are labor intensive as well as fruits and vegetables imported during the United States' off season. These imports also include food commodities such as sugar, coffee, and cocoa. Large swings in the food, feeds, and beverage category can be caused by drought in agricultural areas abroad or in the United States.

The industrial supplies and materials component includes petroleum and a variety of industrial materials. This end-use category regularly stays in a large deficit because of oil imports. However, the deficit can swing sharply due to changes in the price of oil. On the export side, this component is led by chemicals, nonferrous metals, paper, petroleum and products, and coal. However, petroleum product exports partly depend on imported oil. While most of the oil imported into the United States in consumed there, it is interesting that some of the imported oil is exported as refined products.

The "capital goods except autos" component generally stays in surplus since the United States is well known for quality capital equipment. "Capital goods except autos" is led in exports by civilian aircraft along with computers, semiconductors, industrial machinery, and oil drilling, mining, and construction machinery. This end-use category for exports can be volatile because of the aircraft subcomponent. For imports, this category is led by computers and semiconductors.

In contrast to capital goods, the "consumer goods except autos" component and the automobile and parts components are usually in deficit. Foreign producers have made dramatic inroads with American consumers over recent decades. The other goods component primarily includes military goods and low-value shipments. Take a look at the 2008 end-use categories.

Exports and Imports Percent Shares for Census Goods Trade by Principle End-Use Categories, 2008

	Exports	Imports
Foods, feeds, and beverages	8.3	4.2
Industrial supplies	29.8	36.9
Capital goods	36.1	21.6
Automotive vehicles	9.3	11.1
Consumer goods	12.4	23.0
Other goods	4.1	3.1

Services Exports and Imports

The balance of payments portion of the monthly international trade report includes "services exports and imports" while Census data are just for goods. Guess what? The United States actually has a surplus in the trade of services! It is now rare for the United States to have a trade deficit in services. While U.S. residents buy more hard stuff from overseas than we sell to other countries, the United States sells more services to foreigners than it buys from countries overseas. Do you know which categories put the United States in the plus category for a services surplus? Let's see what the major categories are.

Services are shown in seven broad categories. Types of services for imports and exports are the same for six of the seven categories. For the seventh, the export category is "transfers under U.S. military sales contracts" while for imports the category is "direct defense expenditures." The following is a brief description of the types of services included in each category:

◆ Travel: This includes purchases of services and goods by U.S. travelers abroad and by foreign visitors to the United States. Such expenditures are for food, lodging, recreation, gifts, and other items incidental to a foreign visit.

◆ Passenger fares: These are fares paid by residents of one country to residents of other countries. Payments consist of fares paid by U.S. residents to foreign carriers for travel between the United States and foreign countries.

◆ Other transportation: This component includes charges for the transportation of goods by ocean, air, waterway, pipeline, and rail carriers to and from the United States.

◆ Royalties and license fees: These transactions involve intangible assets and proprietary rights such as the use of patents, techniques, processes, formulas, designs, know-how, trademarks, copyrights, franchises, and manufacturing rights. The term "royalties" generally refers to payments for the utilization of copyrights or trademarks, and the term "license fees" generally refers to payments for the use of patents or industrial processes.

◆ Other private services: This category consists of education services, financial services (including commissions and other transactions fees associated with the purchase and sale of securities and noninterest income of banks, and excluding investment income), insurance services, telecommunications services (including transmission services and value-added services), and business, professional, and technical services.

Included in the last group are advertising services; computer and data processing services; database and other information services; research, development, and testing services; management, consulting, and public relations services; legal services; construction, engineering, architectural, and mining services; industrial engineering services; installation, maintenance, and repair of equipment; and other services, including medical services and film and tape rentals.

◆ Transfers under U.S. military sales contracts (*exports only*): These are exports of goods and services in which U.S. government military agencies participate.

◆ Direct defense expenditures (*imports only*): These are expenditures incurred by U.S. military agencies abroad, including expenditures by U.S. personnel, payments of wages to foreign residents, construction expenditures, payments for foreign contractual services, and procurement of foreign goods. These include both goods and services that cannot be separately identified.

◆ U.S. Government miscellaneous services: These are transactions of U.S. government nonmilitary agencies with foreign residents. Most of these transactions involve the provision of services to, or purchase of services from, foreigners, and transfers of some goods are also included.

The two service categories in which the United States really stands out are "other private services" and "royalties and license fees." Yes, the United States is still valued for its education services, financial services, engineering services, and others. If you visit any major university in the United States, you are likely to see a significant presence of foreign students.

Trader Tip _____

The travel component of the services exports and imports can be in surplus, depending on the value of the dollar. When the dollar is weak, lots of Europeans, Japanese, and others find it relatively cheap to visit Disney World and other tourist attractions in the United States. In the meantime, if the dollar is down, U.S. citizens cannot afford those European vacations as much. When the dollar is strong, all of that reverses, boosting the likelihood that the travel component will be in deficit.

Country Data on International Trade

This report not only provides data by end-use category, but also by country and region. Regions covered are North America, Europe (with separate categories for the European Union and for the Euro Area), Pacific Rim Countries, South/Central America, OPEC, Africa, and other countries. The country detail is useful for evaluating appropriate exchange rates between countries. Also, the numbers are handy in political debates over trade policies. Not too many years ago, the biggest deficit for the United States was Japan, but imports from China have grown rapidly; consequently, the current deficit with China far outstrips the deficit with Japan.

Also, the country data indicate that international trade actually is a two-way street. The United States has substantial exports to Canada and Mexico even though the United States has trade deficits with those countries. Take a look at the following table to see exports, imports, and deficits with different countries.

Top 5 U.S. Goods Export-Import Trading Partners in 2008, Values in Millions of Dollars

Exports to	Rank	Value	Percent of Total
Canada	1	261,381.2	20.1
Mexico	2	151,538.6	11.7
China	3	71,457.1	5.5
Japan	4	66,579.2	5.1
Germany	5	54,732.3	4.2
Total Exports		1,300,497.5	

Imports from	Rank	Value	Percent of Total
China	1	337,789.8	16.1
Canada	2	335,555.3	16.0
Mexico	3	215,914.9	10.3
Japan	4	139,248.2	6.6
Germany	5	97,552.9	4.6
Total Imports		2,100,431.6	
Deficit with	**Rank**	**Value**	
China	1	−266,333	
Canada	2	−74,174	
Japan	3	−72,669	
Mexico	4	−64,376	
Germany	5	−42,821	

Market Reaction to the International Trade News Release

Market reaction to this report can be complex. But on the initial release, focus is on the overall deficit and the nonpetroleum goods deficit. Sharp changes in oil prices can cause sizeable shrinkage or widening in the trade deficit. Notice in the following table that the overall trade gap dropped by over $6 billion from November 2008 to January 2009. This reflected sharply lower oil prices that cut the petroleum trade shortfall by about $5 billion. Yet there was little change in the nonpetroleum goods deficit. While the overall narrowing of the trade gap was good for the dollar, the detail indicated that no improvement for manufacturing was seen from exports as exports fell over this period.

This report has a special section on petroleum imports. It includes data on the average price of imported oil as well as the number of barrels imported. Basically, those numbers can help you interpret whether a change in the petroleum balance was price related or not.

Monthly International Trade, January 2009

Billions, U.S. Dollars		Month-Ago		% Change	
	Jan 09	Dec 08	Nov 08	Jan 09	Dec 08
Overall Goods and Services					
Balance	−36.030	−39.900	−42.450	−9.7	−6.0
Exports	124.906	132.517	140.663	−5.7	−5.8
Imports	160.936	172.417	183.114	−6.7	−5.8
Petroleum, Balance	−14.727	−18.790	−19.654	−21.6	−4.4
Exports	3.450	3.507	4.264	−1.6	−17.8
Imports	18.177	22.297	23.917	−18.5	−6.8
Non-Petroleum Goods					
Balance	−31.361	−31.263	−31.992	0.3	−2.3
Exports	79.250	86.114	93.704	−8.0	−8.1
Imports	110.611	117.377	125.696	−5.8	−6.6

Market watchers look at the overall balance for potential impact on the dollar. Typically, a lower deficit boosts the dollar. And analysts check out export and import numbers separately to see the potential impact on U.S. manufacturing. Stronger exports are good for U.S. manufacturing, while imports cut into factory output.

> **Only from an Economist**
>
> A key fact to remember: The trade deficit can still add to economic growth if it's decreasing. A narrowing trade balance adds to GDP growth because it is less of a drain on domestic demand. In contrast, a widening trade deficit subtracts from economic growth. It's not whether the trade balance is negative or positive that affects growth, it's whether it is widening or narrowing that matters.

What are the long-term factors that affect export growth? Broadly, exports gain when the exchange value of the dollar is relatively weaker than that of foreign currencies and when foreign economies are experiencing healthy economic growth. But don't forget that import decisions by buyers overseas are based on specific comparisons between competing products. The U.S. producer must be competitive in price and quality with manufacturers overseas.

Similarly, imports will rise when the exchange value of the dollar is strong, U.S. demand is robust, and prices of foreign products are cheaper than those of competing U.S. goods.

Key Facts About the Import and Export Prices Report

Thus far, the inflation reports we've reviewed have largely focused on domestic prices. Another important question is, "What effect is inflation having on goods that are being imported and exported between countries?" Well, changes in import and export prices provide valuable information on inflation here and abroad. Import price inflation can be seen either as a check on domestic inflation or as a leading indicator for rising import inflation. Export prices are important because U.S. manufacturers have to be competitive to export. On the other hand, if export prices drift upward because of stronger demand, then export prices may be indicative of rising profits.

Therefore, the import and export prices can directly affect the financial markets, such as for the dollar and for bonds. Both markets are sensitive to the risk of import inflation because it erodes the value of any U.S. asset held by either U.S. citizens or foreigners.

Here's what's in the import and export prices report:

◆ Official name: U.S. Import and Export Price Indexes

◆ Release date: Monthly, mid-month for the prior month's data (July release has June data)

◆ Produced by: U.S. Bureau of Labor Statistics, U.S. Department of Labor

◆ Form of data: In indexes. Data are available seasonally adjusted and not seasonally adjusted.

◆ Market watchers focus on: The overall import prices and import prices excluding nonpetroleum imports, month-ago percent changes, and year-ago percent changes (view reports at www.stats.bls.gov/news.release/ximpim.toc.htm)

Import and Export Prices, February 2009

		Month-Ago % Changes		
	Year-Ago %	Dec 08	Jan 09	Feb 09
Imports, all	−12.8	−4.6	−1.2	−0.2
Petroleum imports	−52.4	−25.2	−4.2	3.9
Nonpetroleum imports	−1.9	−1.1	−0.8	−0.6
Exports, all	−4.5	−2.2	0.5	−0.1
Agricultural exports	−15.2	−6.2	6.2	−1.7
Nonagricultural exports	−3.3	−1.9	0.1	0.1
Imports by country of origin				
Canada	−14.4	−4.4	−1.8	−1.6
China	1.0	−0.5	−0.4	−0.5
EU	−2.5	−1.5	0.1	0.0
Latin America	−19.7	−6.1	−1.2	−1.1
Japan	1.9	0.3	0.2	0.2
NICs*	−3.0	−3.2	−2.6	−0.5

Newly industrialized countries.

Data Sources for Import and Export Prices

Just to be clear, let's define import and export prices. Import prices are the prices of goods that are bought in the United States, but produced abroad. Export prices are the prices of goods sold abroad, but produced domestically. The Bureau of Labor Statistics (BLS) collects samples of import and export prices and compiles them into price indexes.

Most of the prices for imports are obtained from the U.S. Customs Service using samples of reports on imports. According to the BLS, the export merchandise prices are obtained from the Canadian Customs Service for exports to Canada and from the Bureau of the Census for exports to the rest of the world. For services, import prices are obtained from a wide range of sources, with data sources for each category researched and developed separately. One example is that the Department of Transportation provides the sample for the air freight price indexes.

The merchandise indexes are published using three different classification systems: Harmonized, Bureau of Economic Analysis (BEA) End Use, and the Standard International Trade Classification (SITC). The Harmonized system was designed to be an international system used for Customs tariff, statistical, and transport documentation purposes. The SITC, also a commodity-based system, was created by the United Nations and was the first classification system used by the International Price Program to publish its price indexes. The End-Use system created by the BEA was designed to categorize items by use or consumption rather than by the more traditional stage of production. You can take a look at the relative importance of import prices in the following table.

Import Prices, End-Use Categories, Relative Importance Percent, January 2009

End-Use Category	Relative Importance, %
Foods, feeds, & beverages	5.096
Industrial supplies & materials	27.753
Capital goods	25.318
Automotive vehicles, parts & engines	14.853
Consumer goods, excluding automotive	26.980
Special indexes:	
Nonpetroleum products	89.109
Petroleum & petroleum products	10.890

Look at the next import prices chart. Markets focus on both the headline import price index and the nonpetroleum import price index. The total import price index is far more volatile due to the inclusion of oil imports.

Import prices: Total vs. Non-petroleum.

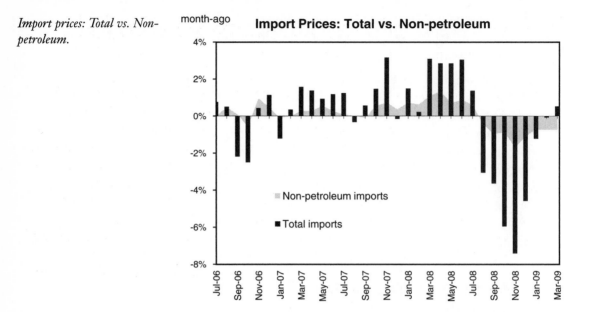

Import Prices: Total vs. Non-petroleum

Market Reaction to the Import and Export Prices News Releases

On the initial release of this report, the import price indexes receive the vast majority of attention. The headline index is heavily influenced by changes in oil prices. If market watchers believe that the trend in oil prices has changed since the reporting period for import prices, the focus will more likely be on nonpetroleum import prices for determining whether import price inflation is damping or worsening U.S. inflation. Higher import price numbers are bad for bond prices and boost interest rates. Higher import prices also can spook equity markets if traders believe the Fed is more likely to raise interest rates due to the report.

However, even the nonpetroleum import price index is heavily laden with commodity types of goods and may not have a direct link to consumer prices. Instead, one can look at one of the end-use categories: consumer goods excluding automotives. This component has a much closer relationship to CPI inflation than the overall import price index.

Although they do not get as much attention as import prices, the export price indexes can have an impact on equities if export prices are rising significantly. Rising export prices can mean higher profits for U.S. manufacturers or farmers. Export prices are put into two broad categories: agricultural exports and nonagricultural exports. To determine a possible impact on stock prices in a particular industry, you would need to determine where the export price strength is. There is no shortage of industry detail on either import or export prices.

Key Facts About the Treasury International Capital Report

If you follow currency, bond, or even stock markets in the United States, wouldn't you like to know what some of the key players are doing? In our more globalized economy, foreigners are increasingly buying and selling U.S. securities. These include stocks, government bonds, government agency bonds, and corporate bonds. Similarly, U.S. citizens have been diversifying investments by investing in foreign securities. An increasingly important factor in worldwide financial markets is how willing foreign investors are to hold or buy U.S. securities. The same holds true for U.S. investors and foreign securities. The amount of money that crosses borders at any given time is an important factor for determining prices of stocks and bonds. And for the United States, there actually is a report that tells you how much money is being spent by foreigners on U.S. securities and by U.S. residents on foreign securities: It's the Treasury International Capital (TIC) report.

TIC data have been around a long time—well over 30 years. But only in recent years have financial markets started to pay attention to this report because of a surge in foreign participation in our markets. Increasingly, the United States has become dependent on foreign investors and governments to buy its federal government debt (Treasuries). In the financial markets, bonds and the dollar are most sensitive to the TIC report. However, equity markets can be affected by TIC numbers if there are signs of foreign investors preferring to move money into or out of the United States due to relative safety in or out of the United States at various times.

The Treasury gives a more detailed definition of TIC. The *Treasury International Capital reporting system* collects data for the United States on cross-border portfolio investment flows and positions between U.S. residents (including U.S.-based branches of firms headquartered in other countries) and foreign residents (including offshore branches of U.S. firms).

Here's what's in the TIC report:

- Official name: Treasury International Capital

- Release date: Monthly, mid-month for two months prior data (July release has May data)

- Produced by: U.S Department of the Treasury

def•i•ni•tion

Treasury International Capital reporting system tracks the flows of financial investments into and out of the United States.

◆ Form of data: In dollars. Data are not seasonally adjusted.

◆ Market watchers focus on: Net domestic securities purchases. But financial issues "of the day" can lead to greater focus on specific detail of the report—perhaps on the purchase of Treasuries or agency bonds (www.treas.gov/tic).

Behind the TIC Data

The TIC data are collected by the Federal Reserve on behalf of the Treasury, but it's also available for use by the Bureau of Economic Analysis. While all three publish TIC data, the primary report comes from the Treasury. The information is primarily collected from banks and broker/dealers of securities in the United States. Some quarterly data are taken from non-banks and non-broker/dealers. More detailed data are collected annually.

The TIC data collection system is specifically designed to capture "U.S.-cross border" financial transactions. That is, it only includes financial transactions that involve both a U.S. resident and a foreign resident. A U.S. resident by definition includes any individual, corporation, or organization located in the United States. But transactions between U.S. residents are not included even for foreign securities transactions. Similarly, transactions solely between foreigners are not included, even for U.S. securities. An example would be a Japanese resident securities broker purchasing U.S. Treasuries from a London-based securities broker. Because many U.S. securities, including U.S. Treasury securities, trade in foreign financial markets, the TIC data will not pick up all foreign transactions in U.S. securities.

Cross-border direct investment activity is excluded from these data. According to the Treasury, direct investment is defined as the ownership or control, directly or indirectly, by one person or by an affiliated group, of 10 percent or more of the voting stock of an incorporated business enterprise, or an equivalent interest in an unincorporated enterprise. Direct investment positions and flows are collected separately by the U.S. Department of Commerce.

Many people follow the TIC country data. Here's what they want to know: What are the financial flows between the United States and specific countries? These data can have an impact on specific exchange rates. However, there is a caveat. The country (or region) detail may not always indicate the actual ultimate owners of U.S. assets or the ultimate obligors of U.S. claims. That is, the foreign party listed in the transaction may just be a middle man. Nonetheless, the country data provide valuable insight into financial transactions between U.S. residents and other countries.

Take a look at the January 2009 Treasury International Capital report.

Treasury International Capital Report, January 2009

Billions, U.S. Dollars	Change in Monthly Level		
	Nov 08	Dec 08	Jan 09
Gross Purchases of U.S. Securities	−945.5	−66.2	−154.3
Gross Sales of U.S. Securities	−922.0	−148.6	−113.2
Domestic Securities Purchases, net	−23.5	82.5	−41.2
Private, net	−3.5	48.1	−35.4
Treasury Bonds, Notes	−33.6	10.7	1.5
Government Agency Bonds	22.7	−13.8	10.1
Corporate Bonds	−1.5	52.7	−46.2
Equities	8.9	−1.6	−0.7
Official, net	−19.9	34.3	−5.7
Treasury Bonds, Notes	−25.1	30.1	−5.8
Government Agency Bonds	5.1	−1.3	5.0
Corporate Bonds	−1.6	4.4	−3.2
Equities	1.7	1.0	−1.6
Gross Purchase of Foreign Securities	−233.6	−58.1	−10.5
Gross Sales of Foreign Securities	−231.6	−36.0	26.1
Foreign Securities Purchased, net	−2.0	−22.2	−36.5
Foreign Bonds, Purchased	−1.6	−0.9	−40.3
Foreign Equities, Purchased	−0.4	−21.2	3.6
Net Long–Term Securities Transactions	−25.5	60.3	−77.7
Other Acquisitions of Long–Term Securities	2.8	1.6	−7.5
Net Foreign Acquisition of Long-Term Securities	−22.76	1.9	−85.2

Market Reaction to the TIC News Release

Market reaction to the TIC report is not easy to boil down. Reactions vary according to what financial markets are more sensitive to any given month. But in general, the primary focus is on "domestic securities purchases, net." This is the difference between foreigners' purchases of U.S. securities and their sales of U.S. securities. It reflects rising or falling demand for U.S. securities overseas.

However, in some months, market attention may be on specific components or specific countries. For example, during 2009, the Chinese government made comments that it might consider diversifying its holdings of government bonds from almost entirely U.S. Treasuries to some mix of holdings. Markets checked TIC reports to see that foreign purchases of Treasuries were holding up and that China actually had not made any changes in its purchasing strategy. Similarly, during the subprime loan crisis, the line for government agency bonds (including Fannie Mae and Freddie Mac) got a lot of attention.

The Least You Need to Know

◆ The international trade report provides important insight into foreign and domestic demand for goods and services.

◆ It is the change in the trade deficit (narrowing or widening) that determines its impact on economic growth (adding or subtracting).

◆ Low or declining import price inflation dampens consumer price inflation in the United States, while high or rising import price inflation adds to consumer price inflation.

◆ The Treasury International Capital (TIC) report provides insight on whether foreigners are more or less willing to buy U.S. securities, which in turn can impact bond yields and the value of the dollar.

Part

Fed Watching: The Best for Last

Well, admit it. You've seen the Federal Reserve's actions on monetary policy make huge headlines—but you didn't quite understand. But now you can know what the financial gurus know—all in bite-size pieces. Who are the key Fed players and what is it the Fed actually changes in the financial markets? What are the key reports from the Fed? It's all here.

And it gets better and better! The Wall Street whiz kids love to talk about how the financial markets give a thumbs-up or thumbs-down on Fed policy. They banter about "fed funds futures," "yield curves," and other exotic terms. But what do they mean? Here's their dark secret: These things are easy to understand once you go through one easy step at a time! You can be the Fed guru!

Chapter 19

The Federal Reserve and Monetary Policy

In This Chapter

- ◆ The purpose of monetary policy
- ◆ The Federal Open Market Committee
- ◆ The Fed's traditional policy tools
- ◆ Where the regional Fed Banks fit in

Remember what a big deal the employment report is for financial markets? While the employment report can rattle markets, when the Federal Reserve (the Fed to you insiders) makes an unexpected interest rate move, that's more like an earthquake!

Yes, nothing gets market attention like a Fed move. And because the Fed is in charge of monetary policy, we first take a look at just what monetary policy is and then talk about how the Fed goes about its business.

What Is Monetary Policy?

Why is there a Federal Reserve? Let's indirectly get to that by first talking about *monetary policy*. As a consumer, don't you like the economy when it's in such good shape that you don't have to worry about it? So what's it like when you aren't worrying about the economy?

You probably have a steady job and business has been very good at the company you work for. Hey, the future looks bright! You've had some fairly decent pay raises in recent years. And when you go to Target, the Gap, or Kroger, you don't notice any significant changes in prices. Life is good! Well, the scenario we just described is exactly why the Fed exists. You also just learned the objectives of monetary policy. The objectives of monetary policy in the United States are healthy, sustainable economic growth and low inflation. In other words, the Fed tries to create the scenario where you have a steady job and life is good!

Monetary policy is the process of the *central bank* controlling the money supply or interest rates to keep economic growth healthy and inflation low. As just mentioned, in the United States, the objectives of the Federal Reserve are healthy economic growth combined with low inflation. The Fed has implemented monetary policy at times by focusing on the growth in the money supply. But currently, when it's time to take charge of the economy, moving interest rates up or down is the Fed's preferred weapon of choice. We talk about money supply more in the next chapter, but for now, money supply is the total amount of money available in the economy. And note that monetary policy differs from fiscal policy. Fiscal policy is legislated policy for government spending, taxation, and government borrowing.

def•i•ni•tion

Monetary policy is the process by which the central bank controls either the money supply or interest rates to achieve specific objectives for the overall economy—typically, low inflation or a combination of low inflation and healthy economic growth.

Central banks, reserve banks, or a monetary authority are responsible for the monetary policy of a country or a group of member states. Another primary responsibility of a central bank is to be the lender of last resort to commercial banks in times of need.

How did the Fed get created? Early in the twentieth century, financial and political leaders decided that they'd had enough of roller-coaster economies where there were booms and then busts. They concluded that private banks alone could not smooth out such harsh ups and downs. In 1913, Congress passed the Federal Reserve Act, and the Federal Reserve System was put in place in 1914.

At the time, the most recent motivation for bringing the Federal Reserve into reality was the Panic of 1907, a financial crisis also known as the 1907 Bankers' Panic, which led to mass withdrawals from banks, a collapse in the stock markets, and widespread bankruptcies among businesses and among state and local governments. The Fed was set up to provide liquidity into financial markets at times of distress. One of the key initial purposes of the Fed was to be a lender of last resort for banks. If an otherwise healthy bank needed emergency cash and couldn't get it any other way, it knew the Fed would be there with a loan to stop any developing panic.

Before we wrap up this introduction, we need to clarify what liquidity is. In general, liquidity in financial markets is an asset that is readily sold at a reasonable market price. There are many willing buyers for liquid assets and you don't have to take a cut in value to sell the asset. The most common liquid assets in the United States are Treasury securities, which are viewed as a safe investment because they are backed by the U.S. government. To sell an illiquid asset (such as an office building or bonds issued by a small company) in a hurry, you have to take a big cut on the price. But when we are talking about the Fed injecting liquidity into financial markets, we generally are talking about cash or reserves given to banks by the Fed. Bank reserves are simply money credited to the bank in its account with the Fed. The bank is then able to use the reserves to lend money to its customers. And banks can loan their unneeded reserves to other banks.

While the Fed has many functions, we focus on monetary policy. But just so you're aware, those other functions include supervision of certain types of commercial banks and bank holding companies, acting as banker for the Treasury when Treasury securities are issued or redeemed, providing oversight for consumer protection laws, and providing services to depository institutions (such as check clearing and transferring of funds), among others.

Trader Tip

While the Fed may be best known for deciding interest rates, it is also one of the best places for consumers to go for consumer finance information. Yes, the Fed takes its role in monitoring consumer credit issues seriously. Before you buy a new home, you should visit the Fed's website or any Fed District Bank's on mortgages and personal finance. To learn how to navigate through mortgages, visit www.federalreserve.gov/consumerinfo/mortgages.htm.

If you are worried about credit card issues, check out www.federalreserve.gov/pubs/consumerhdbk.

The Fed's Monetary Policy Tools

A number of issues affect how the Fed implements monetary policy. Let's summarize what the Fed's main tools are for controlling inflation and maintaining economic growth. Then we'll look at how the Fed implements each.

The traditional monetary policy tools of the Fed are:

◆ Open market operations—or making changes in the fed funds rate

◆ The discount rate

◆ Reserve requirements

There are two relatively recent tools that some see as separate tools, but they may also be seen as an expansion of open market operations. These new tools are:

◆ Payment of interest on reserves

◆ Quantitative easing

We cover the traditional three tools in this chapter along with how payment of interest on reserves fits in with the fed funds rate (details on this are up ahead). Quantitative easing is a new tool, and we cover that in more detail in Chapter 21, on key Fed reports related to the Fed's balance sheet. Before we look at the specific policy tools, let's glance at the two groups of key players: the Federal Reserve Board of Governors and the Federal Reserve District Bank presidents.

The Board of Governors

The Federal Reserve Board of Governors runs the Federal Reserve System from its headquarters in Washington, D.C. There are seven members of the Board of Governors. They are nominated by the president and must be confirmed by the Senate. Each seat on the Board has a full term of 14 years. One term begins every two years, on February 1 of even-numbered years. Those who serve a full term cannot be reappointed. But it is rare for a Board member to serve a full 14-year term—the more lucrative private sector is always beckoning. There are many members appointed to finish an unexpired term and these can be reappointed. All terms end on their statutory date regardless of the date on which the member is sworn into office.

The chairman and the vice chairman of the Board are named by the U.S. president from among the Board members and must be confirmed by the Senate. They serve a term of four years as chairman or vice chairman, but service in these positions does not affect the member's term on the Board.

Only from an Economist

The Fed District boundaries matter to the Board of Governors. Only one member of the Board may come from any one of the 12 Federal Reserve Districts based on language in the Federal Reserve Act. This helps to ensure that no one region of the United States dominates making monetary policy. However, there have been times that presidential selections have been creative in finding a second-home residence in a District not then represented on the Board of Governors.

The District Fed Banks

There are 12 Federal Reserve Banks in addition to the Board of Governors of the Federal Reserve System in Washington, D.C. Fed District Banks were authorized under the Federal Reserve Act of 1913, and are independently chartered by Congress with the purpose of helping the Federal Reserve Board carry out its functions, including monetary policy. Why so many District Banks? Federal Reserve banks are bankers' banks. That is, they provide services to commercial banks, such as providing cash and coin as well as processing checks.

Only from an Economist

Guess which state is the only one to have two Federal Reserve Banks? No, it's not New York, or Illinois, or California. It's Missouri! When the Federal Reserve was being written into law, key help was needed from Missouri Senator James A. Reed to pass the Federal Reserve Act. Reed was on the Senate Banking Committee and was a former Kansas City mayor. Plus, Kansas City was seen as the "Gateway to the West" and had the rail lines to prove it. Today, some would say Denver would make more sense for serving the West, but Denver was not as well developed when the Fed was established.

Here's a little interesting history. During the early part of the 1900s, banks needed to be within a day's ride on a train. The District Bank territories were not drawn so much by state lines but by rail lines. Some Fed District lines split states up, but that is how the rail lines ran. The Fed Districts are named both by the host city and by district number. You can find those district numbers on Federal Reserve notes—it's what you call "cash" in your wallet! The following is a list of the Fed District banks.

- District 1: Boston
- District 2: New York
- District 3: Philadelphia
- District 4: Cleveland
- District 5: Richmond
- District 6: Atlanta
- District 7: Chicago
- District 8: St. Louis
- District 9: Minneapolis
- District 10: Kansas City
- District 11: Dallas
- District 12: San Francisco

The District Bank presidents participate in monetary policy. You're probably wondering how they got to be in that position. Based on the Federal Reserve Act, each District Bank president is appointed by the board of directors of that District Bank for a term of five years. However, the local board's nomination must be approved by the Board of Governors of the Federal Reserve System. While the Board in Washington may make suggestions behind the scenes for whom they think might be a good District Bank president, the local board of directors has a lot of autonomy in picking its own nominee. The terms of all the presidents of the District Banks run concurrently, ending on the last day of February of years numbered 6 and 1 (for example, 2001, 2006, and 2011). However, it is very unusual for a Bank president to not be renominated after a term is completed. A president may be reappointed after serving a full term or an incomplete term. Typically, a District Bank president leaves office only upon mandatory retirement upon becoming 65 years of age (with some exceptions) or due to a decision to move back to the private sector.

Open Market Operations

We've talked about the key players at the Fed—the Fed Board governors and the District Bank presidents. Now, we are going to jump into just what it is they do when conducting monetary policy. We'll start with what the Fed's tools are for monetary policy. The first and primary tool used by the Fed to put monetary policy in motion is open market operations. Sounds pretty complicated, but it boils down to nothing more than interest rates. Open market operations are how the Fed causes short-term interest rates to go up, down, or remain the same. Open market operations are just interest-rate policy! Let's see how the Fed impacts interest rates for monetary policy.

Open market operations are simply purchases and sales of U.S. Treasury and federal agency securities on the open market through the New York Fed's Trading Desk. When the Fed buys Treasury securities, it is in exchange for reserves—money held by banks in their account with the Fed. When the Fed buys Treasuries, it is adding to the supply of reserves on the open market. This pushes the interest rate down for reserves. There is a special name for the interest rate on reserves traded on the open market—the *fed funds rate*. (And no, "fed" is not capitalized; it's short for federal, not the Fed.)

According to the Fed Board, the federal funds rate is the interest rate at which depository institutions (banks) lend excess reserves held at the Federal Reserve to other depository institutions overnight. These loans are for overnight because that is the traditional loan duration when a

def•i•ni•tion

The **fed funds rate** is the interest rate at which banks lend their excess reserve balances with the Fed to other banks overnight.

bank ends the day short of required reserves and has to borrow reserves from another bank. In reality, it is not uncommon that these overnight loans are rolled over for longer periods of time. When the Fed is aggressively buying Treasuries in exchange for reserves, it is lowering the fed funds rate.

What about the reverse? When the Fed sells Treasury securities that it has on its balance sheet, it's taking bank reserves off the open market. This reduces the supply of reserves and pushes up the fed funds rate. One caveat in all this is that the Fed must regularly add reserves to the financial system to keep up with normal economic growth.

Hanging in there? Great! Here's a summary of open market operations:

♦ When the Fed buys Treasury securities, this adds reserves to the financial system and tends to lower the fed funds rate.

♦ When the Fed sells Treasury securities, this withdraws reserves from the financial system and tends to raise the fed funds rate.

Now to the real point: For monetary policy, why do we care about open market operations? It's the impact on interest rates! Lower interest rates spur economic growth. Banks find more eager borrowers—consumers and businesses—at lower interest rates. Consumers borrow more because they can afford to borrow more. Businesses borrow more for that same reason, and also because there are more business opportunities that have a profitable rate of return at low interest rates than at high interest rates.

Only from an Economist

Here's an interesting question: Does the Fed directly cut or raise the rate for a loan such as a car loan or business loan? The answer or answers are no, not directly, and yes, but indirectly. The Fed directly only changes the rate that banks pay to each other. But when their rates change, competition or costs result in similar changes in rates that consumers and businesses pay.

Believe it or not, interest rates that get too low can be too much of a good thing. Interest rates that are too low drive up demand, and all that money floating around boosts inflation. The Fed has to find the right balance between healthy economic growth and low inflation. Over the business cycle (the longer-term ups and downs in economic activity), the Fed may find that some unexpected events require some fine tuning of interest rates. If there are signs of recession, the Fed cuts the fed funds rate. If there are signs of unacceptably high inflation, the Fed raises the fed funds rate.

Open market operations can have one of two objectives. They can be for a specific growth path in reserves or for a specific fed funds rate. During the early 1980s, there was more focus on targeting reserve growth, which gradually shifted to setting a target for the fed funds rate. This is the focus today of open market operations—the fed funds rate. Now, how does the Fed go about deciding on the fed funds rate?

Only from an Economist

What do you call the various policy stances of the Fed? To get out of recession, the Fed cuts interest rates. To cool too-high inflation, the Fed taps the brakes by raising interest rates. Economists have descriptions for these opposite Fed policies: "easing" is when the Fed lowers rates; "tightening" is when the Fed raises rates. Policy is called easy versus tight, expansionary versus contractionary, and accommodative versus restrictive. When the Fed has the policy just right and rates are seen as maintaining steady, noninflationary growth, policy is called "neutral."

The Federal Open Market Committee

The Federal Open Market Committee was established by the Federal Reserve Act as the organization within the Fed that would be responsible for open market operations. That is why it is called the Federal Open Market Committee (FOMC). The FOMC is the Fed's main policy-making body. It meets eight times a year to consider the appropriate fed funds rate to achieve the policy goals of low inflation and healthy economic growth. By law, the FOMC consists of all of the governors of the Federal Reserve Board plus five of the twelve District Bank presidents on a rotating basis (discussed further below). Under the Federal Reserve Act, the FOMC determines its own internal organization separately from the Board of Governors. But by tradition, the FOMC elects the chairman of the Board of Governors as its chairman and the president of the Federal Reserve Bank of New York as its vice chairman.

Although only five of the District Bank presidents have an official vote at the FOMC, all District Bank presidents attend each meeting. This keeps all FOMC members fully apprised of economic conditions in all Fed Districts and encourages a more collegial approach in the making of monetary policy. Because all Bank presidents attend, this necessitates a distinction during the meeting and in the meeting minutes between FOMC "members" and FOMC "participants." Members are only those with official votes. Participants include those with official votes plus the nonvoting District Bank presidents.

The whole point of the FOMC meeting is to assess economic conditions—in general, on economic growth, and on inflation—and then to determine the appropriate fed funds target rate. A few weeks before each FOMC meeting, all of the regional Feds put together a compilation of 12 reports on the regional economies. This report is called the "Beige Book" and is distributed to FOMC participants and the public two weeks before the meeting. The FOMC meeting includes numerous briefings by the Board staff on national economic forecasts, conditions in the financial markets, and special issues.

The meeting reviews two special documents prepared and delivered just prior to the meeting. These are the FOMC "Greenbook" and FOMC "Bluebook." The Greenbook is the Board staff's confidential forecast for the economy. It includes commentary and numbers for GDP and components, employment, unemployment, and personal consumption expenditures (PCE) inflation. Meanwhile, the Bluebook includes the even higher-level classified alternative policy scenarios and outcomes as seen by the Board staff. The Bluebook discusses possible outcomes of higher, lower, or unchanged fed funds rates.

During the meeting, all governors and Bank presidents participate in "go rounds" (participants sit at a massive boardroom table) with each person giving their views on the national and regional economies. Each one is allowed to give an opinion on appropriate monetary policy. Generally, the attitude of Fed officials is that collegial debate is healthy and not personal. Divergent opinions are expected during the FOMC debate.

The final outcome of the meeting is the fed funds target rate decision. The official members vote on the appropriate level for the fed funds target rate. Mostly, the decisions are unanimous as Fed governors and Bank presidents work toward a consensus view. Occasionally there is dissent, but that is rare (we talk more about this situation in Chapter 20).

The bottom line? At the end of each FOMC meeting, financial markets are waiting to see if the Fed changed the fed funds target rate. As seen in the fed funds target chart that follows, the Fed changes the fed funds rate to try to keep economic growth—as seen by monthly employment growth—from being too strong or too weak. The Fed has not always been successful with its timing to keep growth steady and moderate. The payroll numbers below are six-month moving averages.

Fed Funds Target vs. Employment.

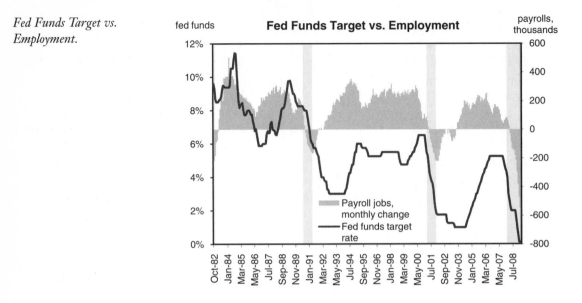

However, the Fed has been more successful in bringing down long-term inflation from highs seen in the 1970s and early 1980s. Because inflation has come down, the needed size of the Fed's target rate changes has come down, too.

Notice in the fed funds and inflations chart below that in the 1990s, the Fed raised interest rates not because inflation had surged substantially, but because early warnings indicated that inflation would rise without the Fed tapping the brakes. Employment growth had been very strong over that period.

Fed Funds Target vs. Inflation.

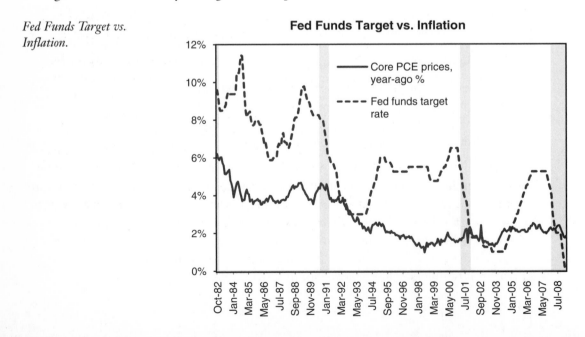

The District Bank Presidents and the FOMC

If all positions for the Board of Governors are filled, there are 12 voting members at the FOMC meeting. The seven governors always have a vote at each FOMC meeting, and the remaining five votes are allocated among the 12 Federal Reserve District Banks on a rotating basis. The New York Fed always has a vote because it is responsible for implementing Fed policy in the financial markets. The Cleveland and Chicago Feds have more frequent voting privileges—alternating each year—than the other District Banks because these two cities were financial powerhouses in the early 1900s when the Federal Reserve was set up. Here's a summary of the voting privileges:

♦ Voting every year: New York

♦ Voting every other year: Cleveland and Chicago

♦ Voting every third year: Boston, Philadelphia, and Richmond in rotation; Atlanta, St. Louis, and Dallas in rotation; Minneapolis, Kansas City, and San Francisco in rotation.

If a voting District president is unable to attend an FOMC meeting, the alternate member is the president of the bank that's scheduled to be a voting member the next year within that rotation group. For the New York Fed, the alternate member is the First Vice President of the New York Fed.

Yes, There Is an FOMC Cycle

We have talked about many of the facets involved with monetary policy. But how do all of the key pieces fit in terms of sequence and timing within the FOCM cycle?

Here's the big picture, schedule-wise, for Fed watchers. The Fed's policy arm—the Federal Open Market Committee—gets together eight times a year in Washington, D.C. For Fed watchers, the first public event in the FOMC cycle is the release of the Beige Book on 2:00 P.M. Eastern Time Wednesday afternoon two weeks before the FOMC meeting. Next in the FOMC schedule is the actual policy announcement or statement, made at about 2:15 P.M. Eastern Time on the last day of the FOMC meeting. Meetings either run one or two days. The statement indicates whether the target rate has gone up, down, or remained the same. Three weeks to the day after the policy meeting, full minutes of the meeting are released to the public with much more detail on why the governors and regional presidents voted as they did.

The cycle on public information on each FOMC decision boils down to this:

◆ The Beige Book is released two weeks before the policy meeting.

◆ The FOMC statement is made public the afternoon the meeting ends.

◆ The FOMC meeting minutes are released three weeks later.

Remember, we're mainly focusing on policy tools in this chapter, but we look at these documents in the next chapter.

Scheduled FOMC meetings tend to be at about the same times each year. These are the last week of January, mid-March, the last week of April, the last week of June, the first week of August, mid-September, the last week of October, and mid-December. FOMC meetings are typically on Tuesdays for single-day meetings and on Tuesday and Wednesday for two-day meetings. The FOMC has, on rare occasion, held emergency meetings to cut the fed funds target rate.

If you want to know more about the FOMC (such as which District Bank presidents are voting this year or in the next two years), go to www.federalreserve.gov/ monetarypolicy/fomc.htm.

The Discount Rate

A lesser-known policy tool—compared to the fed funds rate—is the Fed's discount rate. This is the rate the Fed charges banks for borrowing reserves from the Fed's discount window at regional Federal Reserve Banks. Banks go to the discount window of their local Fed when they are short on required reserves and cannot get fed funds on the private market without paying a very high rate. This may be due to tight credit conditions or because banks with spare reserves are not familiar with the needy bank. The Fed banks have three different credit programs at the discount window: primary, secondary, and seasonal. All loans are fully secured.

Only from an Economist

Why is the discount window called the discount window? Today, the discount window is simply the program of each District Fed Bank to offer special lending to banks that cannot obtain needed reserves on the open market at reasonable cost. During the early days of the Federal Reserve System, a representative of the needy bank would present documents of collateral (such as securities) to a special teller window at the Fed Bank. The value of the collateral would be discounted so as to ensure the Fed would not end up with a loss should the borrowing bank not be able to repay the loan. The name of the discount window came from the practice of the Fed Bank discounting the collateral.

Primary credit is typically available for a period of up to approximately one month to generally sound depository institutions that cannot obtain funding in the market on reasonable terms. Ordinarily, this is relevant only for small institutions that are not well known in the fed funds market by other institutions. On March 17, 2008, the primary credit program was temporarily changed to allow loans for terms of up to 90 days.

The secondary credit program is for depository institutions that do not qualify for primary credit. They are likely experiencing financial difficulties. Loans are typically short term, usually overnight. But secondary credit can be extended for a longer term if it would help the institution return to good health or would be used for an orderly closing of a failing institution. As you'd expect, the interest rate on secondary credit is higher than for primary credit.

Under the seasonal lending program, small depository institutions with a recurring, seasonal need for funds may qualify to borrow from the discount window for up to nine months during the calendar year to meet seasonal borrowing needs of the communities they serve. Institutions with deposits of less than $500 million that experience fluctuations in deposits and loans caused by construction, college, farming, resort, municipal financing, and other seasonal types of business frequently qualify for the seasonal lending program.

While the Fed generally discourages banks from borrowing at the discount window, seasonal borrowing is an exception. However, the Fed generally expects banks to make every effort to get needed reserves through the open market.

In 2003, the Fed changed operating policies in regard to the discount rate. Through 2002, the discount rate was below the fed funds target rate. The idea was that the lower rate would encourage needy banks to go to the window, if appropriate. But some banks went to the window a little too often because of the cheaper rates. So in 2003, the Fed set the main discount rate 100 basis points above the fed funds target rate and created the two discount rate programs: primary credit and secondary credit.

By tradition, the primary credit discount rate is simply called the "discount rate" even though there are actually two regular program discount rates (plus seasonal programs). In the chart that follows, you can see a comparison between the fed funds rate and the discount rate.

Fed Funds Rate vs. Discount Rate.

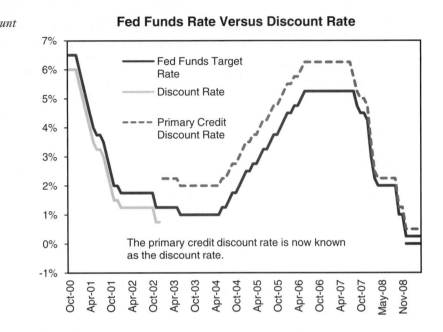

Fed Funds Rate Versus Discount Rate

— Fed Funds Target Rate

— Discount Rate

- - - Primary Credit Discount Rate

The primary credit discount rate is now known as the discount rate.

Trader Tip

When many financial analysts and traders talk about how much interest rates went up or down, they often state that rates went up or down so many "basis points." A basis point is simply one-hundredth of a percentage point. If the yield on a Treasury bond went from 4.20 percent to 4.05 percent, you could say that the interest rate fell 15 basis points. Now you are ready to keep up with the bond traders!

How Is the Discount Rate Determined?

Each District Federal Reserve Bank is required by the Federal Reserve Act to establish the appropriate discount rate at least once every two weeks. The decision to change or keep the discount rate is made not by the District Bank president, but by either the District Bank's local board of directors or the executive committee of the local board of directors. The board of directors typically meets once a month and the executive committee (top management of the local board) meets as needed (usually by teleconference) between board meetings. The bank president, the director of research, or an economist briefs the board or executive committee on current economic conditions and the District Bank president makes a recommendation on the discount rate. Of course, most of the time, the decision is to keep the discount rate unchanged.

But if a District Bank's local board of directors (or executive committee on behalf of the board) does vote to change the discount rate, the Board of Governors must approve the request for a change. Therefore, the District Bank must submit a request to the Board of Governors to change the discount rate. The Board of Governors must approve the request by a majority vote. The Board does not need to wait for a majority of District Banks to ask for a change in the discount rate—it can act on the request of a single District Bank.

The discount rates are the same across all Fed District Banks except for a few days after the Board of Governors approves a request to change the discount rate. When a change is approved, all other District Banks that were not part of the request quickly arrange to have meetings of the local board of directors so they can approve matching requests to change the discount rate.

Today, with the Fed having publicly announced targets for the fed funds rate, changes in the discount rate are usually made at the same time as changes in the fed funds target rate. This is at the end of an FOMC meeting if the fed funds target rate was changed. But this has changed heading into and during the most recent recession as the Fed governors have at times lowered the discount rate separately.

Traditionally, the primary credit discount rate is set at 100 basis points over the federal funds target rate, while the secondary credit rate is set at 150 basis points over the fed funds target rate. But during 2007 and 2008, when the latest financial crisis was at its worst, the Fed reduced this gap down to 25 basis points for the primary credit discount rate. The Fed will likely raise the differential back to 100 basis points during a period of economic health.

How Does the Discount Rate Fit in with Monetary Policy?

The discount rate became far less important in late 1989 when the Fed switched to an explicit target rate for the fed funds rate. For many years previously, the Fed did not announce its target range publicly for some time. The focus was on the money supply and the fed funds rate jumped around more on a weekly basis than now. It was more difficult to judge exactly when the Fed was changing policy. That is, was it tightening or loosening?

But one announcement that the Fed would make immediately was any change in the discount rate. The discount rate would move in the direction of any change in money growth or fed funds targets. During the 1980s, changing the discount rate was known as "ringing the gong" because it sent a loud message to the markets confirming a change in monetary policy.

During the recession that began in 2008, the discount rate regained some of its former glory. While the fed funds target rate is the main focus of monetary policy, the Fed decided that, due to the nature of the credit crunch, it was important to encourage banks to acquire needed capital with additional reserves. The Fed decided that cutting the discount rate helped to add liquidity into financial markets. Also, on March 16, 2008, the Board approved an increase in the maximum maturity of primary credit loans to 90 days (from the previous 30 days), which also added liquidity to the banking system.

When the Fed unwinds its accommodative monetary stance, one place it makes a move is to boost the discount rate gradually back to its traditional 100-basis-points-higher rate . Changing the differential between fed funds and the discount rate is now a permanent tool of the Fed when credit conditions make such a move appropriate.

Brand-New Policy Tool: The Fed Pays Interest on Reserves

The recent financial market crisis and recession resulted in new powers for the Fed. In September 2008, the Emergency Economic Stabilization Act of 2008 gave the Fed authority to pay interest on balances held by or on behalf of banks at Reserve Banks. Earlier, this had been approved by the Financial Services Regulatory Relief Act of 2006, but it was not to begin until October 1, 2011. The more recent legislation accelerated this authority so that it began earlier, on October 1, 2008.

Why is this a big deal for the Fed to pay interest on reserves of banks held at the Fed? This is an important way for the Fed to stabilize the fed funds rate. And we'll see how it helps the Fed with its new policy tool—quantitative easing (I know you're getting curious about this and I promise we'll explore the details in Chapter 21).

For now, let's keep this simple. Banks have basically two kinds of reserves with the Fed: required reserves and excess reserves. Required reserves are those needed to back up bank lending. A bank can't just lend out all of its reserves. Excess reserves are those that are above regulatory requirements. Banks can lend excess reserves but can't lend required reserves. In the past, neither type of reserves was getting interest from the Fed. If excess reserves can be loaned out, the bank makes money. But on any given day for a given bank, demand for its loans might be low. To get any return on the reserves, the bank might offer a very low rate. This can drive down the effective fed funds rate and result in the Fed not keeping the fed funds rate at the target.

In contrast, if the Fed pays interest on excess reserves that is a little below the target rate, this puts a floor on the effective fed funds rate. The bank has no reason to lend excess reserves at a rate below what the Fed is paying. The Fed decided to pay interest on required reserves because banks had long complained that it wasn't fair to be required to set those moneys aside and get no return on them for their stockholders.

Why does the Fed want to pay interest on reserves? This gives the Fed tighter control over the fed funds target rate and more control over monetary policy. Paying interest on excess reserves helps to establish a lower bound on the federal funds rate. This allows the Fed to inject more liquidity into the financial system without the result of the effective fed funds rate falling sharply.

The rate paid on reserves is determined by the Board of Governors and not by the FOMC or District Bank presidents. The rate paid on required reserves is a little higher than the rate paid on excess reserves.

As you can see in the chart that follows, the introduction of interest paid on reserves in October 2008 did start to create a floor for the effective fed funds rate.

> **Only from an Economist**
>
> Want to learn more about interest paid on reserves? Check out the Fed's website: www.federalreserve.gov.

Reserve Requirements

One rarely used tool of the Fed for controlling the money supply is the authority to set reserve requirements. The Fed sets the amount of reserves that banks and thrifts are required to hold against various deposit liabilities. Depository institutions cannot lend out all of their reserves, and required reserves are either vault cash or on deposit with Federal Reserve Banks. Reserve requirements are imposed on commercial banks, savings banks, savings and loan associations, credit unions, and U.S. branches and agencies of foreign banks, among others. Reserve ratios vary according to bank size, type of deposit (savings accounts versus checking accounts), and location (rural banks have lower reserve requirements than urban banks).

How do reserve requirements affect monetary policy? The higher the reserve ratio (the percentage of liabilities or deposits), the less banks and others can expand their loan portfolios. Lower ratios allow for more expansion of credit. The Fed rarely changes reserve requirements and this is not something markets think about. However, if you want to know more, check out the Fed's website on reserve requirements: www.federalreserve.gov/monetarypolicy/reservereq.htm.

We've talked about the key Fed players in monetary policy and the Fed's monetary policy tools. We haven't looked into market reaction yet. That will be in the following chapter when we talk about the actual news releases involved.

The Least You Need to Know

- The Fed's main monetary policy tool is to manipulate short-term interest rates—specifically, the fed funds rate.

- The chief policy group at the Fed is the Federal Open Market Committee or FOMC.

- The FOMC meets eight times a year and consists of the Board of Governors in Washington plus five of the 12 District Bank presidents on a rotating basis.

- The objectives of monetary policy are low inflation and healthy economic growth.

- The Fed started paying interest on reserves held by banks in October 2008, helping to set a floor on the fed funds rate.

20

Fed Reports on the FOMC Meeting

In This Chapter

- ◆ The Beige Book and getting ready for the FOMC
- ◆ The FOMC meeting statement is the Fed's decision
- ◆ The FOMC minutes explains the Fed's decision
- ◆ The Fed's economic forecast

The big event for the Fed is the monetary policy decision at each meeting of the Federal Open Market Committee (FOMC) eight times a year. Three main Fed reports are part of that event, and in this chapter we'll cover a lot about them. For instance, the Beige Book helps prepare the Fed for its decision, the "FOMC meeting statement" is that decision, and the "FOMC meeting minutes" are expected to explain how the decision was made.

Key Facts About the Beige Book

The Beige Book is part of the Fed's policy-making cycle. It is issued to Fed governors, Fed Bank presidents, and the public two weeks before the

FOMC meeting. The Beige Book contains the most up-to-date surveillance on the economy, with the latest economic information collected by the 12 Fed District Banks. How do the District Banks do this? Web-based surveys or tweets? No, the District Bank economists use a traditional method of collecting information—they pick up the phone and dial out! That's right, the Beige Book is a compilation of the District Banks' updates from business contacts in their Fed region.

Each Fed Bank has, over the years, developed long lists of business contacts in banking, real estate, manufacturing, sales, tourism, and so on. Government reports on economic indicators are great, but they take weeks to conduct and publish. The Fed wants the latest information from their business contacts on what's happening right now! And this includes local business leaders' gut feelings on how the economy is going. Do they just call the "big guys"? No, a District Bank adds a contact from the phone book if that business is willing to talk to the Fed. And as a former Fed economist who did the calling, I can tell you that everybody is glad to give their opinion! Also, the District Banks add to their Beige Book list from contacts of District Bank directors.

Think no one is listening to what's going on in your local economy? You're wrong—the Fed is probably one of the most locally oriented government entities when it comes to making policy. Just before they voted on what to do about interest rates at the last policy meeting, odds are they talked to several business people in your area.

> ### Only from an Economist
>
> Why is the Beige Book called that? Because that's the color of its cover in paper form. But going back in history, it started out as the Fed's Red Book. The Red Book was the same idea—a collection of last-minute anecdotal information from business contacts for Fed governors and Bank presidents. But then the Red Book also had confidential numbers from specific companies—such as June sales from Acme Manufacturing or production plans from ABC Manufacturing. The Red Book was shared confidentially with just a few Congressional leaders and when that became known, other members of Congress wanted in. So the Red Book was changed to the Beige Book in 1983, but excluded any company-specific information. And the Beige Book became a public document.

Here's what's in the Beige Book:

- Official name: Summary of Commentary on Current Economic Conditions by Federal Reserve District

- Release date: Eight times a year, on Wednesdays two weeks before each FOMC meeting

- ◆ Produced by: Federal Reserve Board and Federal Reserve District Banks

- ◆ Form of data: Anecdotal information

- ◆ Market watchers focus on: Summary section commentary (view reports at www. federalreserve.gov/monetarypolicy/fomc.htm)

Looking Closer at the Beige Book

The Beige Book is published by the Board of Governors but it is put together by the regional Banks. The District Banks rotate the responsibility of compiling information from all of the banks and then submit the final version to the Board for publication.

Each Beige Book has a standard format. The first part is a national summary of economic conditions as indicated by Fed business contacts. The national summary touches on key areas including consumer spending, tourism, nonfinancial services, manufacturing, real estate, construction, banking, agriculture, natural resources, and prices and wages. Following the national summary, each District Bank has a three-to-four-page summary of District activity.

Market Reaction to the Beige Book

Markets focus on the national summary of the Beige Book. What moves the markets? It depends on what the big issues of the day are for the economy. If credit markets are tight, financial traders will look for signs of whether banks and others are increasing lending or not. If housing is in the tank, the focus will be for signs of improvement in residential real estate. For instance: are real estate brokers reporting more traffic? If inflation is a worry for the Fed, then any comments on higher prices or wages will jump out.

Fed watchers also have a habit of looking to see what key wording the Fed summary section uses for the economy. For example, the March 4, 2009, Beige Book said "national economic conditions deteriorated further" during a period of recession. A notably earlier Beige Book released on March 15, 2006—when the economy was strong—described the pace of expansion as "moderate or steady." Yes, markets react to the overall characterization of the economy if the description is a change from what markets believed.

And guess what? The Fed knows that financial traders focus on such wording. So the Fed is careful to pick wording in all of the Beige Book sections that is not inappropriately excitable for financial markets. That does not mean the Fed mischaracterizes the economy, but simply chooses its words carefully and avoids language that is over the top.

Here are a few more examples of key wording from past Beige Books:

♦ June 17, 1998 (economy was running smoothly): "Overall, the U.S. economy continues its excellent performance. Output and employment are high while inflation is low." Here, the Fed was in steady-as-you-go mode.

♦ June 14, 2000 (pre-recession economy but with inflation pressures): "Reports from the Federal Reserve Districts indicate that solid economic growth continued in April and May, but that signs of some slowing from the rapid pace earlier in the year are also present. … Indications of worsening price inflation, while not widespread, are reported by several Districts. … Contacts across the country report worker shortages and difficulties in recruiting and hiring; half the Districts indicate that labor shortages are constraining output growth." As you can see here, the Fed sometimes has a tough choice balancing economic growth with keeping inflation low.

♦ October 23, 2002 (slowly recovering after recession): "Most Districts reported that economic activity remained sluggish in September and early October. Retail sales were weak across the nation, including some declines in motor vehicle sales from very high levels." The Fed saw the need to keep interest rates low to help economic recovery from the 2001 recession.

Did you know the Beige Book is generally seen as the last word by the Fed before each FOMC meeting? Throughout the year, the Fed chairman, other Fed governors, and District Bank presidents give speeches on the status of the economy. And the speeches provide updates on Fed thinking on the economy and possible policy moves. But one week before each FOMC meeting there is an unofficial "blackout" of Fed speaking engagements so as to not rattle the markets when they are so sensitive to possible interest rate changes. This is the so-called "Fed blackout period." It's all about Fed speeches. The bottom line? The Beige Book, generally, is the last information directly from the Fed about Fed thinking on the economy before the FOMC meeting.

Key Facts About the FOMC Meeting Statement

There are no more tense moments in financial markets than those just before the 2:15 P.M. EST (or EDT) release of the FOMC meeting statement after the end of the FOMC meeting. Lots of money is put on the line by traders when the Fed is in easing or tightening mode. The big question during those phases is how much the Fed is going to cut rates or raise rates. Bond traders take positions on where interest rates will be. Remember, bond prices go in the opposite direction of interest rates, so the

Fed's interest rate decision affects the value of bond portfolios. And equity traders are betting on what interest rates businesses will have while conducting business—and that affects profits.

Here's what's in the FOMC meeting statement:

◆ Official name: The FOMC meeting statement is a "Press Release," dated the day of the FOMC statement

◆ Release date: Eight times a year, approximately the last week of January, mid-March, the last week of April, the last week of June, the first week of August, mid-September, the last week of October, and mid-December

◆ Produced by: Federal Reserve Board of Governors

◆ Form of data: Press release

◆ Market watchers focus on: Any change in the fed funds target rate and changes in emphasis from prior FOMC statements (view reports at www.federalreserve.gov/monetarypolicy/fomccalendars.htm)

Looking Closer at the FOMC Meeting Statement

Remember, the whole point of FOMC is to make a decision about open market operations at the New York Fed's Trading Desk. Does the Desk keep the fed funds rate the same, raise it, or lower it? Technically, the FOMC meeting statement includes instructions for the Desk about what to do. But the Fed knows the whole financial world is reading the statement, too, and much of the language is for the public's benefit rather than for operational instructions for the Trading Desk.

Let's pick apart an FOMC statement from October 29, 2008. This was a relatively standard statement, although it was during a period when the Fed was aggressively cutting interest rates to fight recession. Most FOMC meeting statements are relatively short. It's the minutes that get really long.

The first part of the statement is the policy decision—that is, what the FOMC decided to do with the fed funds target rate. Let's look at some quotes, followed by an explanation of the statement.

◆ "The Federal Open Market Committee decided today to lower its target for the federal funds rate 50 basis points to 1 percent."

Because this is an instruction for the New York Fed's Trading Desk, this part is called the policy directive or simply the directive. The statement typically follows with discussion about views on economic growth and inflation. Here, we see the Fed concluding that economic growth was turning down and that credit availability was a problem.

♦ "The pace of economic activity appears to have slowed markedly, owing importantly to a decline in consumer expenditures. Business equipment spending and industrial production have weakened in recent months, and slowing economic activity in many foreign economies is damping the prospects for U.S. exports. Moreover, the intensification of financial market turmoil is likely to exert additional restraint on spending, partly by further reducing the ability of households and businesses to obtain credit."

What the Fed says about inflation is important. If the Fed is worried about a rebound in inflation, that is seen as limiting how far the Fed will cut rates, or it could result in the Fed raising rates.

♦ "In light of the declines in the prices of energy and other commodities and the weaker prospects for economic activity, the Committee expects inflation to moderate in coming quarters to levels consistent with price stability."

Here, the Fed concludes that declines in oil prices and other commodities and weak economic growth would lead to lower inflation. This means the Fed sees more room for cutting interest rates if needed. Then the FOMC statement typically gives a hint at what direction the Fed is leaning for future policy moves.

♦ "Recent policy actions, including today's rate reduction, coordinated interest rate cuts by central banks, extraordinary liquidity measures, and official steps to strengthen financial systems, should help over time to improve credit conditions and promote a return to moderate economic growth. Nevertheless, downside risks to growth remain. The Committee will monitor economic and financial developments carefully and will act as needed to promote sustainable economic growth and price stability."

This section gives what is known as the Fed's "policy bias." This is not some long-term preference for what goals should be for inflation or GDP growth. Policy bias is simply what the Fed thinks it is more likely to do at the next meeting if a change in policy is needed. Another way to put it is that policy bias is whether the Fed is more worried "right now" about economic growth being too slow (or negative) or inflation rising. Fed policy biases generally are described as "anti-inflation bias," "anti-recession bias," or "neutral bias" (risks are equally balanced, roughly).

In the previous quote from the statement, key words on the policy bias are "downside risks remain," indicating an anti-recession bias and a leaning toward cutting rates again if needed.

The next section in the statement shows how the FOMC members voted—either for the policy action or against it:

> "Voting for the FOMC monetary policy action were: Ben S. Bernanke, Chairman; Timothy F. Geithner, Vice Chairman; Elizabeth A. Duke; Richard W. Fisher; Donald L. Kohn; Randall S. Kroszner; Sandra Pianalto; Charles I. Plosser; Gary H. Stern; and Kevin M. Warsh."

Because FOMC decisions generally are made by consensus and because the Fed likes a united front when possible, most FOMC decisions are unanimous, but not always.

Finally, the FOMC statement has a section on the Board's separate action in approving a change in the discount rate if the fed funds rate was changed at the meeting:

> "In a related action, the Board of Governors unanimously approved a 50-basis-point decrease in the discount rate to $1\frac{1}{4}$ percent. In taking this action, the Board approved the requests submitted by the Boards of Directors of the Federal Reserve Banks of Boston, New York, Cleveland, and San Francisco."

Remember, the Fed almost always moves the discount rate in tandem with the fed funds rate. Only the Board of Governors votes on discount rate changes, but only after a request for a change from one or more District Banks.

An Anti-Inflation Bias Example

What do key portions of the statement look like when the Fed is worried about inflation? An example is the May 10, 2006, meeting statement. The Fed voted to raise the fed funds target by 25 basis points, but still states concern about possible rising inflation pressures. Here's an example of a quote that shows the Fed is worried about inflation:

> "Economic growth has been quite strong so far this year."

> "As yet, the run-up in the prices of energy and other commodities appears to have had only a modest effect on core inflation, ongoing productivity gains have helped to hold the growth of unit labor costs in check, and inflation expectations remain contained. Still, possible increases in resource utilization, in combination with the elevated prices of energy and other commodities, have the potential to add to inflation pressures."

The Committee judges that some further policy firming may yet be needed to address inflation risks, but emphasizes that the extent and timing of any such firming will depend importantly on the evolution of the economic outlook as implied by incoming information.

We see the Fed noting that the economic growth was strong and inflation pressures could be picking up. During periods of extended economic expansion and high resource utilization (that means factories are running full tilt and unemployment is low), the Fed will have an anti-inflation bias, as shown in the above statement.

Dissent at the FOMC

Remember that we said most FOMC votes are unanimous? Well, that means some are not. From time to time, one or more FOMC members dissent because they have a different view on the risks on inflation or economic growth or even over the best way to implement policy changes.

At the August 8, 2006, meeting, the Fed voted to keep the fed funds rate steady at 5¼ percent. The vote was 9 to 1 for the rate to be unchanged. After listing those voting for an unchanged rate, the meeting statement gave the dissenting vote:

> "Voting against was Jeffrey M. Lacker, who preferred an increase of 25 basis points in the federal funds rate target at this meeting."

Federal Reserve Bank of Richmond President Jeffrey Lacker continued to dissent in the same manner for the rest of the FOMC meetings in 2006. Lacker rotated out of a voting position in 2007. Sometimes dissenting positions are ahead of the curve for the next change in the fed funds rate and sometimes not. The next change in the fed funds target was downward on September 18, 2007.

A very interesting dissent on how policy should be implemented occurred at the January 28, 2009, FOMC vote. The Fed in December 2008 had just cut the fed funds target to an historically low range of zero to ¼ percent and in January was looking for additional ways to add liquidity into financial markets (more on that in Chapter 21 on quantitative easing). The overall FOMC voted to continue to expand its balance sheets by new and nontraditional purchases of government agency debt (such as from Fannie Mae and Freddie Mac) and mortgage-backed securities. Guess who was back in the voting rotation? Yes, Richmond's Jeffrey Lacker. This time he dissented because he did not like how the Fed was targeting specific segments of credit markets. Lacker, mentioned in the statement that follows, had what he believed to be a better idea for adding liquidity beyond having a near-zero fed funds rate.

> "Voting against was Jeffrey M. Lacker, who preferred to expand the monetary base at this time by purchasing U.S. Treasury securities rather than through targeted credit programs."

Lacker saw purchasing longer-term Treasuries (in addition to the short-term Treasuries the Fed typically buys) as being less disruptive of credit markets by not showing favoritism to any one segment. This time, Lacker was a prophet rather than just a dissenter. The Fed adopted his position in part by announcing at the very next FOMC meeting that it would indeed improve credit markets by purchasing "up to $300 billion of longer-term Treasury securities over the next six months." But the Fed kept its programs for purchasing other nontraditional securities as well.

Hawks vs. Doves

Occasionally, you'll see or hear the media call certain Fed governors or District Bank presidents *hawks* or *doves*. What does that mean? It's in reference to how trigger happy or not they are to fight inflation. Some are more sensitive to building inflation pressures than other governors or bank presidents.

def•i•ni•tion

A **hawk,** in regard to inflation, is someone (typically in reference to a Fed official) who believes that inflation has a negative impact on business and society and pursues more aggressive monetary policy to keep inflation low. Inflation hawks believe low inflation fosters economic growth.

A **dove,** in regard to inflation, is someone (typically in reference to a Fed official) who believes that inflation is less of a threat and focuses on looser monetary policy to boost economic growth.

While dissents exist often because an FOMC member is worried about staving off recession, most dissents are over not having a strong enough policy against inflation at times. And most dissents come from District Bank presidents and not Board governors. District Bank presidents generally have longer tenure with the Fed than Board governors. They have more experience with business cycles and tend to see the benefits of low inflation more than Board governors. District Bank presidents have closer ties to local bankers and businesses who like low inflation. Some recent well-known inflation hawks have included Dallas Fed President Richard Fisher, Richmond Fed President Jeffrey Lacker, and St. Louis Fed President James Bullard. But sometimes, District Bank presidents fall in the other camp—doves who are more willing to use the fed funds rate to keep growth high. One recent example is San Francisco Fed President Janet Yellen.

Market Reaction to the FOMC Statement

We've covered a lot about the FOMC statement and actually have touched on what markets care about. Let's take a look at the types of questions that concern the market:

♦ Did the FOMC change the fed funds target rate, and if so, by as much as markets expected?

♦ Were there any changes in statement wording that show the Fed changing its views of the economy? For instance, is the recession getting worse or are there signs of rising inflation?

♦ Did the Fed change its policy bias?

♦ Were there any dissenting votes? Did the dissent give any indications of possible changes in future FOMC votes?

Key Facts About the FOMC Meeting Minutes

The highlight of the FOMC cycle, of course, is the meeting statement. But the statement is quite short and does not go into all of the details of why the FOMC made its decision. The FOMC minutes go in depth into the FOMC's thought process.

Historically, the meeting minutes would come out with a long lag. The Fed would release the "previous" meeting's minutes two days after the "latest" FOMC meeting—a lag of six to eight weeks. But then the Fed began a gradual campaign of increased "transparency," in which the public and markets were made more aware of Fed policy more quickly. In 1994, the Fed began announcing its policy statement at the end of each meeting. And then in late 2004, the Fed moved up the release of FOMC minutes to just three weeks after the FOMC meeting! Now the meeting minutes are timely enough to matter to the markets.

Here's what's in the FOMC meeting minutes:

♦ Official name: Minutes of the Federal Open Market Committee

♦ Release date: Eight times a year, three weeks after the FOMC meeting. While the Beige Book is always released on a Wednesday, the FOMC minutes are always released three weeks to the day after the FOMC statement. If the FOMC meeting ends on a Tuesday, the minutes are released on a Tuesday.

- ◆ Produced by: Federal Reserve Board of Governors

- ◆ Form of data: Detailed minutes of the meeting

- ◆ Market watchers focus on: Hints at what the next FOMC policy move will be (view reports at www.federalreserve.gov/monetarypolicy/fomccalendars.htm)

Looking Closer at the FOMC Meeting Minutes

The FOMC meeting minutes are extremely detailed. They start with rather dry (for most) instructions for the Trading Desk on operations, including for actions taken on behalf of the Treasury, such as for foreign currency. The section after the open market operation instructions are what financial markets focus more on. These sections include: Staff Review of the Economic and Financial Situation, Staff Economic Outlook, and Meeting Participants' Views and Committee Policy Action. By "staff," this is the staff of the Board of Governors—generally the Board economists in this context.

Market Reaction to the FOMC Meeting Minutes

Most of the fireworks take place the afternoon the FOMC meeting statement is released. The minutes get market reaction only if there is significantly new insight on Fed thinking contained in the minutes. Analysts focus on changes in the Board's views of the economy and economic outlook. For example, the meeting minutes of the January 27-28, 2009, meeting, released on February 18, painted a picture in which the Board staff economists revised their forecast for economic growth downward sharply.

> "In the forecast prepared for the meeting, the staff revised down its outlook for economic activity in the first half of 2009, as the implications of weaker-than-anticipated economic data releases more than offset an upward revision to the staff's assumption of the amount of forthcoming fiscal stimulus."

The minutes also provide much more detail on the debate between FOMC participants with different views on the economy. Leading up to the adoption of the FOMC directive, there is extensive discussion on current economic conditions and general forecast for economic growth and inflation. You cannot find a better summary of the current U.S. economy than in the FOMC minutes.

Finally, a relatively new facet of the minutes that actually does get market attention is the quarterly economic forecasts of the Board governors and District Bank presidents.

The Fed's Economic Forecast

Historically, the Fed chairman would present the Fed's economic forecasts to Congress twice a year with the Federal Reserve's semi-annual monetary policy report to Congress. In this report (discussed in Chapter 21), the Fed included forecasts for key indicators such as GDP (real and nominal), the PCE price index (because it is preferred to the CPI), and the civilian unemployment rate. These forecasts are not those prepared by the Board staff for each FOMC meeting. Fed District presidents and governors each provide their forecasts, which are compiled to form a consensus or "central tendency." The central tendency forecasts exclude the three highest and three lowest projections for each variable in each year.

On November 20, 2007, the Federal Reserve changed its policy of how frequently and when it would release its forecasts. The Fed now releases economic projections four times a year (every other FOMC meeting). Projections made by members of the Board of Governors and Federal Reserve Bank presidents are published with the minutes of the FOMC meetings scheduled for January, April, June, and October. The forecasts released at the end of January and at the end of June become part of the Fed's semi-annual monetary policy report to Congress.

Markets pay attention to changes in the Fed forecasts. What matters is whether the forecasts are in line with what traders believed the Fed view of the economy to be. With the greater frequency of these forecasts, they provide more timely hints on whether the Fed is likely to make a policy change in the near future.

Take a look at the economic projections chart that follows. Forecasts for real GDP, PCE price inflation, and PCE price inflation excluding food and energy are for fourth-quarter-over-fourth-quarter growth rates. The forecast for the unemployment rate is for each year's fourth quarter average level.

Economic Projections of Federal Reserve Governors and Reserve Bank Presidents January 27–28, 2009, FOMC Meeting Released February 18, 2009

Fourth-Quarter-Over-Fourth-Quarter Percent Changes and Fourth Quarter Average for Unemployment Rate

Central Tendencies	2009	2010	2011
Change in real GDP	–1.3 to -0.5	2.5 to 3.3	3.8 to 5.0
October projection	*–0.2 to 1.1*	*2.3 to 3.2*	*2.8 to 3.6*

Central Tendencies	2009	2010	2011
Unemployment rate	8.5 to 8.8	8.0 to 8.3	6.7 to 7.5
October projection	*7.1 to 7.6*	*6.5 to 7.3*	*5.5 to 6.6*
PCE inflation	0.3 to 1.0	1.0 to 1.5	0.9 to 1.7
October projection	*1.3 to 2.0*	*1.4 to 1.8*	*1.4 to 1.7*
Core PCE inflation	0.9 to 1.1	0.8 to 1.5	0.7 to 1.5
October projection	*1.5 to 2.0*	*1.3 to 1.8*	*1.3 to 1.7*

The Fed added to the forecast traditions with those included in the minutes for the January 27–28, 2009, meeting. For the first time, FOMC participants were asked to provide forecasts for the "longer run." According to the Fed minutes, longer-run projections "represent each participant's assessment of the rate to which each variable would be expected to converge under appropriate monetary policy and in the absence of further shocks to the economy."

In plain English, the long-run forecast gives views on what real GDP growth is sustainable without causing a rise in inflation from low rates. The long-run unemployment rate also is one that is as low as we can get without risking a surge in inflation. Similarly, the long-run forecast for PCE price inflation indicates what the FOMC members believe should be the objective of monetary policy. This last item is especially important. While the Fed has two objectives—healthy economic growth and low inflation—most FOMC participants believe economic growth is best encouraged by a stable economy with low inflation. The long-run inflation forecasts provide a benchmark to compare actual inflation rates to see whether the Fed should be worried about raising rates to lower inflation or not.

Many in the Fed, including Chairman Bernanke, have indicated that they see the benefits of inflation targeting. Some countries actually do announce inflation targets. The argument is that if the public knows what the target is and believes the Fed will maintain inflation within the target in the long run, then inflation expectations are more firmly anchored. The Fed has never adopted official inflation targets, but the new "longer-run" forecasts now appear to include an unofficial inflation target, and this may be as close as the Fed gets to an official inflation target.

Take a look at the Fed central tendency forecasts table that follows. Before the Fed began publishing longer-run forecasts, most viewed the farthest year out in Fed forecasts as indicating long-term Fed preferences. However, some saw the economy taking more than two or three years to return to optimal growth, inflation, and unemployment. The longer-run forecasts are supposed to be achievable within 5 to 10 years. The Fed does not publish a long-run forecast for the core PCE price index because it is believed in the long run the headline and the core PCE price index grow at the same rate.

Fed Central Tendency Forecasts, Longer Run

Change in real GDP	2.5 to 2.7
October projection	*N/A*
Unemployment rate	4.8 to 5.0
October projection	*N/A*
PCE inflation	1.7 to 2.0
October projection	*N/A*

Check out the PCE inflation chart that follows. Based on the combination of farthest-out forecast years and on the longer-run forecast, it is generally believed that the Fed's implicit inflation target for the PCE price index is 1½ to 2 percent at an annualized pace.

PCE Inflation and the Fed's Implicit Inflation Target.

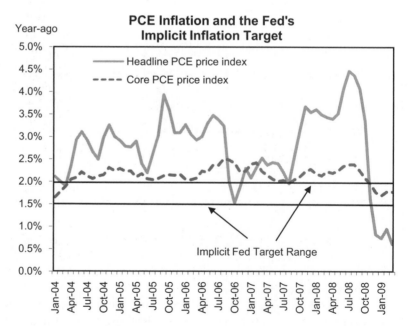

During the latter part of the expansion after the 2001 recession, inflation generally was above the Fed's comfort zone. The recession (beginning in 2008) and lower oil prices brought core inflation back into the Fed's target range. Sharp swings in oil prices have caused overall PCE price inflation to also gyrate quite a bit.

Fed Forecasts over Time

Comparing Fed forecasts over time clearly shows that the Fed adjusted its views of the economy sharply during the early and later phases of the latest recession.

Early in 2008, the Fed did not yet see the dramatic impact of the subprime loan crisis on the economy and so expected economic growth to be moderately healthy. By January 2009, the Fed had seen several financial crises and economic data had worsened, resulting in a sharply lower real GDP forecast for 2009. Each year, the Fed expands the forecast by one year each October FOMC meeting as seen in the fed forecasts and real GDP growth chart.

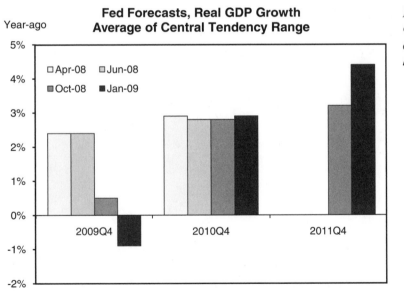

Fed Forecasts, Real GDP Growth, line one; Average of Central Tendency Range, line two.

While the Fed has access to a lot more information than the rest of us, the Fed is not infallible. That's another reason it is good that the Fed publishes its forecasts more frequently. The Fed actually wants the public to know how its views on the economy are changing.

The Least You Need to Know

- ◆ The Beige Book contains up-to-date economic information that's used to make decisions at the FOMC meetings.

- ◆ The FOMC statement is a release that states what economic decisions were made at the FOMC meeting.

- ◆ The FOMC minutes explains the economic decisions made at the FOMC meeting.

- ◆ Markets react if the Fed's forecast isn't in line with what the traders believe to be the Fed's viewpoint of the economy.

Chapter 21

More Fed Reports and Quantitative Easing

In This Chapter

- Monetary Policy Report to the Congress
- Discount rate meeting minutes
- Quantitative easing and the Fed's balance sheet
- How money supply and bank reserves have gained in importance

We've covered the Fed's reports that lead into, cover, and explain monetary policy decisions at each FOMC (Federal Open Market Committee) meeting. But there are a few other reports that are important for Fed watchers and for those who want to see what impact these reports have on financial markets. And guess what? We finally talk more about quantitative easing!

Key Facts About the Monetary Policy Report to the Congress

While the president makes key appointments to the Fed, including picking the chairman, the Fed really is a creature of Congress. The Fed was created by Congress under its constitutional authority to coin money. Congress created the Fed and can change the Fed as it sees fit. However, it should be quickly pointed out that Congress likes letting the Fed make all the tough decisions about interest rates. In fact, if there were a credibility contest between Congress and the Fed, Congress would need lots of PR help and the Fed would still be the clear winner. The Fed is seen as being more interested in focusing on the public good.

On the other hand, Congress likes having the Fed come to Capitol Hill to explain what it's doing. There are two statutorily mandated appearances by the Fed before Congress. These are for the Monetary Policy Report to the Congress twice a year. This report was originally called the Humphrey-Hawkins Report because the requirement to appear before Congress fell under the Full Employment and Balanced Growth Act of 1978, sponsored by Senators Humphrey and Hawkins. That act expired in 2000, but the Fed still reports to Congress twice a year under Section 2B of the Federal Reserve Act.

In late February and in late June, the Fed chair presents the Monetary Policy Report to the Congress and gives testimony to the Senate Committee on Banking, Housing, and Urban Affairs, followed the next day by testimony to the House Committee on Financial Services.

Here's what's in the Monetary Policy Report to the Congress:

- Official name: Monetary Policy Report to the Congress

- Release date: Twice a year, typically the last week of February and mid-July

- Produced by: Federal Reserve Board of Governors

- Form of data: Economic commentary with charts and forecast data (view Monetary Policy reports at www.federalreserve.gov/monetarypolicy/mpr_default. htm)

All of the Federal Reserve Chairman's speeches are posted on the Fed's website, along with those of other Fed governors, at www.federalreserve.gov/newsevents/ speech/2009speech.htm.

Looking Closer at the Monetary Policy Report to the Congress

The Monetary Policy Report to the Congress contains extensive discussions of the state of the U.S. economy and the Fed's policy actions over the past six months. While it is a very useful summary of the economy, there is no new news in this part of the report. Traditionally, what used to provide market excitement was the Fed's semi-annual economic forecasts. In past years, this was the only time that financial markets got to see the Fed's view of where the economy was headed in terms of actual numbers. Now that information is outdated, as the projections are already released in the quarterly forecasts in the FOMC minutes from every other meeting. Today, the only real action is when the Fed chairman testifies before Congress. The Fed chairman's prepared testimony is published separately on the Board of Governors website.

Key Facts About the Discount Rate Meeting Minutes

As discussed in Chapter 19, any changes in the discount rate must be approved by the Federal Reserve Board of Governors after any change is requested by a District Bank. The Board does keep minutes of its meetings to approve or not approve requests for changes. These minutes are a little-known report to financial markets but they can provide valuable insight into policy thoughts of District Banks.

Here's what's in the discount rate meeting minutes:

◆ Official name: Minutes of Board of Governors Discount Rate Meetings

◆ Release date: Irregular, approximately every six to eight weeks

◆ Produced by: Federal Reserve Board of Governors

◆ Form of data: Moderately detailed minutes of the meetings

◆ Market watchers focus on: Number of District Banks requesting discount rate change versus those not requesting (view discount rate meeting minutes at www.federalreserve.gov/monetarypolicy/discountrate.htm)

Looking Closer at the Discount Rate Meeting Minutes

These minutes first report which District Banks have requested a change in the discount rate or have requested maintaining the existing rate. Not all District Banks are on the same schedule for when to consider changing the discount rate, so the minutes report the different times each District Bank submits its discount rate request.

Next, the minutes report the views of the Federal Reserve Bank directors on the status of the economy and why they decided on their request to change the discount rate or keep it unchanged. Here's an example from the January 26, 2009, minutes when the economy was deep in recession:

> "Federal Reserve Bank directors generally agreed that economic conditions had weakened further. Some directors commented that heightened uncertainty over the economic outlook, asset prices, and government efforts to provide liquidity and strengthen financial institutions was adversely affecting financial markets and households' and businesses' spending decisions. Others noted that a credit crunch was restraining economic activity. Most directors viewed inflationary pressures as subsiding in response to falling commodity prices and increased economic slack. With credit conditions in financial markets remaining tight and given the weak economic outlook and the downside risks to that outlook, the directors concluded that very low short-term interest rates remained appropriate. Accordingly, they recommended maintaining the existing primary credit rate."

Then the minutes state the Board of Governors' determination. Generally, the Board defers any change in the discount rate to when the FOMC meets.

Market Reaction to the Discount Rate Meeting Minutes

The discount rate meeting minutes is an off-the-radar report for most of the financial media. But for serious Fed watchers, it provides insight into any developing dissent within the Fed regarding monetary policy. A request for a change in the discount rate is the most common way for District Banks to express displeasure with the majority vote on policy at the FOMC meeting. It also is how local businesses—through their District Bank's board of directors—vocalize their views on monetary policy.

How do we see such dissents? From time to time, the minutes indicate which District Banks are requesting changes in the discount rate that are not approved by the Board of Governors. As an example, the minutes of December 11, 2006, show the Federal Reserve Bank of Richmond being more concerned about inflation. The other 11 District Banks preferred to maintain the existing discount rate. Here's what was reported about the Richmond request:

> "Directors who preferred to increase the primary credit rate did not consider the data to date to present persuasive evidence of slowing inflation. In this light, they believed that additional firming was needed to effect a significant reduction in inflation pressures."

The discount rate request is an important outlet for District Bank sentiment on policy. All District Banks rotate on the FOMC with official votes (except for the New York Fed, which always votes), which means that they don't always have impact on the FOMC vote. But every two weeks, all District Banks can state their views on monetary policy on the discount rate and "send a message" to the Board about what they think. The media really should pay more attention to the discount rate meeting minutes to get more insight into how District Bank presidents are thinking about monetary policy.

Quantitative Easing and the Fed's Balance Sheet

We mentioned in Chapter 19 that a new tool of the Fed is quantitative easing. Let's see what that is and how it shows up in Fed reports.

If you think quantitative easing sounds very technical, you are right. But it can be boiled down to key ideas. So far, we've talked about monetary policy in terms of higher and lower interest rates. That is the traditional approach to monetary policy—raising and lowering the fed funds rate. That is, the Fed trades reserves for short-term Treasury securities. But with the subprime loan crisis starting around 2007, monetary policy moved beyond just interest rates. Especially during 2007 and 2008, credit markets froze up because financial market players were unsure about the quality of many bundled securities, such as for mortgage-backed assets. Banks and other financial institutions did not know what financial assets to trust and were unwilling to lend with those assets as collateral.

To improve financial markets, the Fed cut the fed funds target in December 2008 to a range of zero to one quarter percent, or essentially zero. But the Fed believed more liquidity was needed in the financial markets than would be provided by a near-zero fed funds rate.

Now, we get to the reasons for quantitative easing. After it cut the fed funds rate to essentially zero, the Fed saw the need for two objectives. These were: to keep adding to liquidity overall (money available for lending) and to swap low-quality assets (such as mortgage-backed securities that included subprime loans) for high-quality, highly liquid assets (such as Fed reserves). Quantitative easing is simply a balance sheet strategy for the Fed to do two things. First, the Fed keeps adding liquidity to financial markets without further lowering short-term interest rates by trading Fed reserves for some other asset on the market (in addition to short-term Treasuries). Second, the Fed engages in quantitative easing by buying low-quality assets with high-quality financial assets.

The second part overlaps with the first—with the point being to add to liquidity in part by taking off the market toxic assets of banks. St. Louis Fed President James

Bullard was one of the first Fed officials to start calling this new policy quantitative easing (citing earlier experiences by the Bank of Japan) in a speech on November 20, 2008, titled "Three Funerals and a Wedding:

> "Hint, traditional monetary policy was one of the funerals. In case you're unclear about it, traditional monetary policy is raising or lowering short-term interest rates by swapping reserves for short-term Treasury securities.

> "Whether the FOMC decides to stay on hold at this point or eases further and then stays on hold at some lower level, even zero, may not be the most critical question. The fact is, monetary policy defined as movements in short-term nominal interest rates is coming to an end, at least for now. It's a funeral for a friend.

> "One idea from the Japanese experience is that, with nominal interest rates at very low levels, more attention may have to be paid to quantitative measures of monetary policy."

Bullard's full speech can be found on the St. Louis Fed website at www.stlouisfed.org/news/speeches.html.

Only from an Economist

Quantitative easing means using the Fed's balance sheet to add liquidity without changing interest rates. The Fed swaps reserves for illiquid assets already in the financial markets and for high-quality assets that are longer maturities than the Fed normally buys.

In another speech on March 24, 2009, St. Louis Fed President Bullard went into more explanation about quantitative easing.

> "Since December 2007, the Federal Reserve has established several lending programs to provide liquidity and improve the functioning of key credit markets. The Term Auction Facility, Term Securities Lending Facility, and the Primary Dealer Credit Facility, for example, help ensure that financial institutions have adequate access to short-term credit. The Commercial Paper Funding Facility provides a backstop for the market for high-quality commercial paper. … Finally, over the past year, the Fed has provided loans to support specific financial institutions [Bear Stearns, Citibank, and Bank of America, though not cited by Bullard]. The TAF, CPFF, and swaps in particular have added about $1 trillion to the size of the Fed's balance sheet in recent months. … More recently, the Federal Reserve announced that it would purchase substantial quantities of debt and mortgage-backed securities issued by Fannie Mae and Freddie Mac."

Detailed information about these credit programs can be found on a special Fed web page at www.federalreserve.gov/monetarypolicy/bst.htm.

Later, the Fed announced in March 2009 that it would be buying long-term Treasury securities to add liquidity to financial markets and to bring down longer-term interest rates—more quantitative easing outside the realm of moving short-term interest rates.

How do we keep up with all of these programs? All of these facilities and programs affect the size and composition of the Fed balance sheet—its assets and liabilities. A key point about quantitative easing is that it exists only if the Fed makes it happen. Before September 2008, the Fed offset the sharp increases in its lending to financial institutions by selling Treasury securities in the open market. This drained the rapid growth in reserves and initially kept the new facilities from affecting the overall size of the Fed balance sheet and the growth rate of the monetary base. But in the autumn of 2008, the Fed decided to not offset the surge in reserves from the new credit facilities, and this became quantitative easing. During quantitative easing, if you are a Fed watcher, you have to keep up with quantitative measures of monetary policy.

> **Trader Tip**
>
> While the Fed conducts quantitative easing, the Fed uses its ability to pay interest on bank reserves to keep the fed funds rate from falling below the desired level.

The Fed's quantitative easing can be seen in the surge in total borrowings by depository institutions (mainly banks). The level of borrowings slipped in early 2009 as some financial institutions no longer needed emergency credit obtained during autumn 2008. However, the Fed still was expanding its purchases of longer-term Treasury securities and also for mortgage-backed securities.

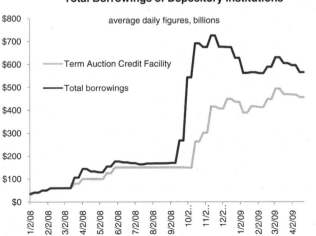

Total Borrowings of Depository Institutions.

Key Facts About Money Supply

Probably the broadest quantitative measure of monetary policy is *money supply*. Money supply, or money stock, is the total amount of money available in an economy at a given time. We care about money supply because it affects how much money and credit are available for spending. Typically, money supply is inversely related to interest rates. The lower interest rates are (notably fed funds), the faster money supply growth is. But with quantitative easing, the Fed can expand or contract money supply without changing the fed funds rate.

def•i•ni•tion

Money supply is the amount of money in circulation at a given time.

There are two key measures of money supply, called M1 and M2. The "Ms" refer to narrower and broader definitions of money supply and you may want to track different definitions. The smaller the M number, the narrower the definition is. The lower the M number, the more liquid (readily spendable) the money is. The Fed has a detailed list of what goes into each of these definitions of money supply but here are the condensed versions.

M1 is the cash in the public's hands, traveler's checks, demand deposits (in checking, not savings) at commercial banks, demand deposits at credit unions, and demand deposits at savings & loan banks. Basically, we are talking about circulating cash plus checking accounts. M1 is the most liquid form of money supply.

M2 is M1 plus savings accounts plus small-denomination time deposits (less than $100,000) plus retail money market mutual funds. A time deposit is a particular type of savings account or certificate of deposit with a fixed term and the deposit can only be withdrawn by giving written notice. IRA and Keogh balances are excluded from M2. Basically, M2 is M1 plus short-term savings accounts.

The Fed currently just tracks money supply numbers for M1, M2—plus a few select types of deposits not found in M2. Previously, the Fed collected and published data for an M3 measure of money supply. M3 consisted of M2 plus large-denomination ($100,000 or more) time deposits; repurchase agreements issued by depository institutions; Eurodollar deposits; and institutional money market mutual funds. The Fed ceased publication of M3 in March 2006 due to the high cost of collecting the additional underlying data and due to a conclusion by the Fed that M3 did not convey additional information about economic activity not already found in M2.

The money supply data are released each week in a Fed statistical report called "H.6" (H is used by the Fed to designate weekly reports) or, more formally, Money Stock Measures.

Here's what's in the H.6 report:

- ◆ Official name: Money Stock Measures

- ◆ Release date: Weekly, Thursday, for the week ending on Monday, two Mondays before

- ◆ Produced by: Federal Reserve Board of Governors

- ◆ Form of data: Dollars, levels, and annualized change from prior week

- ◆ Market watchers focus on: Dollar change in M2 version in money supply from prior week (view money supply reports at www.federalreserve.gov/releases/h6/current/h6.htm)

The following table shows what financial markets focus on for each week's money supply report—the weekly change. This is simply the difference between the latest week's money supply level (in billions of dollars) minus the previous week's level.

Money Supply for Week Ending March 9, 2009

Changes and Levels in Billions of U.S. Dollars

	Week Ending:		
	09-Mar-09	**02-Mar-09**	**23-Feb-09**
M2, Level	8,343.1	8,303.3	8,274.2
Weekly change	39.8	29.1	–4.5
M1, Level	1,577.1	1,561.3	1,544.8
Weekly change	15.8	16.5	–13.4

Tracking Money Supply

The key point about money supply is that it is another way of looking at how much liquidity is in the financial system. It reflects money available for spending. Consumers and businesses don't have to spend all of the money in their checking and savings, but they can't spend at all without having funds in those accounts. Faster money supply growth accommodates more spending. It also can lead to more inflation if money supply grows too fast and allows spending to outstrip growth in what is actually produced by the economy.

Weekly numbers for money supply can be volatile, so it is more important to track a longer trend (monthly or quarterly) to see whether growth in money supply is rising or falling. The M2 definition is better for tracking purposes since it is broader and is still a quite liquid measure of money supply. Although in recent years, financial markets have not given money supply much attention (due to the Fed focusing on interest rates for policy moves), money supply has gotten increased focus during the Fed's shift to quantitative easing. Money supply is where the Fed's additional liquidity injections show up if banks are lending.

The money supply growth chart below shows the Fed letting money supply grow sharply during the latter part of 2008 and into 2009 due to quantitative easing. Notice how much stronger the growth rate is during that period when a shorter period comparison is used (three-months-ago annualized versus year-ago).

Money Supply Growth, M2.

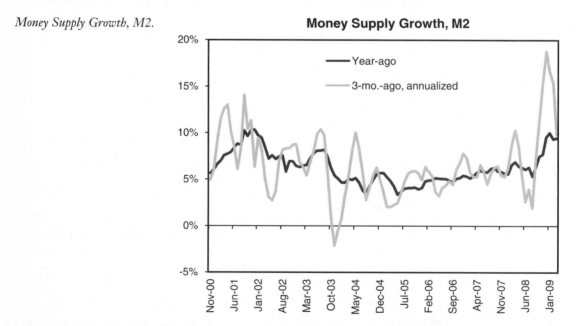

Key Facts About the Reserve Balances and the Monetary Base

Quantitative measures of monetary policy that are related to money supply are reserve balances and monetary base. Banks are required to hold certain reserves in the form of vault cash or reserves with the Fed. These reserves are held against loans made by banks. Excess reserves (above required reserves) can be loaned out and are a source of profits for banks. Banks minimize their excess reserves by making loans. The bottom line? Reserve growth is a source of credit for the economy. Faster growth in bank reserves means loans can grow faster, which also boosts money supply.

The most recognized building block for money supply is the monetary base. The Fed has some adjustments to this definition, but the monetary base is basically total reserves plus the cash component of money supply. The monetary base forms the backbone of how much banks can lend.

At the same time each week (Thursdays at 4:30 P.M. EST), the Fed releases money supply numbers; the Fed also releases data on reserves of depository institutions, including the monetary base.

Here's what's in the H.3 report, or the Aggregate Reserves of Depository Institutions and the Monetary Base:

- Official name: Aggregate Reserves of Depository Institutions and the Monetary Base

- Release date: Weekly, Thursday, for the week ending on Wednesday of the prior week

- Produced by: Federal Reserve Board of Governors

- Form of data: Dollars, levels

- Market watchers focus on: Dollar change in total reserves and monetary base from prior week (view H.3 reports at www.federalreserve.gov/releases/h3/current/h3.htm)

As seen in the monetary base chart that follows, the monetary base surged when the Fed began engaging in quantitative easing in late 2008. Generally, the monetary base grows at a moderate pace, typically ranging from 3 to 6 percent on a year-ago basis. Growth is somewhat higher and lower, respectively, during periods of easy or tight monetary policy. The Fed saw the need for dramatic measures after a resurgence of the credit crisis in late 2008 and autumn crash of the stock market that year. Instead of bumping up growth in the monetary base to the 10 percent vicinity as was the case after the 2001 recession, the Fed in late 2008 boosted the growth rate to an astonishing 100 percent! When the Fed pulls back on quantitative easing, the monetary base will be one of the places you see the impact relatively quickly.

Monetary Base.

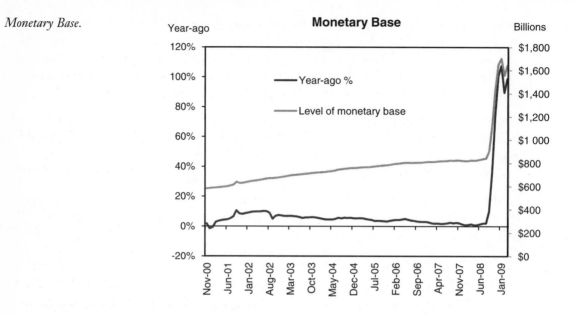

Tracking money supply, the monetary base, and interest rates is important for traders and investors. While the weekly reports put out by the Fed are timely, there is not a lot of context. But there is a publication that collects all of these numbers in one place—though on a monthly basis. One of the most concise reports on money supply, reserves, and related monetary trends is published by the St. Louis Fed. This report, *Monetary Trends,* can be found on the St. Louis Fed's website at www.research. stlouisfed.org/publications/mt/.

Key Facts About Factors Affecting Reserve Balances

Now we get to the nitty-gritty of the Fed's balance sheet. Remember, quantitative easing is all about using the Fed's balance sheet to expand credit. The Fed's H.4.1 report, Factors Affecting Reserve Balances, is probably the most technical weekly report of those addressing Fed balance sheet issues.

Here's what's in the H.4.1 report:

- ◆ Official name: Factors Affecting Reserve Balances

- ◆ Release date: Weekly, Thursday, for the week ending on Wednesday (the day before)

- ◆ Produced by: Federal Reserve Board of Governors

- ◆ Form of data: Dollars, levels, and change from prior week

- ◆ Market watchers focus on: District Bank credit (view the H.4.1 report at www. federalreserve.gov/releases/h41/Current/)

This report has two main sections: the first half shows factors supplying reserves; the second half shows factors absorbing (using) reserves. An example of a factor supplying reserves is U.S. Treasury securities held by the Fed Banks. An example of a factor absorbing reserves is currency in circulation.

Because the Fed went to an interest-rate-targeting method of implementing monetary policy in the mid-1980s, markets have not paid much attention to this report. But it has grown again in importance with quantitative easing. This is the report that shows you how much the special credit programs are growing or contracting. This is also where we first saw the impact of the Fed's quantitative easing in late 2008. When the Fed unwinds its credit easing, you will see the changes first for the special line items in this report.

Since the Fed began creating new credit facilities in 2007 and 2008, it has had to add a number of special line items in the section of the report for factors supplying reserve funds. These special line items have included: term auction credit; primary dealer and other broker-dealer credit; Asset-Backed Commercial Paper Money Market Mutual Fund Liquidity Facility; credit extended to American International Group, Inc.; and Term Asset-Backed Securities Loan Facility. Some of these terms are capitalized because they refer to specific programs created by the Fed (and sometimes in collaboration with the Treasury) to meet specific credit objectives during the recent credit crisis. Odds are there will be other special line items added and later taken out when the programs stop.

The point is that these line items are where quantitative easing showed up first in official reports. When the Fed cuts back on quantitative easing (reducing these special credits), this is where you will see it first.

The Least You Need to Know

- ◆ Requesting changes in the discount rate is one way District Fed Banks can voice displeasure with the direction of monetary policy.

- ◆ Quantitative easing is using the Fed's balance sheet to add liquidity without changing interest rates.

◆ Quantitative easing can show up in changes in bank reserves and in money supply.

◆ The first place you see quantitative easing show up is in the Fed's H.4.1 report on Factors Affecting Reserve Balances.

Chapter 22

What Financial Markets Tell Us About Fed Policy

In This Chapter

◆ Learning about fed funds futures

◆ How the yield curve affects Fed policy

◆ Why the real fed funds rate is important

◆ Understanding the TED spread

There's no shortage of commentary on financial news websites about what the Fed's thinking. Sometimes these sites know what they are talking about, and sometimes, well, they miss the boat entirely! But what are the people who are putting real money on the line saying about the Fed? That is, when traders and investors put their own and their clients' money into the financial markets, what does that say about monetary policy? If you know where to look, the financial markets are "tea leaves" for Fed policy.

Before we jump into fed funds futures, note that there's a difference in this chapter from the "indicator" chapters. In this chapter, the indicator is market data instead of a government report (although some market data can be found published in government reports).

Okay, ready for your last step to becoming a bonafide Fed watcher? It only takes a little bit more work to learn and understand some key secrets of professionals. Relax and read on!

So, What Are Fed Funds Futures?

Here's what's really neat about *fed funds futures*. They sound extremely complicated to understand, but for just figuring out Fed policy implications, they're actually simple. Yes, you can do it and come off as a sophisticated Fed watcher. If you want to actually trade fed funds futures, yes, that's more complicated—and we "aren't going there." But to just understand what they mean for market beliefs on Fed policy, that's easy!

def•i•ni•tion

Fed funds futures are standardized contracts where the owner buys or sells fed funds at a specified date in the future at a specified price.

First, remember from Chapter 19 that the fed funds rate is the rate that U.S. banks charge each other for overnight funds. This rate is typically very close to the Fed's policy rate or target rate unless there are unusual market conditions. Fed funds futures are standardized contracts to buy or sell fed funds at a specified date in the future at a specified price. The price of this futures contract will reflect what the parties to the contract believe the fed funds rate will be for the month of the contract settlement. Therefore, fed funds futures reflect what traders in this market "on average" believe the fed funds target rate will be for the contract month at contract settlement.

Fed funds futures were first offered as one of the many futures contracts traded on the Chicago Board of Trade (CBOT), and the contract has been traded by the CME Group since its acquisition of the CBOT. The contract is settled in cash, based on the average daily fed funds overnight rate for the delivery month. The calculations are based on daily fed funds overnight rates as reported by the Federal Reserve Bank of New York. The net cash settlement is the difference between the final settlement price and the purchase price for the futures contract. But for the purpose of peering into the minds of fed funds futures traders to discover the direction of Fed policy, you only need to focus on prices for the contracts. Fed funds futures trade for as many as 24 months out, but the trading gets very thin beyond about nine months into the future.

The Implied Fed Funds Futures Rate

Now, don't get discouraged, because this is easier than it seems! First, the price paid for a fed funds futures contract tells us what the trader thinks the fed funds rate will be for the contract month. The way fed funds futures prices are quoted explains how one can determine a contract's implicit view of the fed funds rate at the time of the contract settlement. According to the CME Group, the price quote is "100 minus the average daily fed funds overnight rate for the delivery month." In other words, if you believe the fed funds rate will be 2.25 percent for the month of the futures contract, then your bid on the contract is calculated as 100 minus 2.25, which equals 97.75 for the price quote. These are the price quotes—including the settlement for each day—for the various contract months. The expected fed funds rate is implied in the price paid for the futures contract. This implied rate is also called the fed funds futures rate, for a given futures contract.

So if you want to see how professional traders predict the likely Fed policy on interest rates, all you have to do is go to the CME Group web page for fed funds futures, look up the day's settlement price for the various contract months, and "back out" the implied rate with very simple math in a spreadsheet.

Charting Implied Fed Funds for the Big View

Where do you find fed funds futures settlement prices? You can always do a web search for "CME Group," but the direct link to the fed funds futures section is: www.cmegroup.com/trading/interest-rates/stir/30-day-federal-fund.html. Be sure to click on the tab for "Settlements" and when the table for "Daily Settlements for 30-Day Federal Funds Futures" pops up, use the column headed by "Settle."

So you've gone to the website and written down the settlement prices for the contract months going out, say, 12 months. What's the formula to key in so the implied fed funds rate pops up?

Remember, the contract price is:

Price = 100 – Rate

Rearranging the terms, it is:

Rate = 100 – Price

In your spreadsheet, enter in one column the settlement prices for the contract months. In the next column, enter a formula "=100 – x" where "x" is the cell location for that month's settlement price.

The fed funds futures table that follows shows the settlement prices for various contract months at the close of trading on June 25, 2008, and on October 6, 2008. Next to the prices are the implied fed funds rates or *fed funds futures rate*.

def•i•ni•tion

The **fed funds futures rate,** for a given fed funds futures contract, is the fed funds rate implied in the price for that contract. Fed funds futures contracts are based on the formula: 100 minus the expected average effective fed funds rate for the contract month. By knowing the price of the contract, you can calculate the fed funds futures rate: the fed funds futures rate equals 100 minus the price of that futures contract.

Fed Funds Futures, 30-Day

Contract Month	25-Jun-08 Price	Implied Rate	6-Oct-08 Price	Implied Rate
Oct 08	97.735	2.27	98.623	1.38
Nov 08	97.580	2.42	98.645	1.36
Dec 08	97.515	2.49	98.680	1.32
Jan 09	97.415	2.58	98.705	1.30
Feb 09	97.230	2.77	98.715	1.29
Mar 09	97.135	2.86	98.700	1.30
Apr 09	97.045	2.96	98.680	1.32
May 09	96.895	3.11	98.645	1.36
Jun 09	96.850	3.15	98.630	1.37
Jul 09	96.725	3.28	98.545	1.46
Aug 09	96.630	3.37	98.480	1.52
Sep 09	96.535	3.47	98.410	1.59
Oct 09	96.535	3.47	98.280	1.72
Nov 09	96.535	3.47	98.130	1.87
Dec 09	96.535	3.47	98.060	1.94

The fed funds futures rates chart that follows plots the implicit fed funds futures rate for the settlement dates shown in the previous table plus March 18, 2008. The three settlement dates (March 18, June 25, and October 6) represent very different periods in the recent U.S. economy.

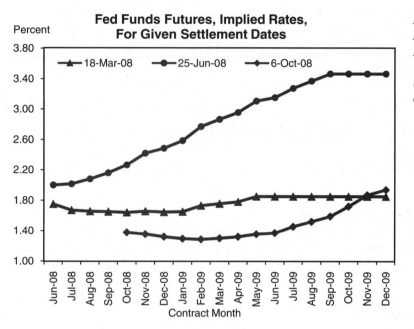

Fed Funds Futures, Implied Rates, For Given Settlement Dates

Fed Funds Futures, Implied Rates, for Given Settlement Dates.

(Source: Data courtesy of CME Group.)

The different trading dates give us insight into how fed funds futures traders viewed likely fed policy. March 18, 2008, was right after the arranged takeover of Bear Stearns by JP Morgan. Economic data had been sluggish, including the then-recent development of declining payroll employment. There were early signs of recession. Fed funds traders were worried about weakness in the credit markets and about slowing economic growth.

The June 2008 numbers reflect a date in which oil prices were spiking, inflation numbers were coming in higher, and it had not become clear that the economy was in recession. The credit markets had appeared to stabilize and a number of Fed officials were rather vocal in their inflation warnings. The fed funds futures market believed the Fed would be tightening in coming months (as seen by the rising implied fed funds rates). Rising inflation was seen as the Fed's worry and traders expected a boost in rates in coming months.

But on October 6, 2008, equities had fallen sharply with the Dow having just posted its largest one-day loss ever. Credit markets were seizing and Lehman Brothers—an investment bank—had gone into bankruptcy. Fed fund futures traders saw the Fed as returning to a mode focusing on providing liquidity to stabilize credit markets and going into recession-fighting mode.

How accurate are fed funds futures for predicting the fed funds rate in coming months? Certainly, all three settlement dates' implied futures rates can't be right. But the charted fed funds futures rates give you a professional opinion about upcoming Fed interest-rate policy. It can also help you understand the behavior of financial markets overall. How many of your friends can talk about the implied fed funds futures rate and actually know what it means?

Yield Curves Tell You What Bond Traders Think About Fed Policy

At that next cocktail party, if your fed funds futures talk doesn't bowl them over, then maybe yield curves will do the trick. Once again, we are talking about market data as indicators. And, once again, this is going to be easy—even easier than implied fed funds rates! We just need to go over some key concepts and then it all comes together. You'll see!

Yield Curve and Treasuries Defined

What is a *yield curve*? The yield curve simply shows short-term interest rates compared to medium-term and long-term interest rates. But the yield curve is based on the same segment of the credit market for all of the different lengths of maturities. The bonds have equal credit quality—the same risk of default across all maturities. You can compare various maturities for Treasuries. Or you could compare, for another example, different maturities of corporate bonds. But you don't mix the interest rates for U.S. Treasuries with those for corporate bonds.

def•i•ni•tion

The **yield curve** is a graph that shows the relationship between interest rates and maturity dates of a bond or debt obligation.

The most common yield curve in the United States is for U.S. Treasury securities. *Treasury securities* are government bonds issued by the United States Department of the Treasury to finance the debt of the U.S. Federal government. They are commonly called Treasuries or Treasurys. Treasury securities have three broad categories based on length of maturity:

- *Treasury bills*—or T-bills—are short-maturity Treasury securities and can have maturities of 4 weeks, 13 weeks, 26 weeks, and 52 weeks. Treasury bills have to have a consistent maturity length (so investors always know what they are getting) and that is why weeks are used instead of months (months have different numbers of days). But for shorthand, these bills are commonly called 1-month T-bills, 3-month T-bills, 6-month T-bills, and 1-year T-bills, even though the actual maturities are based on weeks.

- *Treasury notes*—or T-notes—are medium-term maturity Treasury securities and can have maturity dates of 2, 3, 5, 7, or 10 years.

- *Treasury bonds*—or T-bonds—are long-term maturity Treasury securities and can have maturity dates of 20 or 30 years. Depending on its financing needs, the Treasury may discontinue new issuances of a particular maturity or reinstate a particular maturity.

Anyway, the bottom line is that you now know that different maturities of Treasuries have names you can spout off during half-time chatter during the next NFL football game. Or even during the seventh-inning stretch at a baseball game!

Finding the Market Data for Yield Curves

So how do you go about putting together yield curves so you can see how they have changed over time? First, you can get historical data by going to the Federal Reserve's website for its weekly interest rate publication, known as the "H.15" report and titled "Selected Interest Rates." This report includes many key interest rates, including for the fed funds rate, commercial paper, Treasuries, corporate bonds, state and local bonds, and mortgage rates, among others. There is a weekly report posted each Monday but there are also daily updates for the prior trading day's numbers.

The Federal Reserve's website for this H.15 report is www.federalreserve.gov/ releases/H15/update. This site is about as up-to-date as you can get for a government website—the numbers are never more than one trading day old. And you can download historical data there, too. But if you want *today's* interest rates, then you need to go to private websites. One of the most respected private sites for financial information is Bloomberg.com, which has a specific web page for U.S. Treasuries (along with links for government bonds in other major countries).

The link for today's Treasury rates on Bloomberg.com is www.bloomberg.com/ markets/rates/index.html. The number you are interested in is under the header

"Current Price/Yield." The yield is what you would want to use for the interest rate. These Treasury yield numbers are updated every 15 minutes during trading, but are unchanged on the site after trading stops for the day in the United States.

Key Characteristics of the Normal Yield Curve

A normal yield curve has interest rates rising as the maturity of the bond gets longer. Over the long run or on average, interest rates rise as the maturity of the bond increases. There are a number of fancy-named theories for the shape of the yield curve, but there are two basic reasons behind this normal shape, and they are:

- ◆ Risk: The longer you loan money, the greater the odds that you could lose the money or unexpected inflation could eat up the value of the money.

- ◆ Preference to spend now: People have a tendency to spend or consume now rather than wait. For us to postpone spending, we have to be paid to wait as someone else borrows our money and spends it themselves. And the longer we have to wait, the more we want to be paid.

Fed Policy Effects on the Yield Curve

The factor that can have the fastest and sharpest impact on the shape of the yield curve is changes in Federal Reserve monetary policy. If the Fed is worried about the economy building inflation, then the Fed raises its key policy rate, the fed funds target rate. Short-term interest rates—such as the 3-month Treasury bill—follow the fed funds rate because they have to compete for the same money.

If the Fed is tightening a lot, interest rates on short-term maturities become higher than on long maturities. This is an inverted yield curve. An inverted yield curve is one in which interest rates on short-term debt obligations are higher than on long-maturity bonds. Higher interest rates cut down borrowing by consumers and businesses and, in turn, slow down the economy.

Why do other relative short-term rates (such as the 1-year T-bill or even the 2-year T-note) also rise when the Fed raises the fed funds rate? Even though the fed funds rate is for a very short loan period (typically overnight or up to a month), other short-term rates with longer maturities also increase if financial markets believe the Fed is going to maintain the higher fed funds rate for some time. So if the Fed is expected to keep rates high for a year, then the 1-year T-bill has to compete with the yield on fed funds.

If the Fed is worried about recession, then the Fed cuts the fed funds target rate, pulling down rates on competing short-term Treasuries. We then have a steepened yield curve. A steepened yield curve is one in which short-term rates are significantly lower than for a normal yield curve, resulting in a larger-than-normal difference between short-term and long-term interest rates. Lower interest rates boost borrowing by consumers and businesses and speed up economic growth.

In the treasury yield curves chart that follows, you can see the shapes of the different yield curves.

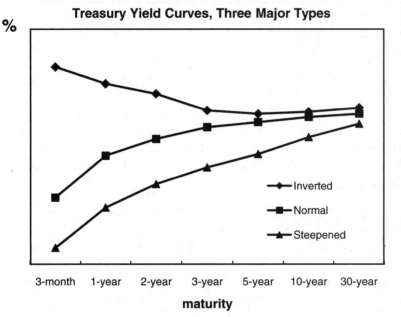

Treasury Yield Curves, Three Major Types.

So it isn't just current Fed policy that is reflected in the yield curve, but also expected Fed policy. No, a 1-month T-bill yield doesn't tell you much about future Fed policy since its maturity basically matches the "now" part of Fed policy and we know what the current fed funds target rate is on any given day. But as maturities get longer, we get more information about market beliefs on Fed policy. Barring temporary, special situations, the yield on the 6-month Treasury bill is going to be very close to what the markets think the fed funds rate will be in six months.

Inflation and the Yield Curve

Investors not only want a return on the money they have loaned, but they want the money they get back to actually have more spending power than when they loaned it out. Put simply: The investor wants to be able to buy more stuff later than he or she would be able to if the money were spent today. The investor does not want inflation to eat up the gains from interest on the bond. So the higher the expected rate of inflation over the period of the loan, the higher the interest rate that will be demanded. Basically, the investor making the loan demands an interest rate that is higher than inflation.

While short-term bills and notes are most heavily affected by short-term changes in Fed policy, long-term bond interest rates are most influenced by changes in expected inflation. Investors expect short-term Fed policy rates to go up and down over the lifetime of a bond and they don't worry about short-term Fed policy. They worry about long-term Fed policy and whether inflation is going to be low or high.

This is why the Fed must have a credible anti-inflation stance. If investors believe the Fed will over the long run do whatever is necessary to keep inflation low, then long-term interest rates will be low. If the Fed is seen as too loose with money for too long, then inflation expectations rise and long-term interest rates rise. So the yield on long-term bonds gives us insight into whether the markets believe the Fed is going to keep inflation low by raising short-term rates when needed. The bottom line is that the yield on long-term bonds tells us whether the Fed is letting inflation expectations rise or is keeping inflation expectations down.

You can see in the following chart comparing bond rates and inflation that in the 1970s and early 1980s, high inflation led to sharply higher bond yields. Long-term rates have since gradually come down due to the Fed's increased credibility on fighting inflation.

Bond Rates and Inflation.

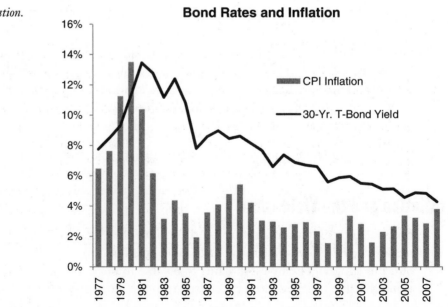

Flight-to-Safety and the Yield Curve

What's one more key factor that can affect yield curves? Flight-to-safety or flight-to-quality. Flight-to-safety is the phenomenon of investors rapidly moving from higher-risk investments to safer investments, such as U.S. Treasuries. Unexpected bad news about the economy can lead investors to protect asset value by getting out of stocks and into Treasuries. There also can be a liquidity issue. Investors may want to have maximum flexibility and will focus on buying short-term Treasuries more so than longer maturities. Flight-to-safety causes the yield curve to fall. Unwinding of flight-to-safety (investors are calmer and feel better about the economy) leads the yield curve up.

Only from an Economist

One component of the index of leading indicators is based on the yield curve concept. We first talked about leading indicators in Chapter 2 while discussing the business cycle. The Conference Board's leading indicators report includes the spread between the 10-year Treasury bond and the effective fed funds rate. An interest rate spread is simply the difference between two interest rates. While not exactly a yield curve, this spread looks at similar issues. The spread in this case is the difference between a long-term interest rate (10-year Treasury bonds) and a short-term rate (fed funds). When the spread is large, that generally means that the Fed has cut interest rates; and when it is small, the Fed has raised interest rates. A large spread means that the economy is about to get a boost from lower short-term interest rates. Similarly, when the yield curve is steep, low interest rates are likely to boost the economy.

Reading Recent Yield Curves

In the Treasury yield curves chart, we see a slightly inverted yield curve for March 1, 2007. The Fed was still in an inflation-fighting mode. The economy was still quite strong on the surface and the markets thought the Fed would be cutting interest rates in coming months, although not by a lot.

By mid-2008, the economy had worsened and the subprime mortgage crisis had carried over into a major meltdown of credit markets in general. The Fed had cut rates sharply back to a more normal yield curve. Oil prices were spiking and financial markets appeared to be stable at that time. So at that point, markets believed the Fed would more likely be raising rates than lowering rates in coming months. Hence the higher 1-year and 2-year interest rates compared to the 3-month rate.

Treasury Yield Curves During Recent Fed Policy Changes.

(Source: Bloomberg Finance LP.)

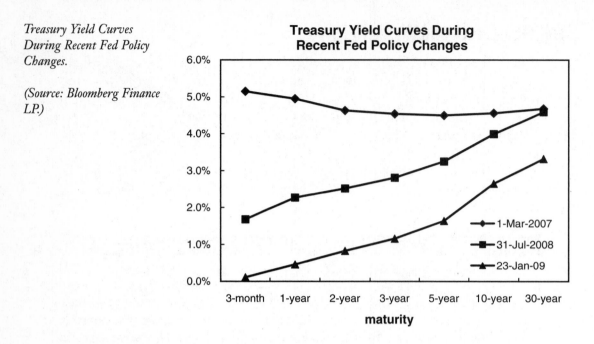

By January 2009, however, the U.S. economy was in deep recession. This was primarily due to a re-emergence of credit markets that weren't working. Also, oil prices had plunged, eliminating fears of rising inflation. The Fed had just cut its target rate to near zero in December 2008, so the January 2009 yield curve represented several factors. It showed market belief that the Fed would be keeping its target rate low for some time. Markets also concluded that inflation was not a threat and that the Fed indeed would raise rates when needed to fight inflation. Thus, the lower long-bond interest rate. But it can't be ignored that many investors feared losses in the stock market and put their money in Treasuries out of flight-to-safety, which also resulted in bumping down the yield curve.

The key takeaways on reading Treasury yield curves are:

♦ Short-term rates tell us where the markets think Fed policy will be in coming months.

♦ Long-term rates tell us whether markets believe the Fed can keep inflation down or not.

The "Real" Fed Funds Rate

Combining market data with inflation reports can give important insight into Fed monetary policy. One factor that helps to determine whether Fed monetary policy is working to slow the economy or to boost growth is the "real fed funds rate." The real fed funds rate is the actual fed funds rate minus the inflation rate or, more specifically, the expected inflation rate. Why is the real fed funds rate an important measure? If inflation is high, then it's easier to pay back the borrowed money. The burden of an interest rate depends on how high inflation is. In fact, if inflation is higher than the interest rate, then the real rate of return is negative. That is, the real cost of borrowing is negative.

In 2008, Chicago Fed President Charles Evans addressed this issue in a speech:

> "To evaluate the stance of policy, I start by focusing on the real fed funds rate—that is, the nominal rate less expected inflation—and where it currently stands relative to a hypothetical longer-run benchmark called the neutral real funds rate. The neutral funds rate is the rate consistent with an economy operating at its potential growth path and with stable inflation. There are many factors and uncertainties involved in assessing the neutral rate. With such caveats in mind, I think the neutral long-run real fed funds rate is somewhere in the neighborhood of 2 to 2½ percent.

> "Real rates above this 2 to 2½ percent neutral point tend to restrict aggregate demand, while real rates below this mark are accommodative and boost aggregate spending. Of course, the real fed funds rate is only one factor affecting liquidity and credit conditions."

By "potential growth path," the Chicago Fed president is referring to the highest possible growth rate for the economy that still has low and stable inflation. What are the key points of the speech?

- First, the "neutral fed funds rate" is the rate consistent with an economy growing at its highest potential rate but still with low and stable inflation.

- Many economists believe the neutral long-run real fed funds rate is somewhere in the neighborhood of 2 to 2½ percent.

- ◆ Real fed funds rates below the neutral fed funds rate are accommodative and boost the economy.

- ◆ Real fed funds rates above the neutral fed funds rate are restrictive and slow the economy.

- ◆ Other factors can also affect liquidity and credit market conditions.

So, How Do I Come Up with Real Fed Funds?

When Fed watchers use the real fed funds approach to analyze how tight or loose Fed policy is, they basically take market data on the fed funds rate and combine that with inflation numbers from government reports. You need these two sets of data: the fed funds rate and an inflation rate. Different economists have different views about which inflation measure is best. But the Fed's choice is the personal consumption expenditures (PCE) price index. You can get the fed funds rate from the Fed's H.15 report (mentioned earlier) and you can get the PCE price index from the Commerce Department's website for the personal income report (as discussed in Chapter 8).

There are two notable issues about calculating the inflation rate: what time frame to use and whether to use "headline" inflation or "core" inflation (excluding food and energy components). For the latter, it's simply best to look at a real fed funds rate using headline inflation and also core inflation. There's really no reason not to do both. Remember from Chapter 8, headline inflation is the overall inflation measure while the core rate excludes food and energy.

For the time frame, many analysts use a year-ago percentage change. However, a year-ago inflation rate may be out of date when taking into account very recent inflation trends. So some like to use an annualized six-months-ago percent change or even an annualized three-months-ago percent change. Whichever time frame you choose, you must use an annualized rate because the fed funds rate is expressed as an annual rate. After you calculate the inflation rate (or two rates, if using headline and core inflation rates) to get the real fed funds rate, simply take the fed funds rate and subtract the inflation rate.

The table that follows shows the numbers involved with calculating two real fed funds rates using headline and core PCE inflation on a year-ago basis.

Calculating the Real Fed Funds Rate

	Fed Funds Target	Headline PCE Price Index	Core PCE Price Index	Headline PCE Inflation	Core PCE Inflation	Real Fed Funds Using Headline	Real Fed Funds Using Core
Oct 07	4.76%	118.635	115.336	3.1%	2.1%	1.6%	2.7%
Nov 07	4.49%	119.349	115.495	3.7%	2.2%	0.8%	2.3%
Dec 07	4.24%	119.678	115.706	3.5%	2.3%	0.7%	2.0%
Jan 08	3.94%	120.052	115.975	3.6%	2.2%	0.3%	1.8%
Feb 08	2.98%	120.212	116.141	3.5%	2.1%	-0.5%	0.8%
Mar 08	2.61%	120.585	116.357	3.4%	2.2%	-0.8%	0.4%
Apr 08	2.28%	120.869	116.532	3.4%	2.2%	-1.1%	0.1%
May 08	1.98%	121.419	116.742	3.5%	2.2%	-1.5%	-0.3%
Jun 08	2.00%	122.346	117.072	4.1%	2.3%	-2.1%	-0.3%
Jul 08	2.01%	123.017	117.286	4.5%	2.4%	-2.5%	-0.4%
Aug 08	2.00%	123.002	117.493	4.4%	2.4%	-2.4%	-0.4%
Sep 08	1.81%	123.106	117.664	4.1%	2.3%	-2.3%	-0.4%
Oct 08	0.97%	122.419	117.657	3.2%	2.0%	-2.2%	-1.0%
Nov 08	0.39%	121.047	117.651	1.4%	1.9%	-1.0%	-1.5%
Dec 08	0.13%	120.434	117.621	0.6%	1.7%	-0.5%	-1.5%

The real fed funds rate chart that follows shows how the rate has varied sharply over business cycles. Based on the real fed funds rate, the Fed was extremely loose with interest rates after the end of the 2001 recession. Many believe that credit was too easy during this period and that's what led to the housing and credit bubble later in the decade.

Real Fed Funds Rate, Nominal Fed Funds Less Year-Ago Inflation***

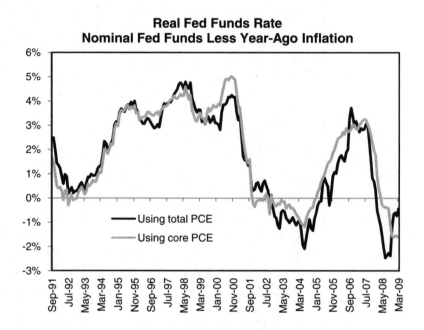

Based on the real fed funds rate, the Fed was even looser in 2008 than during and after the 2001 recession. Fed officials indicated that credit market conditions were severe and called for the very low interest rates.

The TED Spread: Is the Fed Soothing the Markets?

Traditionally, Fed watchers had to worry only about the fed funds rate and maybe the money supply. But in 2008, when the Fed began a quantitative easing strategy (discussed in Chapter 21), financial markets had to expand how they looked to see if Fed policy was working to improve credit markets. In fact, the Fed also changed what it looked at in the credit markets to see if additional credit—or some other action—was needed to sooth the credit markets.

There is one key measure of credit market stability and that's the willingness to lend. This is called the TED spread. TED is short for Treasury-Eurodollar. When the Fed is in a quantitative easing mode, you have to watch the TED spread to see if Fed policy is working.

The TED spread began as the difference between the yield on the Eurodollar minus the yield on the equivalent Treasury bill—a 3-month maturity for both. Today, the TED spread is the difference between the 3-month dollar-denominated LIBOR rate and the 3-month T-bill. LIBOR is the London Interbank Offered Rate and it is a rate at which banks borrow unsecured funds from other banks in the London wholesale money market. The unsecured loans are primarily through the issuance of interbank certificates of deposit. The LIBOR is a daily average of rates that 16 different banks charge each other to lend money in London. But the rate also reflects conditions in credit markets in the United States and worldwide.

But you don't have to worry too much about those details. The key points are that the Treasury is a safe investment and the LIBOR rate is for riskier investments in an important segment of the credit markets. So the TED spread is the yield gap between very, very safe investments versus riskier, but typical, business loans. The TED spread is seen as an indicator of credit risk in the economy. When lenders believe the risk of default is rising, they boost the LIBOR rate. A rise in the LIBOR rate also reflects tighter or less available credit.

The below summarizes what high and low TED spreads tell you about credit markets.

- A high TED spread means that credit markets are nervous about making loans and are charging a premium rate.

- A low TED spread indicates that credit markets feel better about economic conditions and are willing to lend without charging a higher rate.

Over the long term, the TED spread typically has ranged from 30 to 50 basis points. You can see in the weekly TED spread chart below that late in 2008, the TED spread hit historical highs. The daily high (not shown) actually hit 465 basis points on October 10, 2008 (but averaged lower for the week). The surge was due to a collapse in equity markets and lenders fearing the worst from recession. The Fed tends to intervene in credit markets when the TED spread is high. Look for the Fed to inject liquidity when the TED spread jumps.

TED Spread, Weekly.

(Source: Bloomberg Finance LP.)

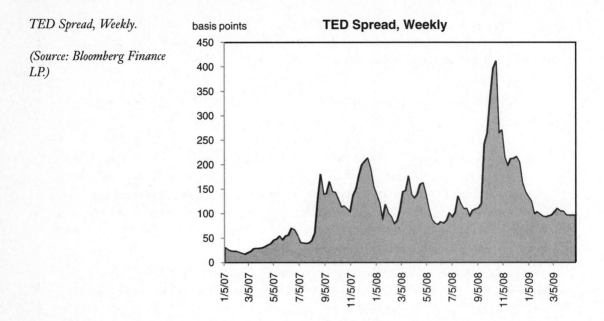

Where can you find data for the TED spread? Glad you asked! Historical data for LIBOR can be purchased at a very low cost at Economagic.com. And as noted before, the 3-month T-bill data can be found in the Fed's daily H.15 report. The LIBOR is posted on Bloomberg.com's website at: www.bloomberg.com/markets/rates/keyrates.html.

The Least You Need to Know

♦ The fed funds futures market is an easy way to learn what professional traders think about where Fed policy is headed.

♦ Yield curves tell us where bond traders think interest rates and long-term inflation are headed.

♦ The real fed funds rates tells us whether the Fed is easing or tightening after taking into account inflation.

♦ The TED spread is an indicator of willingness to lend in the credit markets—and the Fed watches this to see if they need to add more liquidity.

Economic Indicators Glossary

ADP employment report A monthly employment report privately produced by Automatic Data Processing, Inc. (ADP), a payroll and data processing company, that covers private nonfarm payrolls. The survey is based on payroll data processed by ADP, is released two days before the employment situation report, and is used by market watchers to predict government estimates of payroll jobs.

barrel A unit of volume equal to 42 U.S. gallons; for example, a barrel of oil.

basis point In reference to interest rates, one hundredth of a percentage point. If the yield on a Treasury bond went from 4.20 percent to 4.05 percent, you could say that the interest rate fell 15 basis points.

bear market When the stock market is on a downward trend and there is broad-based pessimism about losses continuing in the future.

Beige Book A report prepared by Fed District Banks two weeks prior to each Federal Open Market Committee meeting. The Beige Book is a compilation of the District Banks' updates from business contacts in their Fed regions.

bond Certificate of ownership of debt to be paid by a corporation or government to the holder of the bond, which can be a person, another company, or even another government. Bonds typically have a fixed rate of interest.

Brent   The name of a particular high-grade crude oil produced in the North Sea of the United Kingdom, of slightly lower quality than West Texas Intermediate. Brent is the pricing benchmark for most oil traded internationally.

bull market   When the stock market is on an upward trend and there is a general mood of optimism about continued gains in the future.

Bureau of Economic Analysis (BEA)   An agency within the U.S. Department of Commerce responsible for producing many economic indicators on the U.S. economy, specifically for economic accounts statistics such as the National Income and Product Accounts, which includes gross domestic product and personal income among others.

Bureau of Labor Statistics (BLS)   An agency within the U.S. Department of Labor responsible for producing many economic indicators on labor market conditions (including inflation) within the United States. Some of the economic reports that the BLS is best known for producing are the employment situation, Consumer Price Index, and Producer Price Index.

business cycle   The recurring ups and downs in economic activity experienced by an economy over the long run.

business cycle peak   The last month in which the economy grows overall.

business cycle trough   The last month that economic activity declines.

Business Outlook Survey   A regional (mid-Atlantic states) manufacturing activity index produced by the Federal Reserve Bank of Philadelphia.

capacity utilization rate   The percentage of capacity that a plant or industry is using. It is a measure of how much unused production capability is available to meet an increase in demand.

capital goods   Goods used to produce other goods, structures, or services.

Case-Shiller   A home price index for metropolitan areas in the United States, named for its developers, economists Karl E. Case and Robert J. Shiller. This monthly index—also known as the S&P/Case-Shiller Home Price Index—is a measure of resale price changes for existing single-family homes. This home price index report is a joint product of Standard & Poor's and Fiserv, Inc.

central bank   A government institution that is responsible for the monetary policy of a country or a group of member states. Another primary responsibility of a central bank is to be the lender of last resort to commercial banks in times of need.

Chicago Business Barometer   The headline index of the ISM-Chicago Business Survey.

civilian labor force   The sum of employed and unemployed persons.

coincident indicators   Economic indicators that typically have changes in strength and weakness in line with the timing of the economy's business cycle. While many indicators have leading properties, the Conference Board produces its own specific composite index of leading indicators.

commodity   Any good in a market for which the producer is indiscernible by any differences in the product, because the products are essentially identical. For a specific commodity, any producer's product is completely interchangeable with another producer's product of that commodity. Examples of commodities are wheat and copper.

complementary goods   Products that are used together.

consumer confidence   How optimistic or pessimistic consumers are about current conditions in the economy or how conditions will be in the near future. The Conference Board and the University of Michigan have separate surveys that attempt to measure consumer confidence.

Consumer Confidence Index   A measure of consumers' attitudes toward the economy according to a survey conducted by the Conference Board.

Consumer Price Index (CPI)   A measure of the average change in prices over time of goods and services purchased by households.

Consumer Sentiment Index   A measure of consumers' attitudes toward the economy according to a survey conducted by the Survey Research Center at the University of Michigan.

core inflation   The overall inflation rate for a given inflation indicator but excluding the volatile food and energy components.

currency   Money, and generally the money issued by a particular country's government or used by a particular country's businesses for accounting. For example, the currency used in the United States is the U.S. dollar and the currency used in the United Kingdom is the British pound sterling.

cyclical volatility   The degree to which an economic indicator or sector within the economy rises and falls more than the overall economy during expansion and recession. If an indicator or sector typically rises faster than the economy during expansion and falls faster in recession, it is cyclically volatile.

deflation A downtrend for the general level of prices; overall prices are falling.

diffusion index A measure of how diffuse an indicator's components are or how closely (or not) the components move together.

discount rate The rate the Fed charges banks for borrowing reserves from the Fed's discount window at regional Federal Reserve Banks.

discount window The program of each District Fed Bank to offer special lending to banks that cannot obtain needed reserves on the open market at reasonable cost.

disinflation A slowdown in the rate of inflation; prices still go up, but at a slower rate.

disposable personal income Personal income less personal current taxes. It is the income available to persons for spending or saving.

dove In regard to inflation, someone (typically used in reference to a Fed official) who believes that inflation is less of a threat and focuses on looser monetary policy to boost economic growth.

Dow Industrials A stock market index of 30 of the largest publicly traded companies in the United States. It is compiled by Dow Jones & Company.

durable goods Goods with expected lifetimes of three years or longer.

economic indicators Key statistics about the economy. These statistics are economic measures that help predict growth rates and trends in the economy.

Empire State Manufacturing Survey A regional (New York State) manufacturing activity index produced by the Federal Reserve Bank of New York.

employment cost index (ECI) A measure of the change in the cost of a fixed amount of labor, free from the influence of employment shifts among occupations and industries.

Establishment Survey One of two surveys that form the data in the employment situation report. The Establishment Survey—also called the Payroll Survey—is conducted by the Bureau of Labor Statistics. It is a survey of business establishments to determine the number of payroll jobs each month. The Establishment Survey also produces numbers for average hourly earnings and the average number of hours in the workweek, among others.

existing home sale Occurs when the attorneys have signed off on all of the paperwork, a new name is on the deed, and house keys are exchanged. It's not counted as part of the National Association of Realtors' statistics until it's a "done deal."

expansion   Starts when economic activity resumes growing after the trough of recession, according to the NBER's official definition. As a complementary definition to "recovery" and according to some non-NBER economists, expansion is the growth period after the end recession when the level of economic activity exceeds the prior peak.

factory orders   Orders that are supported by binding legal documents such as signed contracts, letters of award, or letters of intent. Orders can be for immediate or future delivery.

fed funds futures   Standardized contracts in which the owner buys or sells fed funds at a specified date in the future and at a specified price.

fed funds futures rate   The interest rate for a given fed funds futures contract implied in the price for that contract. Fed funds futures contracts are based on the formula 100 minus the expected average effective fed funds rate for the contract month. By knowing the price of the contract, you can calculate the fed funds futures rate: the fed funds futures rate equals 100 minus the price of that futures contract.

fed funds rate   The interest rate at which banks lend their excess reserve balances with the Fed to other banks overnight.

Federal Housing Finance Agency (FHFA)   An independent federal agency created by the U.S. Congress to replace the Federal Housing Finance Board (FHFB) and the Office of Federal Housing Enterprise Oversight (OFHEO), with its primary responsibility being oversight of housing-related government-sponsored enterprises such as Fannie Mae and Freddie Mac. Among economic indicators, FHFA is known for producing the House Price Index (HPI).

Federal Open Market Committee (FOMC)   The policy-making arm of the Federal Reserve. It has eight regularly scheduled meetings and consists of all of the Federal Reserve Board governors plus 5 of the 12 District Bank presidents on a rotating basis.

Federal Reserve, the Fed   The central bank for the United States. The Fed controls monetary policy for the United States, is lender of last resort for commercial banks needing temporary reserves, and has other functions, including supervising the soundness of many commercial banks in the country.

FHFA House Price Index (HPI)   Measures home prices based on home sales that involve conforming, conventional mortgages purchased or securitized by Fannie Mae or Freddie Mac. This is a limited measure of home prices since homes using other types of mortgages are not included.

final sales of domestic product   Equal to GDP less the change in private inventories.

fixed investment   Investment in assets that remain with the company while conducting business. Some fixed investment assets certainly move around (for instance, aircraft for airlines and cars and trucks used by businesses), but they are still retained by the company. Inventory investment is not fixed because these assets move on as they are sold.

flight-to-safety   The phenomenon of investors rapidly moving from higher-risk investments to safer investments, such as U.S. Treasuries, when there is bad news about the economy. Such news can lead investors to protect asset value by getting out of stocks and into Treasuries. There also can be a liquidity issue: investors may want to have maximum flexibility and will focus on buying short-term Treasuries rather than longer maturities.

futures transaction   Purchasing a commodity at a specific price and with a specific month in the future for delivery.

government-sponsored enterprises (GSEs)   A group of financial services corporations created by Congress to improve targeted portions of credit markets and to boost certain segments of the economy. GSEs are involved with a wide variety of credit markets, including for agriculture, student finance, and housing. GSEs generally are privately owned but have either explicit or implicit government backing.

gross domestic product (GDP)   The market value of goods and services produced in the United States. In other words, GDP represents the total production for a country.

hawk   In regard to inflation, someone (typically used in reference to a Fed official) who believes that inflation has a negative impact on business and society and pursues more aggressive monetary policy to keep inflation low. Inflation hawks believe low inflation fosters economic growth.

headline inflation   The overall or total inflation rate for a given inflation indicator, such as for personal consumption expenditure prices, the Consumer Price Index, or the Producer Price Index. This is the number for an inflation indicator that the media gives the most attention.

Household Survey   One of two surveys that form the data in the employment situation report. The Household Survey is conducted by the Bureau of the Census. It is a survey of households on employment status and is from the worker's perspective. The Household Survey is best known for producing the unemployment rate each month.

Housing Market Index   A measure of homebuilder optimism about housing markets. It is based on a survey that the National Association of Home Builders sends to a panel of its homebuilder members. Builders are asked to rate housing market conditions based on their experiences.

housing permit   An authorization by the municipality or other local government for a builder to begin construction on one or more housing units.

housing starts   The number of residential units on which construction has actually begun.

housing unit   A house, an apartment, a group of rooms, or a single room intended for occupancy as separate living quarters; each unit must have its own entrance to the outside of the building or to a common hall.

ICSC-Goldman Sachs Chain Store Sales   A weekly report on sales by major department stores in the United States, produced by the International Council of Shopping Centers (ICSC) and Goldman Sachs, an investment bank.

industrial production index   A measure of the real output of the manufacturing, mining, and electric and gas utilities industries in the United States.

inflation   A general trend of rising prices for goods and services in the economy.

inventories   Materials and supplies, work in process, finished goods, and goods held by businesses for resale.

ISM manufacturing index   A national manufacturing activity index released by the Institute for Supply Management, which reflects a survey of purchasing executives from about 300 industrial companies. Being released on the first business day of each month, financial markets see this index's news release as the first major indicator of the month.

ISM non-manufacturing index   A national non-manufacturing activity index released by the Institute for Supply Management, which reflects a survey of purchasing executives from about 400 non-manufacturing companies.

ISM-Chicago Business Survey   A regional (Chicago, Illinois, metropolitan area) survey of both manufacturing and non-manufacturing activity index produced by Kingsbury International, LTD, and the Institute for Supply Management-Chicago, Inc.

jobless claims   A measure of the number of unemployed produced weekly by the U.S. Department of Labor. Data are for those initially filing for unemployment benefits under state unemployment programs and for continuing claims.

lagging indicators   Indicators that have peaks and troughs that typically occur after the highs and lows of the overall business cycle. While many indicators have lagging properties, the Conference Board produces its own specific composite index of lagging indicators.

leading economic indicators, index of   An economic indicator that is designed to give advance warning of turning points in the economy such as for going into and coming out of recession. It has ten component indicators that tend to lead the economy and is produced by The Conference Board.

leading indicators   Economic indicators that typically have changes in strength and weakness ahead of the timing of the economy's business cycle. While many indicators have leading properties, the Conference Board produces its own specific composite index of leading indicators.

LIBOR (London Interbank Offered Rate)   A rate at which banks borrow unsecured funds from other banks in the London wholesale money market. The LIBOR is a daily average of rates that 16 different banks charge each other to lend money in London, but the rate also reflects conditions in credit markets in the United States and worldwide.

mass layoff   A company-specific economic event when 50 or more initial claims for unemployment insurance benefits are filed against an employer during a five-week period. Mass layoff data are published monthly by the Bureau of Labor Statistics.

misery index   The unemployment rate plus the inflation rate.

monetary policy   The process by which the central bank controls either the money supply or interest rates to achieve specific objectives for the overall economy—typically, low inflation or a combination of low inflation and healthy economic growth.

Monetary Policy Report to the Congress   The Federal Reserve's semi-annual report to Congress on the status of monetary policy and the economy.

money supply   The amount of money in circulation at a given time.

Monster Employment Index   A measure of employer online recruitment activity; is seen as a leading indicator of changes in the strength of the job market. It is produced by Monster Worldwide, Inc., of monster.com fame.

National Bureau of Economic Research (NBER)   A nonprofit economic research group that is best known for setting official peak and trough dates for business cycles in the United States.

net exports   The difference between exports and imports of goods and services.

new single-family home sale   Takes place when a deposit is taken or sales agreement is signed.

nominal GDP   The current-dollar GDP.

nondurable goods   Goods with expected lifetimes of less than three years.

nonrevolving credit   Installment loans with fixed payments.

nonstore retailers   Retailers that do not operate from fixed, point-of-sale locations.

North American Industry Classification System (NAICS)   A statistical classification system used by national statistical agencies in Canada, Mexico, and the United States for the purpose of collecting, analyzing, and publishing statistical data related to the countries' business economies. In the United States, NAICS has largely replaced the older Standard Industrial Classification (SIC) system. Examples of indicators using NAICS include retail sales, factory orders, and industrial production, among others.

not in the labor force   Those who aren't in either the employed or unemployed categories.

OPEC (Organization of Petroleum Exporting Countries)   An intergovernmental organization whose stated objective is to coordinate and unify petroleum policies among member countries. That is, OPEC attempts to coordinate oil production and prices among its members.

open market operations   The Federal Reserve's purchasing and selling of securities in the open market through the New York Fed to raise or lower interest rates or to increase or decrease liquidity in financial markets. The Fed generally buys or sells United States Treasuries when conducting open market operations, but has expanded to other securities such as GSE debt and mortgage-backed securities.

Pending Home Sales Index   A measure of home sales produced by the National Association of Realtors. A pending home sale occurs when a seller accepts a sales contract on a property and it is recorded into a Multiple Listing Service (MLS) as a "pending home sale."

personal consumption expenditures (PCEs)   The purchases of goods and services, by persons and nonprofit institutions, that primarily serve households.

personal income   Monies individuals get for their labor (salary and wages), for owning their own business (proprietor income), for someone using an individual's property (rent), and for financial investments (interest and dividends)—plus private and government aid.

Producer Price Index A measure of inflation at the producer level. It is based on average changes in prices received by domestic producers for their output.

productivity For labor, this is the ratio of the output of goods and services to the labor hours used in the production of that output; basically, higher output per hour means labor is more productive.

quantitative easing A balance sheet strategy for the Fed to keep adding liquidity to financial markets without further lowering short-term interest rates by trading Fed reserves for some other asset on the market (in addition to short-term Treasuries).

real fed funds rate The actual fed funds rate minus the inflation rate.

real GDP Inflation-adjusted GDP.

real investments Physical assets intended to produce goods or services. Such assets are buildings, such as manufacturing plants, apartment complexes, and hospitals. Physical assets are generally considered by economists to include software and intellectual property. Real investments are in contrast to paper investments such as stocks and bonds.

recession A significant decline in economic activity that permeates the economy and lasts more than a few months.

recovery The part of the expansion phase that occurs immediately after the business cycle trough, in which the economy is growing but has not reached a level of activity matching the prior peak.

Redbook A weekly measure—formally known as Johnson Redbook—of sales at chain stores, discounters, and department stores, as collected by Redbook Research, Inc., of New York.

retail and food services store sales Sales of firms in the United States that sell merchandise and related services to final consumers.

revolving credit A type of credit that does not have a fixed number of payments. A revolving line of credit has a fixed amount of credit available for which the customer pays a commitment fee and is then allowed to use the funds when they are needed. One type of revolving credit used by consumers is credit cards.

seasonal adjustment A statistical technique that attempts to measure and remove the influences of predictable seasonal patterns to reveal underlying trends in an indicator from month to month.

sector fundamentals   The underlying factors for each sector that determine sector growth rates. GDP divides the expenditure view of the economy into relatively tidy categories that have common factors affecting that sector's growth.

single-family home sale   Occurs when a deposit is taken or sales agreement is signed.

social insurance   Programs by the government that support individuals during unemployment and other times of need as specified by legislation. Social insurance programs include unemployment insurance, Social Security, Medicare, and Medicaid, among others.

source data   Economic indicators and surveys that are available early and are used by a statistical agency (such as the Commerce Department) to calculate another economic indicator that is published later.

spot transaction   A transaction for a commodity that's available for immediate delivery.

stock   Certificate of ownership in a company. Stocks also are called "equities." Stocks are generally bought and sold on a stock exchange such as the New York Stock Exchange. The collective market of these stock exchanges is called the stock market.

store retailers   Retailers that operate from a physical, or fixed point-of-sale, location.

subprime loans   Loans offered to borrowers who do not meet prime underwriting guidelines. These borrowers might have low credit ratings or, for some other reason, have a higher perceived risk of default. They may have a history of loan delinquency or default, a recorded bankruptcy, or limited debt experience. Subprime lending is found in a variety of credit types (including mortgages, auto loans, and credit cards), but in the media in recent years has been used in reference to mortgages.

TED spread   The difference between the 3-month dollar-denominated LIBOR rate and the 3-month T-bill. Originally, this spread was the difference between the yields on the 3-month Euro-dollar and the 3-month T-bill, hence the name "TED" for Treasury-Eurodollar.

thrifts   These are special savings banks also known as savings and loans institutions. Thrifts have had special regulatory status in the United States and traditionally have been required to have the vast majority of loans in mortgages.

trade balance   The difference between dollar values of exports and imports.

Treasury bills Known as T-bills, these mature in one year or less and are issued with maturity dates in weekly increments, such as for 26 weeks.

Treasury bonds Known as T-bonds, these mature in 20 to 30 years.

Treasury notes Known as T-notes, these mature in 2 to 10 years.

Treasury securities Government bonds issued by the United States Department of the Treasury and are used to finance the debt of the U.S. Federal government.

unemployment claims Claims made by unemployed persons who wish to receive unemployment benefits.

unemployment rate The percent of the labor force who are unemployed.

unit labor costs A measure of how much labor costs go into one unit of production. From the productivity report produced by the U.S. Department of Labor, it is defined as total labor compensation divided by real output.

value of construction put in place A measure of the value of construction installed or erected at a site during a given period.

West Texas Intermediate The name of a particular high-grade crude oil produced in the United States.

yield curve A graph that shows the relationship between interest rates and maturity dates of a bond or debt obligation. For example, using Treasury securities for a given date, one might compare yields on a 3-month T-bill, a 2-year T-note, a 5-year T-note, a 7-year T-note, a 10-year T-bond, and a 30-year T-bond. There are similar yield curves for other types of bonds (such as corporate or municipal).

Index

W-X

V

Y-Z